Coach's Guide

to AER's Recreational Archery Curriculum

Note to AER Students

This manual was designed to be used in support of your learning to teach this curriculum as well as being designed for use as a reference, so you will find some repetition of topics.

Suggestions for improvement are most welcome.

Copyright 2010
Archery Education Resources
3712 North Broadway, #285
Chicago. IL 60613
ISBN 978-0-9821471-4-6

AER Coach's Guide
Table of Contents

Coach's Guide (Introduction) 11

Archer's Guide (Annotated) i

Preface i

Getting Started v

The Olympic-Style Track
- Introduction 1
- Signposts—Stage I Getting Started
    - Archery Safety 1
        - *Good Behavior is Expected* 1
        - *The Whistle System* 2
        - *Good Behavior is Expected Everywhere* 2
        - *The Range Rules Must Be Obeyed* 3
    - Basic Archery Form 3
        - *Taking Your Stance* 3
        - *Standing Well* 3
        - *Keeping Your Shoulders Down* 5
        - *Setting Your Bow Hand* 5
        - *Positioning Your Head* 6
        - *Drawing the String* 6
        - *Finding Your Anchor Position* 7
        - *Following Through* 8
        - *Getting In Line* 8
        - *"Grouping" Your Shots* 8
        - *Aiming "Off the Point"* 9

- **Signposts—Stage II Getting Better** 12
  - Intermediate Archery Form 13
    - *Bracing Your Bow* 13
    - *Modifying Your Stance* 13
    - *Modifying Your Posture* 14
    - *Using a Finger Tab* 14
    - *Modern Bow Hand Technique* 16
    - *Drawing Smoothly* 16
    - *Anchors Away?* 16
    - *Stabilizing the Shot* 17
    - *Adding a Sling* 18
    - *Still Following Through* 19
    - *Lining Up* 19
    - *Step-by-Step* 20
    - *Using a Bow Sight* 24
    - *String Alignment* 26
    - *Equipment Inspection* 27
    - *Grouping Better* 29
  - Stage II Mental Aspects 29
    - *Talking to Yourself* 30
    - *Goals* 31
- **Signposts—Stage III Achieving Mastery** 33
  - Advanced Archery Skills 33
    - *Tuning* 33
    - *Bare Shaft Tuning* 33
    - *Fully Sighting In* 38
    - *String Alignment II* 39
    - *Shooting Cool* 39
    - *Clickers* 40
    - *Shooting Rhythmically* 41
    - *Scoring* 42
  - Stage III Mental Aspects 43

- *Journaling* 43
- *Getting Help from Others* 44
- *Imagine This* 45
- *Affirmations* 46
- *Shot Thoughts* 47
- *More on Goals* 47
- Signposts—Stage IV Owning the Sport 49
  - Finishing Your Kit 49
    - *Changing Gear* 50
  - Refining Your Archery Skills 51
    - *Advanced Tuning* 51
    - *Mastering the Clicker* 52
    - *Archery Gear Maintenance* 52
    - *Scoring* 53
  - Stage IV Mental Aspects 53

The Compound Track

- Introduction 57
- Signposts—Stage I Getting Started 57
  - Archery Safety 57
    - *Good Behavior is Expected* 57
    - *The Whistle System* 58
    - *Good Behavior is Expected Everywhere* 58
    - *The Range Rules Must Be Obeyed* 59
  - Basic Archery Form 59
    - *Taking Your Stance* 59
    - *Standing Well* 59
    - *Keeping Your Shoulders Down* 61
    - *Setting Your Bow Hand* 61
    - *Positioning Your Head* 62
    - *Drawing the String* 63
    - *Finding Your Anchor Position* 63

- *Following Through* 64
- *Getting In Line* 64
- *"Grouping" Your Shots* 64
- *Aiming "Off the Point"* 65
- **Signposts—Stage II Getting Better** 68
    - Intermediate Archery Form 69
        - *Modifying Your Stance* 69
        - *Modifying Your Posture* 70
        - *Using a Finger Tab* 70
        - *Modern Bow Hand Technique* 72
        - *Drawing Smoothly* 72
        - *Anchors Away?* 73
        - *Stabilizing the Shot* 74
        - *Adding a Sling* 75
        - *Still Following Through* 75
        - *Lining Up* 76
        - *Step-by-Step* 76
        - *Using a Bow Sight* 81
        - *String Alignment* 83
        - *Using a Release Aid* 84
        - *Equipment Inspection* 86
        - *Grouping Better* 88
    - Stage II Mental Aspects 88
        - *Talking to Yourself* 88
        - *Goals* 89
- **Signposts—Stage III Achieving Mastery** 91
    - Advanced Archery Skills 91
        - *Peeping Through the String* 91
        - *Mastering Your Release Aid* 92
        - *Fully Sighting In* 93
        - *Shooting Cool* 95
        - *Tuning* 95

- *Bare Shaft Tuning* 96
- *Shooting Rhythmically* 99
- *Scoring* 100
- Stage III Mental Aspects 100
  - *Journaling* 100
  - *Getting Help from Others* 102
  - *Imagine This* 102
  - *Affirmations* 103
  - *Shot Thoughts* 104
  - *More on Goals* 105
- Signposts—Stage IV Owning the Sport 107
  - Refining Your Archery Skills 107
    - *Finishing Your Kit* 107
    - *Advanced Tuning* 108
    - *Archery Gear Maintenance* 110
    - *Scoring* 110
    - *Getting the Point* 110
    - *Walking the String* 111
  - Stage IV Mental Aspects 112

The Traditional Track
- Introduction 117
- Signposts—Stage I Getting Started
  - Archery Safety 117
    - *Good Behavior is Expected* 117
    - *The Whistle System* 117
    - *Good Behavior is Expected Everywhere* 118
    - *The Range Rules Must Be Obeyed* 118
  - Basic Archery Form 120
    - *Taking Your Stance* 120
    - *Standing Well* 120
    - *Keeping Your Shoulders Down* 120

- *Setting Your Bow Hand* 121
- *Positioning Your Head* 122
- *Drawing the String* 122
- *Finding Your Anchor Position* 123
- *Following Through* 123
- *Getting In Line* 124
- *"Grouping" Your Shots* 124
- *Aiming "Off the Point"* 125

- **Signposts—Stage II Getting Better** 128
  - Intermediate Archery Form 129
    - *Modifying Your Stance* 129
    - *Modifying Your Posture* 130
    - *Using a Finger Tab* 130
    - *Longbow Bowhand Technique* 131
    - *Drawing Smoothly* 132
    - *Anchors Away?* 133
    - *Still Following Through* 133
    - *Lining Up* 134
    - *Step-by-Step* 134
    - *Using the Point* 139
    - *Walking the String* 140
    - *String Alignment* 142
    - *Bracing the Bow* 143
    - *Equipment Inspection* 144
    - *Grouping Better* 146
  - Stage II Mental Aspects 146
    - *Talking to Yourself* 146
    - *Goals* 147

- **Signposts—Stage III Achieving Mastery** 149
  - Advanced Archery Skills 149
    - *Tuning* 149
    - *Blank Bale Testing* 149

- *Bare Shaft Tuning* 150
- *Shooting Cool* 153
- *Shooting Rhythmically* 154
- *Scoring* 155
- Stage III Mental Aspects 155
  - *Journaling* 156
  - *Getting Help from Others* 157
  - *Imagine This* 157
  - *Affirmations* 158
  - *Shot Thoughts* 159
  - *More on Goals* 160
- Signposts—Stage IV Owning the Sport 162
  - Finishing Your Kit 162
    - *Changing Gear* 163
  - Refining Your Archery Skills 163
    - *Advanced Tuning* 163
    - *Archery Gear Maintenance* 165
    - *Scoring* 165
  - Stage IV Mental Aspects 166

Appendices (Archer's Guide) 169
- Types of Styles/Targets/Scoring 169
  - NFAA Shooting Styles (Chart) 170
- Glossary 173
- Scores, Scoring, and Competition 177
- Some Individual Competition Rounds 179

Appendices (Coach's Guide) 185
- The First Three Arrows 185
- Setting Up Bow Accessories 185
  - Bow Sights 185
  - Kinds of Bow Sights 185

- • Pin Sights 186
- • Target Sights 187
- • Using Bow Sights 188
- • Quivers 189
- • Release Aids 189
- • Finger Tabs 190
- • Kisser Buttons 190
- **Equipment Maintenance and Repair** 191
  - • Checking Arrows 191
  - • Installing and Replacing Nocks 188
  - • Fletching Arrows 191
  - • Installing and Replacing Points 191
  - • Replacing a Center Serving 191
  - • Serving on a Nocking Point 191
  - • Making the Nocking Point Fit the Nock 192
  - • Installing a Peep Sight 192
  - • Adding a D-Loop to a Compound Serving 192
  - • The Rest of the Book 192
- **Training with Release Aids (Compound Only)** 192
  - • The Preliminaries 192
  - • Release Aid Training 193
- **Eye Dominance** 193
- **On Stances** 194
  - • There is Nothing Wrong with the Square Stance 194
  - • The Other Stances 194
  - • Stance Rules 197
  - • Fine Tuning a Stance 197
- **More on Bow Sights** 198
  - • Extending Sights 198
  - • More on Pin Sights 199
- **Bow Fitting** 201
- **Bow Setup** 201

- **Setting Up a New Recurve Bow** 201
  - Assembling the Bow 201
  - Setting the Nocking Point Location 202
  - Setting the Centershot 203
  - The First Shots 203
- **Setting Up a New Longbow** 204
  - Setting the Brace Height 204
  - Setting the Nocking Point Location 204
  - The Arrow Rest 205
  - The First Shots 205
- **Setting Up a New Compound Bow** 205
  - Assembling the Bow 205
  - Setting the Nocking Point Location 206
  - Setting the Centershot 206
  - The First Shots 207
  - Mechanical Complications 207
- **Bow and Arrow Tuning** 207
  - What is Tuning? 208
- **Tuning Concepts** 208
  - Bow/Arrow Fitting 208
  - Bow/Arrow Setup 209
  - Bow/Arrow Tuning 210
- **AER Archery Drills** 211
  - Shoulders Up/Shoulders Down Drill 211
  - Rotate That Elbow Drill 211
  - Elbow Rotation Test 212
  - Arm Relaxation Drill 212
  - Finger Release Drill 213
  - Back Tension Drill #1 213
  - Back Tension Drill #2 213
  - Back Tension Drill #3 214
  - Blank Bale Routines 214

- • Mirror Drill 215
- **AER Basic Coaching Approaches** 215
- **AER Coaching Principles** 216
- **Field Archery** 218
- **Anatomy of an Archery Session** 219
  - • First Third Modules 219
  - • Second Third Modules 219
  - • Final Third Modules 220
- **Making Evaluations** 220
- **Equipment You Can Make** 222

Archery Education Resources
Recreational Archery Curriculum
Coach's Guide

Introduction
Before you begin looking through this Guide to the AER Recreational Archery Curriculum, you may also want to have your *AER Beginner Archery Class Instructor Guide* and *AER Program Guide* handy as well.

All of what is in the *AER Archer's Guide* is here in this book but with a great deal more detail, plus suggested drills and exercises, and additional resources and references as well. We recommend you read this Guide with a highlighter in hand as it is chock full of information, some of which will be more important to you.

Because of students having access to the *AER Archer's Guide*, some of your students will have quite a bit of prior knowledge and some will not. Therefore, it is recommended that when questions are asked, you begin with questions of your own, possibly most frequently "Have you read that section of the *Archer's Guide*?"

Individual Curriculum Plans
Everything you will be doing with your student-archers is integrated into a personalized Individual Curriculum Plan (ICP). Extra copies of each of the plans can be downloaded from the AER Coach's Website. All of the steps the archers need to take are on the plan including short descriptions of all *Signposts*. You are expected to be able to lead your students through performing all of the tasks on the plan and help them customize the plan to fit their needs and interests. In an AER Introductory Archery Course, all the students need is the Individual Curriculum Plan which comes free when they sign up for the course. The *AER Archer's Guide* is for people who want more information, such as the archers themselves, parents of younger archers, etc. There is even a mode for those who might want to go it alone (*see Self Study Mode below*).

You will keep an ICP for each archer you are working with as well as providing them with a copy for them to track their own progress. We recommend you keep your copies in a three ring binder with dividers for each class. Look on the AER

What's all of this space down here for? Well, later we provide exact duplicate pages of the entire *The Complete Archer's Guide* and we have annotated many of those pages with tips on how to teach this curriculum. You are encouraged to make notes on any unused space!

Notes _____

_____

_____

_____

_____

website (*www.archeryeducationresources.com*) as we plan to sell binders with dividers set up for this purpose

If a student leaves your program, they take their plan (your copy) with them. If you want copies of their plan before they are surrendered, you are allowed to photocopy them for professional purposes only, not to be released for publication, etc. without the permission of the student-athlete.

Tracks

Archers will choose to be on one of three *Tracks*: Olympic-Style Archery, Compound Archery, or Traditional Archery. Each *Track* has step-by-step instructions and ways to measure students' progress. Once they have chosen a *Track*, though, they are not stuck there! They can change *Tracks* at any time, although it is not recommended they change often as they may have to do some backtracking and will almost certainly have to acquire new archery equipment, but no one will have to start from scratch. There are so many exciting ways to shoot arrows, we don't want anyone to miss any of the fun.

Olympic-style	Compound	Traditional
This will focus on developing good basic form, in stages, that will allow archers to progress toward elite form as older youths/adults.	This will include both "fingers" and "release aid" forms but primarily "unlimited" categories as the others will be encompassed en route.	This will include classic longbow (self- or laminated bows) as well as modern longbow (FITA Barebow).

Rationale The rationale for the ICPs and *Tracks* is that young archers begin their archery experiences at any age between about eight and eighteen years old. Consequently, the curriculum cannot be rigid, like a school structure in which all eight-year olds are in the third grade. In addition, archers have widely varying desires as to what they want to get out of archery as well as widely varying aptitudes for the sport, consequently a self-paced system seems desirable. Archery offers a variety of configurations (styles) to pursue, so allowance needs to be made for these aspects of personal taste. Archers also cannot choose between the various

Notes _____
_____
_____
_____
_____
_____
_____
_____

styles/forms of archery without knowing what they are and experiencing them, so a wide exposure of beginning archers to the possibilities is to be encouraged. Archers are also likely to move from place to place, so having a system that is easily transportable from program to program, even from state to state, is desirable.

Stages

In each *Track* there are four *Stages*: Stage 1: Getting Started, Stage II: Getting Better, Stage III: Achieving Mastery, and Stage IV: Owning the Sport. These Stages will take students, even if they have never shot an arrow before, up to the point where they are good enough to compete on the national level. After a student completes the requirements for a *Stage*, there are downloadable, customizable certificates of completion on the AER website (*www.archeryeducationresources.com*) for you to print out and award to your students.

Signposts

Each *Stage* has *Signposts* that tell the archers what we want them to do, what to do next, and how well they have to do it to move along the *Track* from *Stage* to *Stage*. What's a *Signpost*? Here is an example:

4. Obeys all safety rules (written/oral) .... ☐ Sometimes ☐ Often ☐ Always
   Even though rules are occasionally violated when they are being learned, there can be no violations for several weeks before an "always" can be given. *Must achieve "Always" to advance to the next Stage.*

Once a *Signpost's* form or execution element has been taught, your role as AER Archery Coach is to evaluate your students, either on some regular basis or whenever they want and you have the time. If they are struggling with some element of making a shot or you have seen them demonstrate their competence only a few times, you may give a "Sometimes" rating. If, class after class, they demonstrate their mastery of this *Signpost*, you will give them an "Often" rating. When, in your opinion, they do this without fail, they will receive an "Always" rating. They may collect all three ratings before they are done or jump right to "Often" when they are evaluated. (Jumping right to "Always" is not allowed as multiple evaluations are required for the assessment.) We will supply the criteria you will use to judge student-archer competence as we go along.

Notes _____

_____

_____

_____

_____

_____

_____

The example *Signpost* (above) is particularly important in that it requires an "Always" rating before students can move to the next *Stage*. In general, students need "Often" ratings to move on, but not necessarily on all *Signposts* as some may not apply to them. In *Stage I* and *Stage II* all archers will do almost all *Signposts*. After that you and your students can skip or edit *Signposts* based on their particular situation.

Coaching

As an AER Archery Coach you are expected to be able to explain everything in more detail, and give your student-archers specific exercises and drills to help them with what they are working on at the moment and, in general, help them through the process. The primary purpose of *This Guide* is to provide you with support for these tasks.

Coaching Principles Archery is best learned when archers are primed to learn, which is when they are immersed in it. Consequently you must be alert to "teaching moments" that occur when student-archers first notice some element of their own form or express dissatisfaction or discontent with the way things are going. We also follow the "One Next Thing" coaching structure in that an archer can only consciously concentrate on one thing at a time, so we give archers only one thing to work on at a time. (Each *Signpost* is a "next thing.")

Student-archers will be encouraged to make their own decisions, in consultation with their parents if underage, and informed by you, the coach. They will also be discouraged from making *Track* changes frivolously, but if the goal is to have student-archers become independent, we cannot start by ignoring their independence.

A rock bottom principle is that it is okay for a student to pursue archery just "for fun." To exclude these students would also exclude the possibility that they could change their minds. We earnestly believe that competition is part of the fun and a big part of what can be learned, but it is just a part, not the whole. AER is an inclusive, not an exclusive, organization.

Please consult the Appendices for AER archery-specific coaching principles.

Competition

Student-athletes may begin competing on any *Track* and at any *Stage* (assuming

Notes _____

_____

_____

_____

_____

_____

_____

such competitions and competition categories are available). But any student-athlete wanting to represent the program (as part of a competitive team or to be able to wear an AER shirt while competing, for examples) must have both competition and deportment goals for each competition.

Competition Goals are, at first, simple process-oriented goals, for example, "maintain a strong bow arm for at least 80% of shots taken." Later, goals may become more extensive and complicated but should always emphasize process, not outcome (*e.g.* score or "winning").

Deportment Goals are goals based on behavior at the tournament, such as "no advice will be given to other archers" or "no trash talking will occur on the field." A recommended goal for first competitions will always be "to have fun."

These goal sheets will be signed by both archer and coach before time and a "report card" will be created by both the archer and the coach giving grades (A, B, C, etc.) for how well each goal was met, after the competition. Competition Goal Sheets are available for download and printing in the Coaches Section of the AER website (*www.archeryeducationresources.com*).

Self Study Mode

For those students who are not attending an AER Archery Course because: there isn't one near them, they'd rather work alone, they are home schooled, whatever the reason, we have a Self Study Mode available. This is more complicated and more expensive because participants have to buy reference works and acquire all of their own equipment, even targets, and find a safe place to shoot . . . but if that is what they want to do, we think this is a good way to do it.

This Guide

This Guide has been designed to be useful in training you to use this curriculum as well as being a reference later; consequently there is more than a little repetition. There is also considerable overlap between the *Tracks*, and many of the *Stage I* and *Stage II Signposts* are essentially identical.

Navigation Essentially what you have in hand is the *Archer's Guide*, but with comments, notes, and additional appendices. This is so you can know what they (might) have read as well as having the information you need for a particular part

Notes

of a *Stage* in their Curriculum Plan. All notes and references can be found in the margins (in AER Red).

In this guide you will be provided:
- when and how to introduce clickers
- when and how to introduce bow/finger/wrist slings
- when and how to introduce stabilizers
- when and how to introduce bow sights
- when and how to introduce release aids
- when and how to introduce finger tabs
- when and how to adjust draw weight
- when and how to change arrows
- when and how to adjust shooting distances
- when and how to introduce field archery
- when and how to perform *Signpost* evaluations
- how to tune bows/arrows
- what basic rounds are shot by archers of these styles
- how to locate information on the internet (especially the AER website which we are going to load up for you)

Also don't forget your basic instructor and program guides have useful information in them, such as:
- how to keep track of all of the paperwork
- standard forms for record keeping and informing participants (rules, insurances, etc.)

. . . and lots more, too.

AER operates on a "continuous improvement" basis, so if you find mistakes in any of our products or you have suggestions as to how we might make this better and more helpful, please contact us.

Please be aware that this is not the only way to teach archery, but it is *a* way, the very best we could come up with. If you think you know of a better way to teach something, please accept the challenge to prove it. If you think you can do so, we will be setting up part of the AER website (*www.archeryeducationresources.com*) where you can share what you have learned and, in future versions of this curriculum, we will change what we recommend to reflect best practices (with full attribution for your contribution, of course).

Notes _____

Other Guides

Whole books have been written on single topics that we will be addressing and it is quite impractical to address these topics in the same level of detail here. So, we are recommending a number of very helpful resources to you. Many will be available for free on our website (the Easton Arrow Tuning Manual, helpful magazine articles, etc.). There are some books, though, that we recommend you read and these will be made available on the AER website. Here are our recommendations:

All Tracks

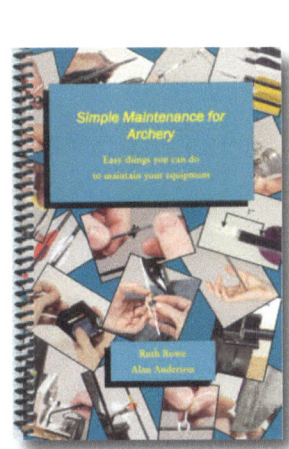

Simple Maintenance for Archery
by Alan Anderson and Ruth Rowe

This is a great little book that has step-by-step instructions (with photos) on how to do almost all maintenance on bows and arrows. It is highly recommended, in fact, all archers and coaches need a copy of this book.

Easton Arrow Tuning and Maintenance Guide
by Easton Archery

Easton Archery makes the vast majority of aluminum and aluminum-carbon arrow shafts in the world. This tuning guide is a free download (from all over the place as well as the AER website). Though it has come out in a number of editions, the earlier editions are more appropriate for what we are doing (the most recent goes into the tuning of $600/dozen Olympic arrows). This guide covers all of the aspects of how to select arrow shafts, build arrows, and tune them. Highly recommended resource.

With Winning in Mind
by Lanny Bassham

There is no better place to start to learn about the mental game of archery (even though the author was a rifle marksman). This little book has sold over 100,000 copies to archers, golfers, dog agility trainers, and beauty pageant competitors. Obviously its contents have application to more things than archery. Highly recommended.

Traditional Track

You may or may not have a great many traditional archery students and you, your-

Notes

self, may or may not be interested in traditional archery. Here two sources from which to learn the basics. Most people can get by with the first.

Beginner's Guide to Traditional Archery
by Brian J. Sorrells

This is a basic little book that has a bit of a bowhunting slant, but it shows you the difference between the bowhunting form of traditional archery as it compares to the target form. There is a little section on basic tuning. A good place to start.

Traditional Archery
by Sam Fadala

This is a step up from "Beginner's Guide to Traditional Archery" and likewise covers all of the basics.

Olympic-Style Track

You are very likely to get quite a few Olympic-style archery students, so there are more recommendations.

Handbook of Modern Recurve Tuning
by Richard A. Cockrell

This is a step-by-step guide to tuning recurve bows. It is designed to be used as a reference and includes a set of instructions for each task.

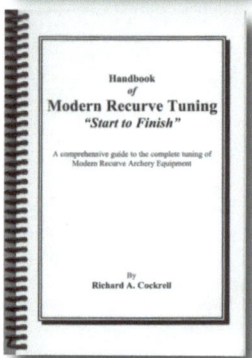

Fundamentals of Recurve Target Archery
by Ruth Rowe

Ruth Rowe covers all of the basics of shooting Olympic-style from a coach's vantage point. This book is not as comprehensive as "The Simple Art of Winning," but maybe not as overwhelming, either.

The Simple Art of Winning
by Rick McKinney

This is the "bible" of Olympic-style archery (American-style). Written by a three-time World Champion and two-time Olympic silver medalist.

Notes _____

Compound Track

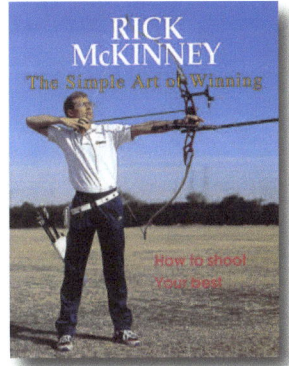

Compound archery is the most popular form of archery in the U.S., so you should expect quite a few Compound Track students, but from the simple fact that compound bows are really quite heavy, many youths begin with lighter recurve bows and switch to a compound bow when their arm and shoulder muscles develop to be able to hold them in place at full draw. Because compound bows use mechanical advantage to launch arrows, tuning and adjusting them is a much more mechanical process, so these books are a bit more "engineery" than the others.

Tuning Your Compound Bow, 4th Ed.
by Larry Wise

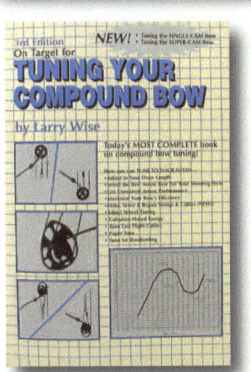

Compound bows are mechanical contraptions and professional archer, coach, and bow mechanic Larry Wise walks you though all of the details. Covers bows (all styles of compounds) and arrows. Will be intimidating to those new to compound bows, but start by skimming to find the basics and skip over the more complicated bits.

Core Archery
by Larry Wise

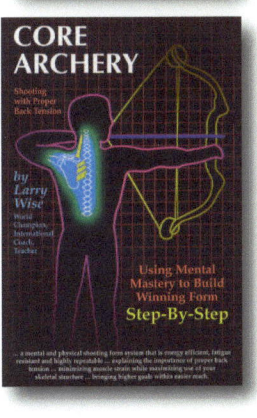

This little book not only covers compound bow shooting form but all of the bio-mechanical reasons for why we shoot them they way we do. There is no better book on compound bow shooting form and execution.

We do not recommend that you rush out and buy all of these books. If you are on a budget, try your local library first. See if you can borrow a copy of a book you are interested in from another coach. Read it and, if you find it helpful, acquire your own copy. "Try before you buy" is not only a guide to investing in archery equipment, but archery books, too. As we said, if you find the book valuable, by a copy as a "thank you" to the author, then pass your old copy on to a new coach.

A key element in becoming a better coach is that you are always "becoming" a better coach, meaning that the learning never stops.

The AER Team
www.archeryeducationresources.com

Notes

Beginning on the next page is the **The Complete Archer's Guide to the AER Recreational Archery Curriculum** which has been annotated to help you teach the curriculum.

The only difference is the page size (to allow space for the comments). Even the page numbers are the same as in the Archer's Guide so that you can refer students who own that book to specific pages you want them to read.

The *Archer's Guide* is available (without the annotations) for purchase by your students at:

www.archeryeducationresources.com
and
Amazon.com.

Archery Education Resources
Recreational Archery Curriculum
Preface

Introduction

When we comment on a topic, it will be in red type in the margin . . . just like this . . .

If you are reading this it is probably because you have taken an archery class or got a dose of archery at summer camp or even at school and you would like to get really, really good at it. Well, congratulations, this is the beginning of your path to archery excellence!

What you will find on these pages are descriptions of everything you have to do to become an excellent, even an elite, archer. Here are some of the key features:

Individual Curriculum Plans

Everything is integrated into your own personalized Individual Curriculum Plan (ICP). All of the steps you need to take are on the plan. including very short descriptions of all *Signposts*. Your AER Archery Coach will lead you through performing all of the tasks on the plan and will help you customize it to fit your needs and interests. In an AER Archery Course, all you need is the Individual Curriculum Plan which comes free when you sign up for the course. This book is not required but is offered to those of you who want more information and for those who might want to go it alone (*see Self Study Mode below*).

Tracks

You can follow any of three *Tracks*: Olympic-Style Archery, Compound Archery, or Traditional Archery. Each *Track* has step-by-step instructions and ways to measure your progress. And once you have chosen a *Track*, you are not stuck there! You can change *Tracks* at any time, although it is not recommended you change often as you may have to do some backtracking and acquire new archery equipment (but you will not have to

An Olympic-Style Archer.

. . . or even down here!

Notes _____

start over). There are so many exciting ways to shoot arrows, we don't want you to miss any of the fun.

The Olympic-Style Track addresses the only style of archery used in the Olympic Games.

Here you start with a recurve bow and sequentially add things like stabilizers, bow sights, cushion plungers, and clickers until you have a full kit. Along the way you learn the ins and outs of making every accessory an accuracy enhancing tool.

The Compound Track If you are more interested in shooting a compound bow, we offer two modes of compound instruction—shooting with your fingers on the string or with a mechanical release aid. From the foundation you build, you can select any one of the dozens of different styles of compound bow shooting.

You start with a bare compound bow and sequentially add things like stabilizers, bow sights, launcher rests, and release aids until you have a full kit. You will learn how to place every arrow just where you want it.

A Compound Archer

The Traditional Track addresses not only the style of Robin Hood, but includes "modern traditional" (FITA Barebow), too.

A Traditional Archer

Whether you like the historically famous wood bows of centuries ago or their high tech, modern equivalents, you will learn how to shoot with incredible accuracy in a step-by-step process.

We recommend that archers choosing the *Traditional Track* and who do not yet have their own equipment, start out using program recurve bows.

Compound Track archers can start with a *Genesis* (or *Genesis*-type or "zero letoff") bow, if they can handle the mass of the bow. *Olympic-Style Track* archers start with recurve bows. In fact, all can start (through *Stage I*) with recurve bows to good effect.

A FITA Barebow Archer

Notes _____

Disabled Archers

Student-archers are expected to acquire their own equipment before they begin *Stage II* (either by purchase or loan or trade or . . .).

Stages

In each track there are four *Stages*: Stage 1: Getting Started, Stage II: Getting Better, Stage III: Achieving Mastery, and Stage IV: Owning the Sport. These *Stages* will take you, even if you have never shot an arrow before, up to the point where you are good enough to compete on the national level.

This manual covers all three *Tracks* and each *Stage* of them. Whichever *Track* is selected, you will start out with archery's most basic configuration: bow and arrow. You will learn archery safety, basic archery posture, and how to execute a shot. From then on, as you shoot arrows, we will help you improve your form and execution to produce accurate results and in no time at all you will have made it out of the *Stage* you are in and on to the next *Stage*.

Signposts

Each *Stage* consists of *Signposts* that tell you what to do, what to do next, and how well you have to do to move along the *Track* from *Stage* to *Stage*. What's a *Signpost*? Here is an example:

4. Obeys all safety rules (written/oral) . . . . . . ☐ Sometimes ☐ Often ☐ Always
   Even though rules are occasionally violated when they are being learned, there can be no violations for several weeks before an "always" can be given. *Must achieve "Always" to advance to the next Stage.*

Once a *Signpost's* form or execution element has been taught, your AER Archery Coach will evaluate you regularly or whenever you want and he has the time. If you are struggling with an element or you have only been able to demonstrate your competence a few times, you may receive a "Sometimes." If, class after class, you demonstrate your mastery of this *Signpost*, you will receive an "Often" rating. When, in the opinion of your Coach, you do this without fail, you will receive an "Always" rating. This example *Signpost* is particularly important as it requires an "Always" rating before you can move to the next Stage. In general, you need "Often" ratings to move on,

Be cautious—don't sign off archers at the "Always" level too easily, especially here. Safety is the #1 overarching goal. Insist on the rules being followed. Make notes on a student's ICP when safety rules are violated after being taught. There is no rush to safety . . . and students should not get the impression that they must achieve the *Signposts* in numerical order. They may be working on all of the *Signposts* in a *Stage* simultaneously. This *Signpost* (*Stage I*, #4) is assumed to be included in every subsequent Stage as students are to get an "Always" before moving on to *Stage II*. Accept no backsliding in the later *Stages* with students saying things like "I already did that!" This curriculum exists to encourage learning and once things are learned, they should become permanent behaviors.

Notes _____

_____

_____

_____

_____

_____

_____

but not necessarily on all *Signposts* as some may not apply to you. You and your Coach can skip or edit *Signposts* based on your particular situation.

Coaches

If you are part of an AER Archery Course using this curriculum, you will also have an AER Archery Coach trained in how to teach you what you need to learn and help you figure out whether you have learned enough to move on to new aspects of archery. Your AER Archery Coach can explain everything in more detail, give you specific exercises and drills to help you with what you are working on at the moment and, in general, help you through the process.

Self Study Mode

For those of you who are not attending an AER Archery Course because: there isn't one near you, you'd rather work alone, you are home schooled, whatever the reason, we have a Self Study Mode available. This is more complicated and more expensive because you have to buy reference works and you will have to acquire all of your own equipment, even targets, but if that is what you want to do, this is the best way to do it.

The AER Team
www.archeryeducationresources.com

It is encouraged that you say "I don't know . . ." when you are asked a question you can't answer. We hope you will add ". . . but, I will try to find out." Do watch out for students with insatiable curiosity, though. It is smart for you to ask how important it is that your student get an answer to their question. You could spend quite a bit of your time trying a satisfy what is idle curiosity. You can also throw the question back to the student to see if they can find an answer to their own question, from an Internet search, for example.

Notes _____

_____

_____

_____

_____

_____

_____

_____

Getting Started

Step 1 Pick a Track The first decision you have to make is to pick a *Track*. There are literally dozens of different styles and configurations of bows and arrows, but the three AER *Tracks* cover the core information and techniques needed for any of them.

The Olympic-Style Track addresses the only style of archery used in the Olympic Games.

Here you start with a recurve bow and sequentially add things like stabilizers, bow sights, cushion plungers, and clickers until you have a full kit. Along the way you learn the ins and outs of making every accessory an accuracy enhancing tool.

The Compound Track If you are more interested in shooting a compound bow, we offer two modes of compound instruction—shooting with your fingers on the string or with a mechanical release aid. From the foundation you build, you can select any one of the many different styles of compound bow shooting.

You start with a bare compound bow and sequentially add things like stabilizers, bow sights, launcher rests, and release aids until you have a full kit. You will learn how to place every arrow just where you want it.

The Traditional Track addresses not only the style of Robin Hood, but modern traditional style (FITA Barebow), too.

Whether you like the historically famous wood bows of centuries ago or all of their high-tech modern equivalents, you will learn how to shoot with incredible accuracy in a step-by-step process.

Step 2 Start Shooting AER believes that archery is fun and we start in the first *Stage* of every *Track* with shooting arrows, lots of arrows. Archery sessions include games, drills, mock competitions, real competitions, and fun! The sheer fun of shooting arrows is never lost. Even if you get frustrated from time to time, we will emphasize the fun involved while we get you out of your slump and you are back on *Track*.

This manual covers all three *Tracks* and each *Stage* of them. Because of this you can sneak a peek at what the other *Tracks* are learning. You can look ahead to see what will happen next in your *Track*, but most importantly you can get help understanding what you need to do to become a first-rate archer, step-by-step.

Notes _____
_____
_____
_____
_____
_____
_____

Whichever *Track* you select you will start out with archery's most basic configuration: bow and arrow. You will learn about archery safety, about basic archery posture, and how to execute a shot. From then on, as you shoot arrows, we will help you improve your form and execution to produce accurate results and in no time at all you will have made it out of the *Stage* you are in and on to the next *Stage*.

Let's get started!

Archery Education Resources
Recreational Archery Curriculum
Olympic-style Track

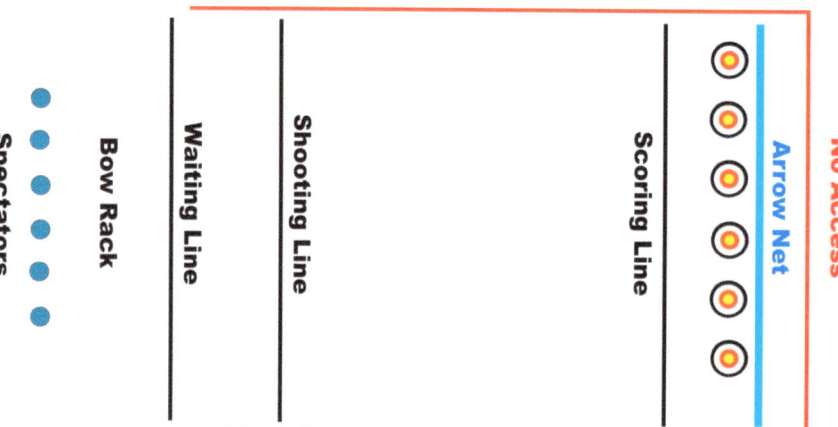

This diagram shows a typical layout for an indoor archery range. Archers are expected to be behind the waiting line when it is not their turn to shoot . . . behaving well.

Archery Education Resources
Recreational Archery Curriculum
Olympic-Style Track

Introduction

There is a great deal of excitement in archery circles every four years when archery is contested in the Olympic Games. And Olympic-style archery is even more popular in other countries, such as Korea, France, Italy, and India. There are also other "world stage" events, such as national championships and world championships. While only a few people get to contest archery in major stadiums, archery is contested in smaller sites all over. Our classes are conducted at Parks and Recreation Centers, public school grounds and gymnasiums, and occasionally at permanent archery ranges. And whether the shooting area is set up temporarily or is permanent, it is set up as a target range, because this creates a safe environment in which to practice archery and, after all, Olympic-style archery is contested on target ranges (although Olympic-style archery is recognized in field archery, too). The first topic in AER archery classes is always orientation and safety. Safety will continue to be a topic as we help you build safe archery habits, because you don't have to think about a habit, it is just something you do.

Coaches are expected to teach all of the safety aspects covered in the AER Beginning Archery Class Instructor Guide. *Adherence to the safety rules surrounding pulling arrows —the most dangerous aspect of archery—is paramount. You need to have a zero-tolerance attitude toward safety violations.* Signpost *evaluations of "Often" should be delayed several lessons for any infraction.*

Signposts—Stage I Getting Started

Archery Safety

In every *Stage* of every *Track* our most important concern is your safety. Archery is a safe sport because safe behaviors are developed into habits and the nice thing about habits is you don't have to think about them, they are just something you do. Consequently all of the safety *Signposts* apply to all of the *Tracks* and all of the *Stages* and all require "Always" ratings for you to proceed forward. But don't fret about this, being safe is just part of having fun!

Good Behavior Is Expected The expectation is that when you are waiting behind the waiting line (*see diagram at left*), that you will do nothing dangerous, nor will you cause any discomfort for other archers. The *Signpost* that you will be

Notes _____

_____

_____

_____

_____

_____

_____

evaluated on looks like this:

1. Exhibits good behavior
   when not on shooting line .... ☐ Sometimes ☐ Often ☐ Always
   Other archers and archery equipment treated respectfully while staying behind the waiting line.
   Must achieve "Always" to advance to the next Stage.

The Whistle System The system used to direct a group of archers is called the "Whistle System." Here are the whistle system commands:

The Whistle System

Two Blasts	Archers may come to the shooting line.
One Blast	Archers may place an arrow on their bows and begin shooting.
Three Blasts	Archers may walk to the target to retrieve their arrows.
Five or More Blasts	Emergency letdown! Stop immediately and wait for instructions.

This system is used all over the world at every level of archery (even at the World Championships and the Olympic games), although at competitions an air horn rather than a whistle may be used. A "letdown" from full or partial draw is performed by pointing the arrow at the floor/ground (outdoors) or the target immediately in front of you (indoors) and easing the string back to it's undrawn position. In an "emergency letdown" you also take the arrow off of the bow and place it back in its quiver. The *Signpost* that you will be evaluated on looks like this:

2. Understands and
   follows the whistle system .... ☐ Sometimes ☐ Often ☐ Always
   Knows and obeys all four whistle system commands. *Must achieve "Always" to advance to the next Stage.*

Good Behavior Is Expected Everywhere Just as you are expected to behave in a safe and polite manner when off of the shooting line, the same is true when you are on the shooting line. Trying to distract another archer during a contest is unsportsmanlike and, in general, one doesn't even speak to other archers when "on the line." Here is your *Signpost*:

3. Exhibits good behavior
   when on shooting line .... ☐ Sometimes ☐ Often ☐ Always
   Does not talk to, or interfere with, other archers on the line. *Must achieve "Always" to advance to the next Stage.*

You are empowered to add to the Range Rules (for *your* classes, anyway)! If you are having a particular problem, write a new rule to deal with it. Remember to be positive and to state the behavior allowed, not the behavior forbidden, e.g. "Arrows always point to the target" rather than "never point an arrow at a person." Later you can remove the rule or keep it if it has particular utility. An ideal set of rules doesn't exist, but whatever they are they should be short, and positive, etc.

Notes _____

_____

_____

_____

_____

Usually the idea of good behavior only has to be explained to the 8-12 year-old set, but there are exceptions. If a student has trouble meeting this *Signpost*, ask the sponsor or site staff if he/she has a history of such behavior. Being forewarned is also being forearmed.

The Whistle System was changed in 2008, specifically the "Emergency Letdown" signal was changed from "four or more" blasts to "five or more." Some older materials may not reflect the change and, since it is not a major change, no fuss need be made.

During FITA competitions, if one archer complains about the behavior of another archer, it is taken seriously. A judge can monitor the situation and if the offending archer is judged to have deliberately tried to disadvantage another archer, he/she can be disqualified. For our purpose, this is only good manners. People talking trash on the line in a mean-spirited manner can only lead to a "no fun" situation which conflicts with our second overarching goal.

When you are evaluating *Signposts*, always focus on the Stage an archer is in. Here your archer is quite a beginner, so a high level of performance is not expected. What is expected is that the archer places his feet carefully and doesn't move them thereafter. The exact spacing, angle, etc. may vary (a little) and the student could still get an "Often" or "Always." More precision is expected later.

The Range Safety Rules Must Be Obeyed There are actually quite a few safety rules that apply when you are shooting arrows on a target range. We encourage coaches to post the standard "range rules" so you have an opportunity to read them. Some rules will be given only orally, so you need to listen carefully as there is no tolerance for violations of safety rules. A typical set of range rules is supplied on the next page.

The *Signpost* involved follows. The safety *Signposts* have not been duplicated at each *Stage* as always behaving safely is a requirement to pass out of the first stage. All safety rules will be enforced at each *Stage* of your program.

4. Obeys all safety rules (written/oral) .... ☐ Sometimes ☐ Often ☐ Always
   Even though rules are occasionally violated when they are being learned, there can be no violations for several weeks before an "always" can be given. *Must achieve "Always" to advance to the next Stage.*

Basic Archery Form

The other major component of *Stage I* is achieving good basic archery form and execution. This is done with the only equipment being a bow and arrows (and an armguard, which is mandatory archery safety equipment).

Taking Your Stance The first part of any archery shot involves placing your feet properly; this is called "taking your stance." The stance everyone starts with is called the "square stance." In this stance your feet are about shoulder width apart with the tips of your shoes lying on a line that leads to the center of the target. (The line isn't there, you have to imagine it.) The line that is there, the shooting line, is supposed to be "straddled," that is you have one foot in front of the line and one foot behind.

Note that this puts you sideways to the target, which is good because that's the best way to shoot arrows. Turning your body either left or right at this stage will interfere with your making good shots, so it is important to not move your feet after you have taken your stance. Here is the associated *Signpost*:

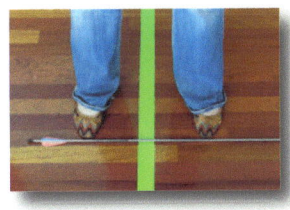

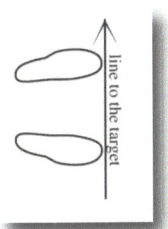

In a square stance the tips of your toes are on a line to the center of the target.

1. Adopts a square stance .... ☐ Sometimes ☐ Often ☐ Always
   Tips of shoes make line to center of target, feet shoulder-width apart, straddling the shooting line.

Standing Well The next step is to have good posture, which is not what your Mom or the military wants from you. You need to stand straight and relaxed. Your

Notes _____

_____

_____

_____

_____

_____

Archery Range Rules

1. Know and obey all range commands.
2. Keep your arrows in your quiver until you are told to shoot.
3. Always wear your arm guard and finger tab.
4. Only use the arrows the instructor gave you and remember what they look like.
5. Always keep your arrows pointed down or toward the target.
6. If you drop an arrow, leave it on the ground until you are told to get your arrows.
7. Always walk at the archery range.

Archery Range Whistle Commands
Two Blasts "Archers to the Shooting Line."
One Blast "Begin Shooting."
Three Blasts "Walk forward and get your arrows."
Four or More Blasts "Stop shooting immediately! Wait for instructions!"

Archery Range Procedures
- Stand behind the waiting line until you hear two (2) whistle blasts or "Archers to the shooting line." Take your bow and straddle the shooting line.
- Keep your arrows in your quiver until you hear one (1) whistle blast.
- After you have shot all of your arrows, step back from the shooting line, set your bow on the rack, and wait behind the waiting line.
- After everyone is done shooting and is behind the waiting line, the instructor will blow the whistle three (3) times, then walk forward to the target line.

Pulling Your Arrows
- Two archers at a time from each target may go forward from the target line to pull their arrows.
- Stand to the side of the target and make sure that no one is standing behind your arrows.
- Pull your arrows out, one at a time, and put them into your quiver.
- After you have pulled all of your arrows, return to the waiting line.

Notes _____
_____
_____
_____
_____
_____
_____
_____

Younger archers tend to elevate their shoulders, neck, and head when they draw the bow (re "Standing Well"). Watch for this. Encourage them to keep their upper body "down." Reason: elevating the chest and shoulders restricts the ability of the back muscles to come into play while drawing the bow (as they are involved in the elevating).

Also see the comment below.

knees are neither bent nor locked back. Your chest is not puffed out, it is relaxed downward. Here is the associated *Signpost*:

2. Exhibits good archery posture .... ☐ Sometimes ☐ Often ☐ Always
   Stands relaxed and straight up and down, doesn't lean left or right, forward or backward. Knees straight but not locked.

Keeping Your Shoulders Down A particular part of archery posture that has its own Signpost involves your shoulders. Your shoulders are to be "down." If you don't know what this means ask your coach about the *AER Shoulders Up, Shoulders Down Drill*. We are not telling you why this is done this way; if you are curious, ask your coach. (In general, we are organizing your skeleton and muscles to work together most effectively.) The *Signpost* here is:

3. Keeps shoulders low .... ☐ Sometimes ☐ Often ☐ Always
   Shoulders are in the "down" position throughout shot.

Setting Your Bow Hand One of the spots beginner's struggle is in placing their bow hand onto the bow. The spot on the bow where this happens is called the "grip," and it looks much the same as the grip on a pistol, but you neither hold it like a pistol, nor do you "grip" or squeeze the bow. You don't want to squeeze the grip area of the bow because doing that doesn't help you draw the bow; in fact squeezing the bow detracts from your ability to pull the bowstring. (It makes you stiff and weak!) Holding a bow like a pistol puts the back of the hand parallel with the bow, which causes the archer's elbow to turn inward (sideways), very close to the path the bowstring takes when it is "loosed." So close, in fact, that it is easy for the string to whack your elbow that way and your armguard won't protect it as it is protecting your forearm, not your elbow!

To set your bowhand correctly, you start with your hand relaxed, flat, and with your palm facing the floor/ground. You slide your hand (between thumb and first finger) into the "throat" (deepest part) of the grip. Then you bend your wrist down onto the bow and relax your fingers (they do not wrap around the bow). The knuckles of your bow hand are now at about a 45° angle to the ground, which is one way for you to check to see that you've got it right (*see photos*). The bow actually sits on the pad of your thumb and doesn't touch the other half of your hand. When you do this you

It is not "normal" to raise a bow while keeping the shoulders "down." One has to exert some effort to keep them down. This is a primary reason why they are to do the steps of the shot sequence as separate steps. (Note—They aren't introduced to shot sequences until *Stage II*, but you are guiding them that way all along.) During the "Raise the Bow" step, one makes a conscious effort to keep the shoulders "down." This is very hard to learn if one is simultaneously drawing the bow. Make sure students don't "draw on the way up" . . . until they can draw with their shoulders "down" as a matter of habit. Introduce the *AER Shoulders Up, Shoulders Down Drill* here if you haven't already done so.

Notes _____

_____

_____

_____

will find that your elbow has rotated away from the path of the bowstring and out of harm's way.

There are a few people who are very, very flexible and who can adopt this bow hand yet still have their elbow sideways. These archers need to learn how to rotate their elbows out of the way. Here is a test to see if you are one of these people: take a bow and set your bow hand properly, then hold the bow out as if you were going to shoot (don't use an arrow as you won't be shooting). Then bend the elbow of your bow arm. The bow should swing around and come up against your chest (*see photo right*). If it does, you are good to go. If the bow swings up in an arc toward your head, ask your coach about the *AER Elbow Rotation Drill*. Rotating your elbow will become one of the steps you will need to do to safely shoot arrows. Please, whacking your elbow is not a nice way to learn this! Do the test and find out whether you are doing it right or not.

Here's your *Signpost*:

BAD

GOOD

4. Exhibits good bow hand .... ☐ Sometimes ☐ Often ☐ Always
   Bow hand is relaxed, in proper position with bow sitting on pad of thumb, fingers curled slightly and relaxed.

Positioning Your Head Another posture element that gets its own *Signpost* is head position. Since you are standing sideways to the target, you must turn your head to look over your shoulder to see the target. This is correct archery posture. On the other hand, tilting your head at all makes everything more difficult. Student-archers often do this in an attempt to "look down the arrow" as a way to aim. This technique does not work for a number of reasons, the primary one being that as soon as the arrow comes off of the bow, it falls, therefore it cannot hit the point sighted at. At very close distances, like where we begin shooting arrows, the amount the arrow falls is very small leading to the impression that "this works" but, as you move back from the target, the arrow will impact lower and lower compared to the aiming point. The idea of using the arrow to aim with is not a bad idea as you will see later, but the technique of looking down the shaft plainly does not work. Here is your *Signpost*:

5. Exhibits good head position through shot .... ☐ Sometimes ☐ Often ☐ Always
   Head is turned toward target erect, neither tilted nor dipped.

The bowhand is a major problem area for students. It can be compounded by the use of wooden-handled recurve bows, which have thick grip areas which in turn make it hard for smaller students to get a proper bow hand on them. Lack of a good bow hand is a major cause of bruised bow arms. Show students the elbow bending test as a way of emphasizing that they can check themselves from time to time.

Tilted heads can be made erect with a finger. Use just one finger to reposition your archer's head properly. Once they have found out what the correct position is (and have resisted the urge to look down the arrow) they will be able to replicate it fairly easily.

Notes _____

_____

_____

Beginners need to know how to start (finger and elbow placement), how to pull (using their back muscles to rotate their draw shoulder with some torso rotation thrown in), and where they are going (to their firm anchor position). At the same time they are supposed to maintain their good archery posture! So, this is quite a complex task. In general, the more complex the task, the more time it takes to master, so you should not be too quick to give "Oftens" and "Always" here.

Drawing the String There are people who are very cautious and do things carefully and slowly. Others, more exuberant in nature, rush everything. Archery is done somewhere in the middle. If you are slow and cautious, it might take you ten seconds to draw the bow. This is too slow—your muscles are getting tired even as you pull and the longer it takes, the more tired you will be when the pull required gets greater toward the end of the draw. Energetic folks tend to yank the string back; you can recognize them because their arrows tend to fall off of their arrow rest when they pull without caution. It should take only 1-2 seconds to draw the string. This is not rushed, nor is it slow. It is smooth and strong. In the beginning you may take longer than this, 2-3 seconds, because you are still learning to get the bowstring all the way back to where it belongs. This is okay, but the goal is to draw the string in a smooth, strong, and controlled fashion.

This is done with the draw elbow level with the draw hand.

Here is the *Signpost* for drawing the string:

6. Draws the bow smoothly and in rhythm .... ☐ Sometimes ☐ Often ☐ Always
   Bow string is drawn smoothly and quickly without hurrying, draw elbow is high.

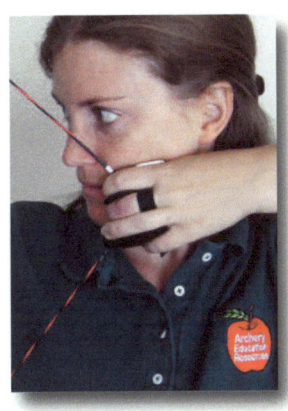

Finding Your Anchor Position An "anchor" position in archery refers to the position of your drawing hand with regard to your body. Over the years there have been many anchors, from behind the ear to down at the chest, but for consistent accuracy, the anchor position must bring the bow string in front of your aiming eye. You will be taught two anchors—a *high* anchor first and a *low*, or Olympic-style, anchor later.

The high anchor is found by pressing your draw hand against your face such that the tip of your index finger is positioned in the corner of your mouth and your top finger wraps around your cheek bone (*see photo*). If you have difficulty finding this position, your coach will help you find it, first without a bow and then with a bow. This is the *Signpost* for finding your anchor position:

7. Exhibits a reasonably tight anchor .... ☐ Sometimes ☐ Often ☐ Always
   Anchor position is consistent with draw hand pressed against face (high anchor) bringing the string in front of the aiming eye.

Many students, young and old, are hesitant to have something unknown (like a bowstring and the end of an arrow) right next to their eyes or face (or glasses). Others it doesn't bother. So, it may take some patience with the sensitive ones, which is entirely their due. And once they are convinced it won't hurt them, they become fine with it.

The biggest bugaboo is having the thumb of the draw hand "up" which equates to "in the way." The thumb must be held "down" so it ends up under the jaw at anchor. Then it can be relaxed. Having the thumb in any "up" position blocks the hand from achieving a tight anchor. Having the pad of the draw hand thumb on the little fingernail positions both thumb and little finger correctly. After anchor has been found, these can be relaxed.

Notes _____

Following Through Bowlers follow through, golfers follow through, baseball batters follow through, and . . . archers follow through. The archery "followthrough" form element is simply to maintain your body position after each arrow is shot for at least one second. A key part of this, because your bow hand is relaxed, is that your bow will rock gently in your hand after the bow string is released. This rocking is an indicator that tells you how well you executed the release of the string and held your followthrough position by how regular it is. (Does it happen the same way each time?) This is the *Signpost* for following through:

8. Exhibits good followthrough .... ☐ Sometimes ☐ Often ☐ Always
   After the string is released, bow arm stays up and draw hand moves backward along face.

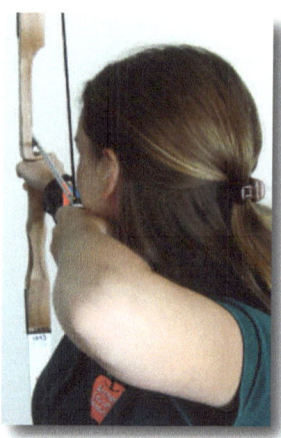

Good alignment (top) is essential for consistency; poor alignment (below) causes "plucked" releases (bottom) and poor consistency.

Getting in Line This *Signpost* holds the key for consistent accuracy. In order for everything to work in this style, your draw elbow has to be in line with your arrow at full draw (*see photos*). It is that simple. Most beginners start with their draw elbows too low and sticking out away from them. As you progress your elbow needs to get "in line" as this alignment with the arrow allows your fingers to slip from the string in the most relaxed manner. (Tense draw fingers can cause arrows to fly sideways!) The sooner you can get into this position, the sooner everything else comes together to make great shots.

A key element in archery is achieving good form as quickly as possible because you do not want to practice doing it wrong! At some time or other in school one of your teachers had you rewrite each of your misspelled words on an assignment ten times. This is a fairly good rule of thumb: if you practice something *incorrectly*, it will take ten times the work doing it *correctly* to fix the incorrect execution. So, if you shoot arrows 10 times incorrectly, it takes 100 correct shots to make doing it correctly somewhat of a habit (1000 incorrect shots requires 10,000 correct ones!). So, never settle for doing something "any old way." If it is not right, start over.

This is the *Signpost* for achieving good alignment:

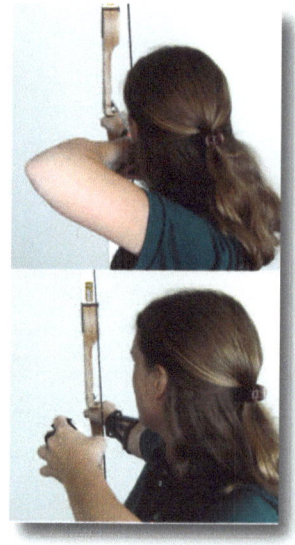

9. Exhibits good alignment .... ☐ Sometimes ☐ Often ☐ Always
   At full draw, draw elbow lines up with the arrow line extended backward.

"Grouping" Your Shots When anyone first begins shooting arrows, we celebrate all "bull's eyes." But as time goes on, the goal is not just hitting the target's cen-

If the bow hand is relaxed the bow will "bow" (as in to "take a bow") and it takes about 1-2 seconds for it to do so, so one of the cues you can use is "Hold your form until the bow 'bows.'" This is a good indicator of how long to hold their followthroughs as the amount of time is constant (as opposed to "until the arrow hits the target" in which it is not) and it encourages good form. The same will be true when stabilizers are introduced, but the top limb will "bow" forward instead of backward as it will now.

Line, line, line! Alignment is the key to good form and accuracy (Getting In Line). If the draw elbow is behind the arrow, the forces in the bow and archer's body are arrayed properly and the draw wrist and hand can be relaxed and the fingers can come off the string as a unit. If there is a "kink" in the alignment, there is no relaxation and no smooth release. A ragged release causes the string to swing wildly (you can see this in slow-motion video) and arrows to fly all over the place. The importance of line cannot be emphasized too much—to coaches. Athletes should not be thinking about "line" as it is too abstract; their cues/shot thoughts are "reach to the target" (bow arm) and "swing elbow backward" (draw arm), both of which contribute to good line.

You can encourage students to keep track of their groups by asking them "How big are your groups, normally?" They often will not include "flyers" (arrows that don't group) at the beginning, which is okay . . . in the beginning. Archers typically use phrases like "I am holding the red" (all arrows in the red and gold (7-10 rings) or "I usually hold the five ring" (all arrows in the blue, red, and gold or 5-10 rings. Most people specify the yardage, too, but that comes later. As time goes on, more and more attention will be paid to the size of the groups. Right now attention is being paid to the act of grouping arrows and less so to their location. The key point is: if they can group their arrows they can move the group into the center with aiming techniques. If they can't group (a sign of inconsistent form), then aiming doesn't matter, so reasonable "grouping" must precede learning to aim.

ter, it is hitting it consistently, which is why the concept of "grouping" is introduced here. Shooting arrows that all land in (roughly) one place is even more important than hitting those bull's eyes, because if you can shoot arrows so they land all in the same place you can move those arrows to a new place using an aiming technique. (Most people prefer the center as a landing location.) But, if you can't "group" your arrows and you get a bull's eye, the next arrow will be somewhere else and each subsequent arrow in yet another location.

So, how do you get "good groups?" Grouping is an outcome of consistency; grouping is the outcome of doing the same thing, the same way, over and over. There is a very old saying: "Repetition is the Mother of Learning." This is true in archery, but repetition without good form and execution is worse than not practicing! You must strive to "do it right" over and over.

Be aware, though, that there is not a lot of "trying" involved. (Actually "trying too hard" blocks making progress in archery.) The target gives you feedback: either the arrows are in nice, tight groups, or they are not. If you are reasonably careful about how you shoot, even moderate amounts of practice will result in good groups in very little time.

Here is your first target-oriented *Signpost*:

10. Shoots good groups consistently .... ☐ Sometimes ☐ Often ☐ Always
   Three arrow groups fit into an eight inch circle two ends out of three at 10 yards. Must achieve "Often" to advance to the next Stage.

Aiming "Off the Point" Back when we addressed where an archer needs to put his or her head, the wrong idea of aiming by looking down the arrow shaft was mentioned. The idea of using the arrow was good but the wrong part (the shaft) was being used. An accurate aiming system, that needs no additional equipment attached to the bow, is the technique of *aiming off the point* (the arrow point).

Because we shoot arrows up into the air so they can arc down into the target (due to the large effect gravity has on relatively slow flying arrows), we hold the rear end of the arrow down under our aiming eye so that the arrow shaft points upward. If you are executing shots with good alignment, a soft bow hand, and a decent followthrough, your arrows will rarely miss left or right of a vertical centerline on the target. (We use a clock face for orientation on circular targets. The very top of the tar-

Notes _____
_____
_____
_____
_____
_____
_____

get is 12 o'clock, the bottom is 6 o'clock, the left edge 9 o'clock, and the right edge is 3 o'clock (*see diagram*). We can then specify any location on the target by naming the ring and the time, *e.g.* 6:30 in the red or 11 o'clock in the 3-ring. So, if you meet the requirements mentioned, your arrows will be in a narrow band from 12 o'clock to 6 o'clock and rarely left or right of that band. You will have solved the "windage problem" which is "How do I aim left and right?"

The other question: "How do I aim up and down?" is called the "elevation problem" and is more difficult to solve. You can do it by shooting many hundreds of arrows at each of a great many different distances and let your brain do the math, or you can use an aiming technique like "aiming off the point."

Here is how it works. Imagine that you are about to release the string on a perfect shot, one in which the arrow will strike the target dead center. Now imagine what you are seeing through your aiming eye just before the arrow is shot. This is called your "sight picture." Because you are focused on the target, the target is about the only thing you will notice, but in your field of view is part of the bow and also part of the arrow. The point of the arrow in your sight picture is in some position relative to the image of the target, *e.g.* blue ring at 6 o'clock. (If you haven't mastered all of the previous steps or if your bow and arrows aren't perfectly matched (and this typically is the case with borrowed or program equipment) you may be to one side or the other of that 12 o'clock—6 o'clock line; in any case, it is somewhere on or near the target). You release the arrow and it goes right into the center. Ah, but you want to do it again, don't you? Are their any clues as to how to get your body and bow back into that perfect full draw position time after time? The answer is "the position of the arrow point in your sight picture." *If your foot positions, posture, and shot execution are exactly the same and the arrow point is at the exact same place in your sight picture, the arrow will land in the same location.* This is aiming off the point.

There is one distance at which if you put the point onto the center of the target in your sight picture, the arrow goes into the center. This is called "point blank range." Archers now usually refer to it as being at their "point on target" distance or their

Notes _____

This point of aim diagram is from a pamphlet printed in 1932. The technique was invented in the mid-1800s.

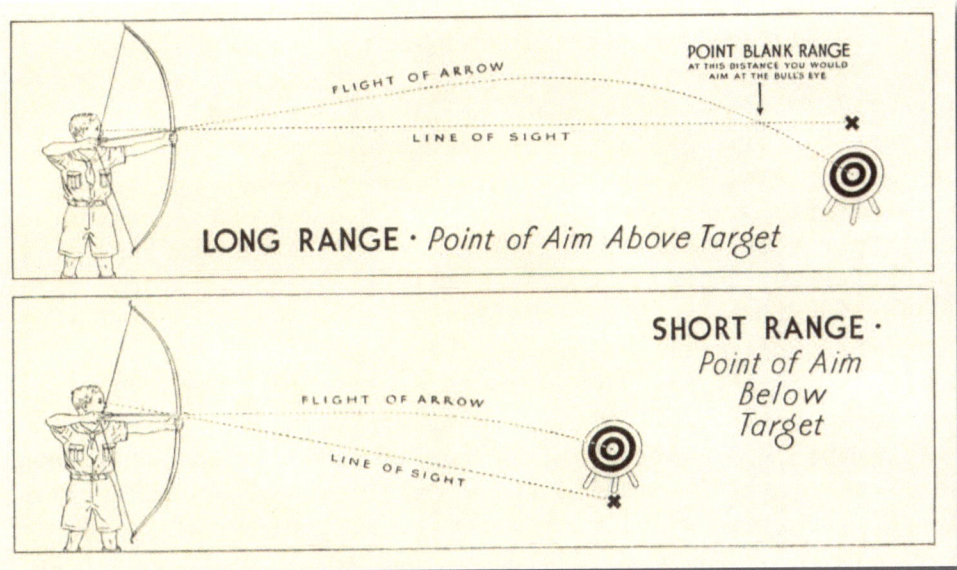

To answer the question, "I am going to use a bow sight, why do I have to learn this?" is obviously, "You don't have to." But, this is fun. It teaches part of the aiming technique needed to use a bow sight well, and it doesn't require all of the fiddling needed when setting up a bow sight to use. One possible tongue-in-cheek rejoinder is "It's boring to shoot just one way!"

"point on" for short. At closer distances than the point-on-target-distance, the point of aim is lower than the center and at longer distances than the point-on-target-distance, the point of aim is higher on the target. At very short distances, the POA (point of aim) may be on the ground or floor and for much longer distances it may be up on the wall or the hill, or trees on top of the hill (*see the diagram*)!

This is the *Signpost* for aiming off of the point:

11. Uses arrow point to aim with .... ☐ Sometimes ☐ Often ☐ Always
    Must be able to find and use a point of aim for at least one distance (7-15 yards).

Notes _____
_____
_____
_____
_____
_____
_____

Signposts—Stage II Getting Better
Must have completed requirements of Stage I before beginning.

Congratulations! By making it out of *Stage I* you are now quite a good archer. You know how to stand, fit an arrow to the string, raise the bow, draw it smoothly, release the shot cleanly and follow through . . . and your arrows go mostly into the center of the target at shorter distances. You can stop at this point and enjoy archery for the rest of your life this way. But, after you have acknowledged that you have come a long way, you might feel like there is more to learn . . . and there is. If you want to keep going then you need to learn *intermediate archery form* and in order for you to do so you must acquire your own equipment.

The equipment you need is the same equipment you have been using: bow, arrows, and armguard, but there is more you will have to get as you go (finger tab, bow sight, stabilizer(s), cushion plungers, clickers). The reason you need your own equipment is the equipment needs to be fitted to you. For example, now that your draw length has become somewhat regular, you don't need extra-long arrows (used by beginners for safety). You may need to adjust the bowstring's length or even change it for one made differently or from different materials. If you intend buying your own gear, ask your AER Archery Coach if he/she does "Bow Fittings." This is a service in the form of a private lesson that measures you up for the equipment style you favor, so that you will know exactly what to buy as well as where you can shop and what you can reasonably expect to pay.

If you are borrowing equipment, the same criteria apply, so consult your coach as to what exactly you need to acquire.

When you have your own equipment, the first thing you are going to want to do is set it up correctly. The first step is to set the brace/string height (twisting the string to make it shorter increases the brace/string height, untwisting the string decreases it—note that new strings tend to stretch somewhat and have to be twisted from time to time to keep them the same length) and placing a nocking point locator (like on your class bow) on the string. If this has not been done when you acquired your equipment, your Coach will assist you. Then you can start shooting your way through the next *Stage*.

Now You Need Your Own ...

bow

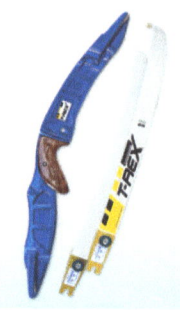

arrows

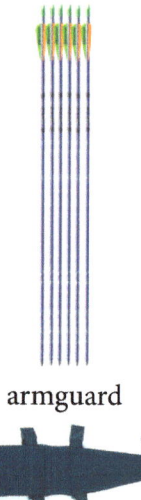

armguard

Notes _____

_____

_____

_____

_____

_____

_____

Intermediate Archery Form

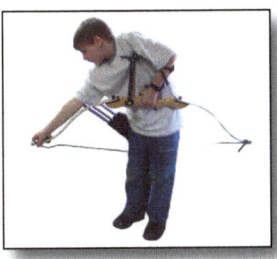

Bracing Your Bow Now that you have your own bow, it is time to learn how to *brace*, or string, your bow. There are quite a few ways to brace a bow (set the string into position); but only one way, the safest way, is recommended—using a bow stringer. Your coach will demonstrate how to do this safely (*see photo*) and then ask you to do it a couple of times to be sure you are doing it correctly. From that point onward, you can brace your own bow. You will want to acquire your own bowstringer for this purpose. This is the *Signpost* for being able to brace your bow:

1. Able to brace the bow .... ☐ Sometimes ☐ Often ☐ Always
   Able to brace and unbrace bow safely using a bowstringer.

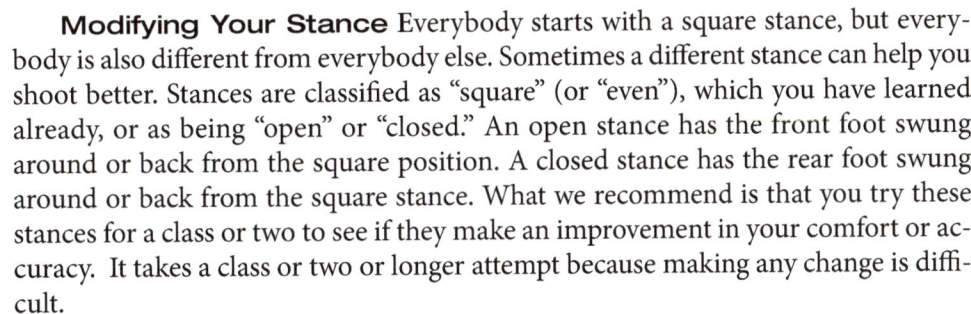

Modifying Your Stance Everybody starts with a square stance, but everybody is also different from everybody else. Sometimes a different stance can help you shoot better. Stances are classified as "square" (or "even"), which you have learned already, or as being "open" or "closed." An open stance has the front foot swung around or back from the square position. A closed stance has the rear foot swung around or back from the square stance. What we recommend is that you try these stances for a class or two to see if they make an improvement in your comfort or accuracy. It takes a class or two or longer attempt because making any change is difficult.

A basic AER learning principle is: *anytime you change something, your archery gets worse before it gets better*. Because archery is a repetition sport, you have had many repetitions of your archery shot making it comfortable and "normal." Whenever you make a change, it feels uncomfortable and "not normal" which automatically makes you worse! It takes a fair number of repetitions to overcome this effect and make the new way seem at least reasonable. And you can't evaluate whether the change was good or bad until you have taken many shots. If the "result" of the change is your archery gets worse and then gets better than when you started, it is a good change. If it gets worse and never gets back to where you were before the change, it is a bad change. But without a fair chance, you will never make any changes. Don't be a archer who says, "I tried that for ten minutes and it wasn't as good!" Nothing in archery will be better after only ten minutes of trying. (Of course, if something creates pain, we recommend you stop doing it immediately!)

Stances (from bottom to top) can be "square," or "open," or "closed," or "wide open" or done other ways (not shown).

All AER archery students must use a bowstringer to brace their bows, no exceptions!

See the Appendix *On Stances* for more detail. Be aware that because the square stance is taught to beginners, many seem to think it is the "baby stance." Nothing could be further from the truth. The square stance can be used by one and all for a great many purposes and for a great many styles, which is why it is taught first. If student doesn't want to experiment with a new stance, this *Signpost* may be skipped until later or altogether.

Notes _____
_____
_____

If you try, say, an open stance and it doesn't work for you, don't go straight to a closed stance and try that. Return to your "normal" square stance for several lessons and get back to the feel of "normal" before you try the closed stance (or anything else).

Generally, an open stance is the most popular stance (although popularity is not a guarantee of anything as every individual is unique) and a closed stance makes it easier to get into line. So, if you are struggling with getting or keeping good alignment, try the closed stance. If you want to look like all of the other archers, try the open stance.

But realize, you do not have to change your stance! In fact, unless you have certain evidence that a different stance works better for you, changing is not recommended. But if you don't try the other options you will never know if there is a better archery stance out there for you.

A prime criterion to evaluate form changes is "Can it be done the same way, each and every shot?" This is your *Signpost* if you modify your stance:

2. Adopts a personal stance consistently .... ☐ Sometimes ☐ Often ☐ Always
   If open or closed stance is adopted, must adopt that stance consistently.

Modifying Your Posture A refinement of the form you have learned so far is the *hip tuck* or "hip tilt." If you rotate your hips slightly (bottom of your hips is rotated forward), your back becomes flat (*see photos*) and your center of gravity drops slightly. The flat back allows your back muscles (instrumental in drawing the bowstring) freer reign and the lower center of gravity makes you more stable (less tendency to sway back and forth as you shoot). While this is a small change, so are all of the others as you build better form, but the sum of many small changes can be a big improvement in score! Here is the *Signpost* for your refined archery posture:

3. Exhibits good archery posture .... ☐ Sometimes ☐ Often ☐ Always
   Stands relaxed and straight up and down, doesn't lean left or right, forward or backward. Knees straight but not locked. Shoulders down. Small of back flat.

Using a Finger Tab Bows used in beginner classes are very light drawing. As you gain experience the amount of draw weight you can handle goes up. But as the draw weight goes up, so does the tension on the bowstring along with the pressure

Without the hip tuck, the archer's back is hollow; with it, it is flat.

This "flat back" produced by the hip tuck (Modify Your Posture) gives a more rounded back which, in turn, gives the archer's back muscles more range of motion to draw the bow. A stiff, military "chest out" posture uses much of the back muscles' range of motion to puff out the chest and does nothing to help an archer in his/her task, so it is to be avoided.

Notes _____

_____

_____

_____

it creates on your fingers during the draw. At very high draw weights, this pressure can damage the nerves in your fingers. Long before that would happen, the discomfort of shooting leads to some form of finger protection. The vast majority of target archers use a finger tab for this purpose. In addition to protecting your draw fingers, tabs also provide a slick surface for the string to slide from.

It makes no sense to stint when buying a tab because they do not cost much. The most expensive tabs cost almost $30, but a very good tab (the *Black Widow* tab made by the Wilson Brothers is our recommendation—*bottom in photo*) typically can be had for around $10, if not under $10. If you are a very serious archer, you may want to buy two, not because they wear out fast but they are small enough to get lost and you want to have a backup tab. If you alternate days using them, the two tabs will be near identical in their performance (both will be "broken in" to the same extent). There are many styles of tabs, even from a single manufacturer, so consult with your coach or read the catalogs or online information carefully.

At the same time you break in a new tab, you will probably want to try a "split-finger" placement on the bowstring. This usually happens when you begin to shoot longer distances (outdoors). Placing one finger above the arrow (the other two below) instead of all three below the arrow and using the same anchor position, effectively lowers the back end of the arrow the width of your top finger. This is actually a great deal. The effect is to point the arrow upward more and thus greater "cast" or distance can be had. The *Black Widow* tab has leather flaps between the top two fingers that protect your fingers from developing calluses and reduce "finger pinch," that is pinching the arrow between your top two fingers. The reason you were started "three fingers under" was that beginners tend to tense their hands when they draw, which if you use a "split-finger" position from the start a) causes the fingers to pinch the arrow and b) causes the string and the arrow to rotate away from (and fall off of!) the bow. This is very frustrating for beginning archers. The "three fingers under" approach eliminates this source of frustration and once beginning archers learn to relax their draw hands while drawing, a change to split finger is possible.

This is the *Signpost* for using a finger tab:

Finger tabs can be sources of problems but also sources of information. Tabs need to be fitted (trimmed if necessary; the tab's material must wrap around the top and bottom fingers somewhat as the string wraps around them) and worn snuggly. The draw fingers still need to be held in a fixed position (typically touching one another and the arrow), but without tension. As tabs wear, the indentations and wear patterns on the tab can tell you how that tab is being used. For example, if the indentation from the string is narrow, this indicates the tab being placed consistently on the string; if wide, maybe the archer is a little careless at this. The position of the indentation shows you where the string is regarding the fingers (you have to see where the archer wears his tab, of course) and the depth of the indentation shows you where the pressure is greatest and least. See *The Magic Release* by Don Rabska in the Coach Resources section of the AER website.

Notes

4. Uses an archery tab correctly .... ☐ Sometimes ☐ Often ☐ Always
   Can put on a fitted archery tab and use it properly as a guide to placing fingers on string.

Modern Bowhand Technique Recurve bow grips come in a number of styles. There are even companies that make custom grips to fit the best-selling bows. And many expert archers modify their bow's grip using auto body dent filler, tennis racquet wraps, tape, and other substances it make it exactly as they want. Rather than complicate matters unnecessarily, fine tuning of the grip of your bow will be left until later. There is only one exception to this recommendation: if the (removable) grip supplied with your bow really doesn't fit your hand or is quite uncomfortable, take it off. You can then wrap the grip area with "tennis racquet tape" to make a softer surface to place your hand. (Note—You do not want a sticky or non-slip surface there; you want your hand to slide into place.)

This is the *Signpost* for your new bow hand position:

5. Exhibits good bow hand .... ☐ Sometimes ☐ Often ☐ Always
   Bow hand is relaxed, with bow sitting on pad of thumb, fingers curled slightly and relaxed.

Drawing Smoothly There is little you have to change to bring your draw up to intermediate archer standards, if you have worked to get a quick, smooth draw in the previous *Stage*. If you have changed your finger position to "split-finger" and changed your bowhand positioning and have more draw weight to handle, then it will take some time for all of those elements to become comfortable again. Then with a little focus on your draw, you can get back to full draw position with the smooth, controlled, and quick draw you had using a lighter-drawing program bow. This *Signpost* is worded the same as before because the goal is the same, but reaching the goal will take some time and effort as things have changed a little bit:

6. Draws the bow smoothly and in rhythm ..... ☐ Sometimes ☐ Often ☐ Always
   Bow string is drawn smoothly and quickly without hurrying, draw elbow is high.

Anchors Away? It was mentioned in *Stage I* that there are other anchors and that you would be learning two. It is time to learn a *low* anchor. This typically happens as you move to longer distances (as with the split-finger string grip). Moving your anchor position from alongside your face to under your jaw lowers the back

In order for an archer to be relaxed (a requirement for performance) the draw must be smooth and strong, under control. Yanking on the string is a sign of fatigue (or cluelessness). Shaking while drawing or at full draw is a sign of being "overbowed"(too much draw weight), which pretty much kills any chance of achieving good form. Archers should be able to draw their bows smoothly and seemingly effortlessly with the bow held straight up and down (arrow level, pointed at target). Any other draw (higher, lower, draw elbow too low, etc.) is dangerous in the event of a premature loose of the string. If archers struggle to draw, they need less draw weight—this is an absolute.

There is no part of archery that is more "personal" than the grip area of the archer's bow. After the string is loosed, the arrow is still on the string and the bow still in the bow hand (the only remaining point of contact!) for about 20 milliseconds. This doesn't seem like much time, but if the bow is placed improperly in the bow hand or if the bow hand is not relaxed, there are forces being exerted on the grip that are acting when the string is let go. (The official term is "pre-loaded bow hand torque.") So, this is one area of the bow that archers will customize. This issue is de-emphasized early in the program.

Notes _____

_____

_____

_____

_____

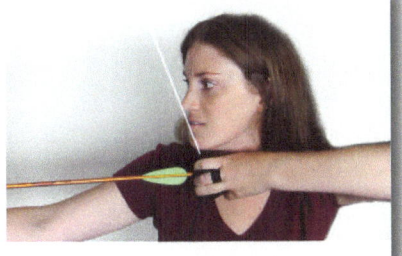

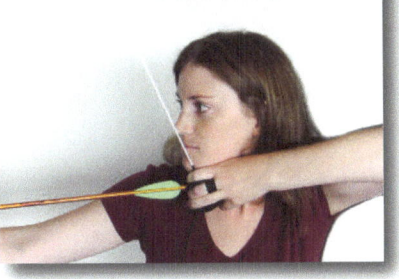

end of the arrow far more than any other change you are making. It creates much greater "cast" (distance shot) because of this.

To execute the low or "Olympic-style anchor use a light-drawing practice bow at first (even without arrows; just draw, anchor, and then let down the string—then repeat until comfortable). What you will find is that your head position has to be modified slightly. You must raise your chin a fraction of an inch. If you do not, your chin can block off your new hand position. The bow is drawn to slightly (1-2 inches, max) below the chin, then you "find your anchor" by raising your hand up until it presses against the bottom edge of your jaw (*see the photos*). Some people draw until the bowstring touches the corner of their chin before they raise their draw hand, and they say that, in this manner, they know whether they have drawn the string the correct distance. You do not want the bowstring any farther back (along the edge of your jaw) as the string will then drag on the skin of your face and worse, cause the arrow to fly offline!

Obviously, if this lower anchor gives you greater distance, it is less useful at short distance. Adult Olympic-style archers do not shoot anything shorter than 30 meters (about 33 yards) outdoors but field archers shoot arrows as close as at ten yards or so, so field archers will often use the high anchor for short shots and the low anchor for the long ones. So, it is best to practice both. (If you are not interested in field archery, you can just shoot the low anchor.)

This is the *Signpost* for evaluating your new low anchor:

7. Exhibits Tight Anchor .... ☐ Sometimes ☐ Often ☐ Always
Anchor position is consistent with draw hand pressed against jaw (low anchor) bringing the string in front of the aiming eye.

Stabilizing the Shot It is time to add a stabilizer to your bow. You are starting with a single "long rod" stabilizer because almost everyone uses one (for good reasons). You can modify the long rod setup with "V Bars" and/or other additional stabilizers later.

When you add a long stabilizer, it changes the feel of the bow greatly. Beginners must exercise extra care as you are not used to having that long thing sticking out in front and it is all too easy to hit people with it by swinging

Many beginners struggle with the anchor position as it requires the draw hand to be pressed firmly against the cheek (high anchor) or against the under jaw (low anchor). Hovering/floating the anchor hand is a major source of poor group sizes. The goal is to get the bowstring right in front of the aiming eye and "pressing the flesh" is a requirement for this and for the stability of the position. Head position cannot be affected by this. Note that this does not apply to compound archers shooting mechanical release aids. The anchor position of a release aid is closer to a "touch point" than it is a firm anchor (due to the peep sight being the thing that keeps its position from shot to shot). Be very cautious in applying technique from one kind of bow to others that are quite different (recurve bows and longbows are much alike, but compound bows, due to their let-off, can be very different).

Notes

your bow around too quickly.

Start getting used to it by drawing your bow on a target (at short distance) and then letting down. Repeat this several times before trying a shot. Start at short distance because adding the stabilizer changes the impact points of your arrows; in other words, all of your points of aim will have to be relearned. Now shoot some arrows, gradually getting back to the longer distances you were shooting at before the stabilizer was introduced.

If the stabilizer was borrowed just for a while so you could learn to use one, you will need to acquire your own. If you want to shoot a recurve bow without a stabilizer and bow sight, that is called FITA Barebow style and that style is covered mostly on the *Traditional Track*. So, if you change your mind about shooting Olympic-style, you will need to change *Tracks*. If you are unsure as to whether you want to shoot with a stabilizer, etc., keep going for a while as you are still adding things and you haven't experienced the full setup yet.

This is the *Signpost* for shooting with a stabilizer:

8. Shoots comfortably with a stabilizer .... ☐ Sometimes ☐ Often ☐ Always
   A long rod makes a bow easier to hold steady at full draw and through release.

Adding a Sling Most people shoot with some kind of "sling." It might be a finger sling, or a wrist sling, or a bow sling. Most Olympic-style archers choose finger or wrist slings, while most compound archers like the simplicity of a bow sling (*see photos*).

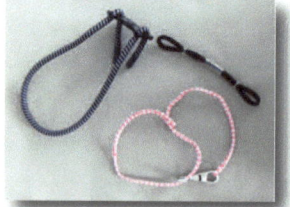
Bow slings (top left) attach to the bow and you put your hand through the loop before gripping the bow; finger slings (top right) connect bow thumb and first finger; wrist slings (bottom) go around the wrist, around the bow and hook back to the loop.

What the sling does is make it okay for you to have a relaxed bow hand throughout the entire shot. Even though you have been taught this is the correct way to shoot, sometimes subconsciously/unknowingly you are concerned about dropping the bow (which *is* embarrassing) and will involuntarily squeeze the grip. This tension is undesirable.

To get used to a finger sling or wrist sling (whichever you choose) put the sling on and then hold your bow out at arm's length and let go of it! When you do this, the bow will be caught by the sling! This may be a little dramatic, but you have just made the point to your subconscious mind that you cannot drop your bow if you are using your sling. Now, it can relax its vigilance regarding that happening.

You must use your sling for each and every shot you take from now on, no ex-

Some take readily to a stabilizer, others do not. Adding a stabilizer affects where the arrow hits the target and this change may create the impression "This thing is no good." For those who get this impression you can try some blank bale shooting—eyes closed—short range. This actually emphasizes the objectionable "feel" of the stabilizer, which can result in it being accepted quicker because what is being blocked out is the influence of the target and the inevitable judging of the shot by where it lands. Alternatively, you can try introducing the sling (below) and then go back to trying a stabilizer. Sometimes the lack of acceptance can be related to a feeling that the student is going to awkward by the stabilizer) and be embarrassed.

A sling is not absolutely necessary (the 2008 Men's Olympic Champion doesn't use one) but the vast majority of Olympic-style archers use them. If an archer's bow hand position is weak, they may be holding on to the bow, resulting in the feeling that they do not need a sling. Which is really an argument for working more on their bowhand position, not for whether to use a sling. An exercise to teach proper bow hand position is to kneel in front of an archer (and toward the bow side) as they shoot over your shoulder without a sling. (There is a question of trust here—or there should be!) Everything done properly results in the bow flying out of the archer's hand (which you are there to catch, of course)! They should be able to do this three shots in a row. Note that this is an advanced exercise and should not be done casually.

In the Appendix—*Making Your Own Gear* you learn how to make inexpensive wrist slings you can give away, use for a fundraiser, whatever. Check it out.

Also, do have your archers "drop their bows" (see the text immediately above) from time to time to reinforce to their subconscious minds that they do not have to "grab the bow" when an arrow is shot.

Following through can be practiced while dry-firing the bow! The archer has to be on the shooting line, but has no arrow in her bow. The bow is held in the position it would be while aiming, except that the draw is 2-3 inches (max!). The string is loosed and the bow makes its "bow." Another way to do this that is more realistic is to attach a loop of string to the nocking point. The size of the loop = draw length – brace height. Then the archer puts her fingers through the loop and assumes full draw position (which results in 1-2 inches of draw—if not, shorten the loop). The string is loosed and the followthrough ensues.

ceptions! You are creating a new habit.

This is the *Signpost* for shooting with a sling:

9. Shoots comfortably with a sling .... ☐ Sometimes ☐ Often ☐ Always
Uses a finger/wrist sling comfortably and easily.

Still Following Through There is a little you need to modify in your followthrough. The difference is that with a long rod stabilizer, your bow will tend to gently rock forward upon releasing the shot, instead of rocking backward as it did before. But the same rationale applies: the followthrough gives feedback about the latter stages of the shot through its consistency.

This *Signpost* is included because it is easy to let the followthrough work it's way back into the release. For example, one bad habit is called "dropping your bow arm." This happens to compound bow archers more often because their bows are so heavy, but whether the cause is due to the weight of the bow or not, the flaw is to allow the bow to drop down immediately after the shot. The problem with this is: shoot drop, shoot drop, shoot drop can easily become: shoot drop, shoot drop, drop shoot (ooops)! So, an archer does well at the time of releasing the string to be thinking about doing the followthrough correctly.

This is the *Signpost* for following through:

10. Exhibits good followthrough .... ☐ Sometimes ☐ Often ☐ Always
After the string is released, bow arm stays up as the bow jumps straight out into bow sling, then "bows," and draw hand moves backward along face.

Lining Up Alignment is, like the followthrough, something that you cannot just set and forget. Focus on it needs to be continual. You can check your own alignment with a mirror (an inexpensive closet door mirror propped against a wall will do) or you can ask your coach or even another knowledgeable archer to check it for you from time to time. The goal is to always have your elbow in or past line, and having your elbow on average slightly behind the arrow line is very desirable.

This is the *Signpost* for getting into good or better line:

11. Exhibits good alignment .... ☐ Sometimes ☐ Often ☐ Always
At full draw, draw elbow lines up with or is slightly behind the arrow line extended backward.

The alignment goal for Olympic-style archers is to get their draw elbows' behind arrow line. This is insurance for having the arrow ahead of line (the dreaded "flying elbow") which is a major cause of "plucking" the string. (See *Pluck, Pluck, Pluck* by Steve Ruis in the Coach Resources section of the AER website (*www.archeryeducationresources.com*).) Archers are not robots, so if they are typically "in line" there are small percentages of the time when they will be behind and ahead of line—behind is okay, ahead is not. If the archer's elbow is typically behind arrow line, there are small percentages of the time when they will be even farther behind line or be "just in line"—both of which are okay.

Notes _____

_____

_____

_____

Step-by-Step The key to consistent accuracy is to get accurate and then get consistent. Getting accurate with bow and arrow involves getting good form and good execution. Getting consistent is largely a mental task of being focused on doing things the same way each time. Being focused means not letting your mind drift. The question is: "How can I do this?" The answer is "With a strong mental program."

The start of the mental game in archery begins with what is called a *shot sequence* or a *shot routine*. This is simply a list of the things you do to make a good archery shot. At first a basic set of steps is learned, then as time goes on you will modify the sequence by changing steps or adding or removing steps until it is your personal shot sequence.

Learning the basic shot sequence is the goal of this *Signpost*, but keep in mind that a shot sequence is just a tool. The ultimate goal is to learn to use it to guarantee consistency. Here is what a shot sequence is to be used for:
- practice of the sequence ensures all of the steps are done (and in the right order).
- the sequence provides a common set of terms for discussions with your coach.
- each step of the sequence has physical and mental checks to occupy your mind.
- the sequence can be used to diagnose problems in your shot.
- the sequence is the foundation upon which your mental program will be built.

The last point is a little vague, but here is the rule that makes it work: *if anything, anything at all—mental or physical—intrudes from a prior step or from your environment, you must let down and start over*. So, for example, if you are about to draw the bow but your feet/stance feels funny, you must let down. Without this discipline, it will be very hard to improve at all. Shooting a bad shot requires ten good shots to wash away its influence. Not shooting a shot that feels wrong (somehow) actually will help you shoot good shots in the long run!

> **The Rule of Discipline**
> *If anything, anything at all—mental or physical—intrudes from a prior step or from your environment, you must let down and start over.*

A Basic Shot Sequence On the next three pages we present a basic shot sequence to use shooting any kind of bow. You will personalize it later.

Here is the basic sequence of steps that result in a well-shot arrow (*see photo sequence next three pages*):

Notes

Having the entire class doing the basic sequence either with mimetics (play acting) or with stretch bands while shouting out the names of the steps is not a bad idea at all. With younger students, be aware that they may want to snap other students when they loose their stretch bands. This is not to be tolerated—ever. Alternatively, you can walk around with a clipboard/binder and ask individual students to "stand and deliver" a shot sequence performance. There are AER Basic Shot Sequence handouts available for downloading in the Coach Resources section of the AER website (www.archeryeducation-resources.com). Students with the Archer's Guide have the photos to learn from.

Take Your Stance
Place your feet shoulder width apart, with your toes on line to target (a square stance), legs are straight (neither bent nor locked back at knees), shoulders are down, chest is down, head is balanced on top of spine and turned toward target; everything is relaxed.

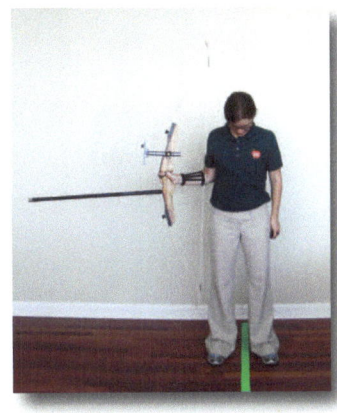

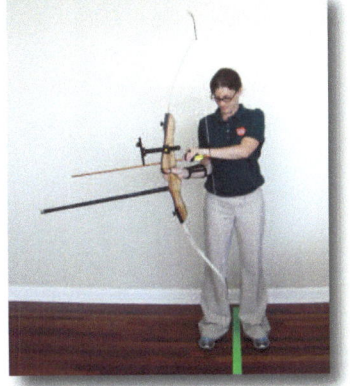

Nock an Arrow
Check to *hear* arrow snap onto the string, *see* that arrow is on arrow rest, and *see* that the index vane is pointing away from the bow. (Later, check to see if clicker is over arrow, if clicker is used.)

Set Your Hands
(*Draw Hand*) Fingers wrap around string in a "deep hook" (slightly behind first joint of fingers) and *not* on the fingertips; thumb reaches down to touch little finger tip. One to two inches of draw keeps hands from moving to different positions. (*Bow Hand*) Palm flat to ground is slid into the grip's throat, then wrist is bent until bow sits upon the pad of the thumb. Other fingers are relaxed (curled); see that bowhand knuckles make 45° angle to ground.

Notes _____

Raise the Bow
Maintaining slight draw of string, bow is raised to a height at which draw hand is between chin and eye level, bow hand brings sight aperture to top of target or arrow point to top of target. Draw elbow must be as high or higher than draw hand.

Draw the String
Maintaining high draw elbow, string is drawn to just under the anchor position. All muscles except shoulder and back muscles need to be as relaxed as possible with no extra tension. Both shoulders need to be kept in "down" position.

Find Your Anchor
Move your draw hand to its anchor position (here high anchor is being used). Draw hand must be firmly pressed against bone. String must be visible in aiming eye. Increase tense feeling between shoulder blades by moving the draw elbow around toward the back.

Notes _____

Aim

Move the bowsight aperture/arrow point to where desired and increase the tense feeling between shoulder blades by moving draw elbow around toward the back. Relax. Check to see aperture/arrow point are steady (not necessarily still). Once learned, aiming is natural and easy. (Later you will first check string alignment and adjust.)

Release the String

Continue to increase tense feeling between your shoulder blades by moving your draw elbow around toward the back as the fingers of the draw hand are relaxed. Stop holding string. This is not so much an activity as it is the stopping of the effort to keep fingers curled.

Follow Through

Allow bow to rock forward (if long stabilizer used) or back (if no stabilizer is used) while maintaining the position of the bow arm and both shoulders until the shot is completed. Due to the squeezing of the shoulder blades together, the draw hand's fingertips should finish moving when just below ear.

Notes _____

1. Take Your Stance
2. Nock an Arrow
3. Set Your Hands
4. Raise the Bow
5. Draw the String
6. Find Your Anchor
7. Aim
8. Release the String
9. Follow Through

This list consists of short phrases that are indicative of what is being done. For each step of a shot sequence there are physical things to check. Each step also provides a touch point, a point in time where certain physical sensations are checked. In the long run, you will develop the "feel" of what makes good shots and what makes dissapointing ones.

After each shot, all you need do is reset physically by taking a deep breath and letting it out and reset mentally by "letting go" of the previous shot. What "letting go" means is that if you think you did something wrong, plan to focus on what you need to do right in your next shot. If you did everything right, enjoy the shot and whatever the case, *stop thinking about that shot*. If you want to think of this as a separate step, do so. This is just a beginning sequence; it can be shortened or lengthened as you desire.

This is the *Signpost* for learning a basic shot sequence:

12. Knows and can demonstrate
    steps in shot sequence .... ☐ Sometimes ☐ Often ☐ Always
    Using a light-drawing bow or stretch band, can demonstrate steps in whatever shot sequence has been adopted.

Using A Bow Sight It has taken this long to introduce a bow sight because until a beginning archer has fairly steady form, the focus on aiming that is inherent in the use of a bow sight can detract from learning good form. Here you will focus on the kind of sights used in Olympic-style shooting—target/moveable sights. After the sight is properly set up and bolted onto your bow, you can begin "sighting in."

See the Appendix—The Ins and Outs of Bow Sights for a more detailed treatment of bow sights.

Sighting In "Sighting in," which is discovering which sight aperture positions

Notes _____

_____

_____

_____

_____

_____

_____

correspond to which target distances, is started at close range. This is a distance at which you have a good point of aim (*e.g.* 10 yards/meters or so). You begin by shooting by point of aim (POA) while ignoring the bow sight's aperture/pin, then after several successful shots in a row, notice the position of the sight aperture in your sight picture just before you shoot. The aperture is then moved until when sighting POA correctly, the aperture is centered on the target in your field of vision. The two sight pictures now represent the same "aim" and either should result in arrows landing in the center of the target. As you become accustomed to using the sight's aperture to aim with, you can then move back incrementally (no more than five yards at a time) and shoot *without moving the aperture*. As you move back the arrows impact lower, note how much lower the arrows hit. Before adjusting the aperture for this new distance, be sure to write down the aperture position for the previous distance, either as a scale reading or by marking it's position on a blank piece of tape affixed to the sight.

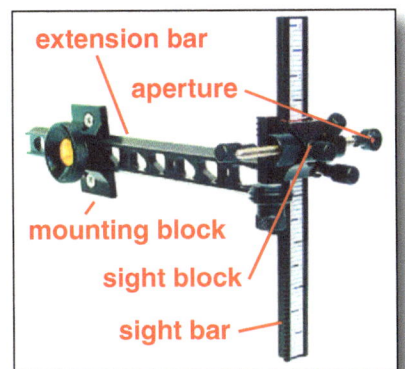

Typically one gets sight markings/readings for each ten yards or meters of distance you shoot (10, 20, 30, 40 yards, etc.). Getting at distances that are in between those settings requires a bit of imagination. The gaps between 10 and 20 yards and 20 and 30 yards, for example, are not the same. You can't just split the difference between your 20 and 30 yard marks to get twenty five! But you will get a close approximation, so you can fill in the "half way" marks with just a little testing and adjusting. Since target contests are shot at distances that have a five yard/meter increment at its smallest (5, 10, 15, 20, 25, 30, etc.) that's all you need for target archery. If you intend to shoot field archery you will need sight markings for every 1 yard of distance you are shooting! To start with if you have all of the "fives" you can estimate (interpolate) the others fairly well. For later, there are computer programs that allow you to print custom sight tapes or sight setting lists for each and every yard of your bow's capacity!

Meters or Yards? Should you "sight in" in meters or yards? The answer depends on the types of rounds you shoot. If the rounds specify distances in meters (typical for international competition) then meters is more convenient. If the rounds specify distances in yards (typical for U.S. field archery competitions, for example) then yards is more convenient. If you want to shoot both, pick one or the other and then here's

Notes

a simple conversion table (make all of the distance conversions before hand and write them down because doing math while shooting arrows is not a good idea):

Yards ▶	Meters	Meters ▶	Yards
10	9.14	10	10.94
20	18.29	20	21.87
30	27.43	30	32.95
40	36.58	40	43.75
50	45.72	50	54.92
60	54.86	60	65.90
70	64.01	70	76.88
80	73.15	80	87.49
90	82.30	90	98.85

If you want to do the calculations yourself:
1 yard = 0.9144 meters
1 meter = 1.0936 yards

This is the *Signpost* for beginning to use a bow sight:

13. Uses bow sight to aim with .... ☐ Sometimes ☐ Often ☐ Always
Can aim bow using a simple target/moveable bow sight.

String Alignment There is another use for fixing the positions of things in your sight picture; it is called *string alignment*. This technique enables you to fine tune the windage (left-right) of a shot. In your sight picture all along there has been part of your bow, part of your arrow, and . . . part of the bowstring. Most people pay no attention to the bowstring because it is so close to your aiming eye that it is very fuzzy (it is out of focus). But if you do pay attention to it, it enables you to keep your head and your bow in the same relationship to one another. And if you are keeping your head straight up and down (no tilt!), you will be keeping your bow straight up and down, too.

You may have seen pictures of traditional hunters tilting their bows quite a bit. This is called *canting the bow*, and when you are aiming off of the point there is very

With a 10# bow, you can draw and anchor facing a student to show them the position of the bowstring in front of your eye (no arrow!). Make sure you can see the string in your sight picture, that you are looking along the inside edge of the string (the edge closest to you), and that you are lined up with the string over the arrow rest. Warn students before doing this as it can be disconcerting.

Notes _____
_____
_____
_____
_____
_____
_____
_____

little effect on your shot, but if you are using a bow sight on a bow there is a big effect! In target archery, for the greatest accuracy you want the bow to be at the same angle each and every shot. Straight up and down is an angle you can find reliably (as gravity is your guide), which is something hard to say for other angles.

Aligning the string is simply lining up the fuzzy string image with something on the bow, such as the inside edge of the sight aperture or the arrow. Many people don't want to use the arrow because the string gets in the way of seeing the point, but you get the idea. If you practice lining up the string after you get to full draw each arrow you shoot, it will become a habit and less and less time will need to be devoted to it.

Start with a light drawing bow (10#), get to your full draw position, and look for the string in your sight picture. Play with it, see if you can get it to line up at various points on the bow or your bow hand. Don't stay at full draw so long you get fatigued. Let down, rest for 30 seconds, and start over. After you get used to seeing the bowstring in your sight picture, try some shots at a close in target with your bow. Be consistent in your placement of the string in your sight picture.

This is the *Signpost* for aligning the string:

14. Can identify string in sight picture
    and align string with bow .... ☐ Sometimes ☐ Often ☐ Always
    Able to identify position of bowstring in sight picture at full draw and adjust accordingly.

Equipment Inspection No matter how good your equipment is, it does suffer wear and tear. It is necessary for you to inspect your equipment often, even between shots! Every time you brace your bow, pull back the string a couple of inches and let go; it should twang nicely. Your ear is capable of detecting changes in that "twang." If your bow sounds different, it may indicate a stretched or defective bowstring or that your bow has changed. If your ear detects a significant difference in the "twang" of your bow upon bracing or your brace height measurement shows a large difference, here is how to test your bow for damage. On a folded towel or soft carpet, lay the bow down so you can pull the string while holding the bow down with your foot (*see photo*). This way, if the bow breaks (all bows can break!), the pieces will fly into the floor instead of into you! Draw the bow smoothly and listen for any sounds the bow

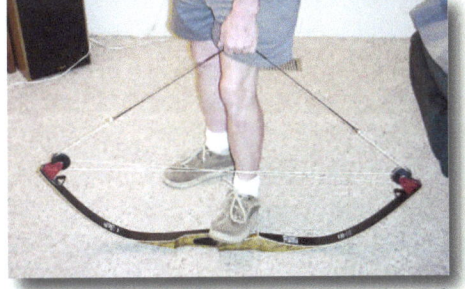
Don't just pull a suspicious bow using normal form—do a "safety pull test" instead as is being shown with this old compound bow.

See the Appendix—
Equipment Maintenance and Repair.

Notes _____

makes. If you hear any kind of cracking sound, let down and take your bow to a good archery shop to see if it can be repaired. If you hear no sound, draw the bow 1-2 inches past your normal draw length. If still no sounds, then the bow is probably sound and the problem is more than likely with the string. Try replacing the string to see if it restores things to the prior condition.

Inspecting Strings Strings that have broken strands sticking out obviously need to be replaced. When archers buy bowstrings they often buy two to make sure they have a "backup" in case the primary string fails. They set each string up with nock locators in the same places with enough twists to make the two strings the exact same length. Both are "shot in," that is quite a number of shots are taken with each (to do this just change strings each day you shoot), the "spare" is stored in a plastic bag in a safe place with a safety pin holding the two loops together (so the twists won't come out).

Checking Brace Height A check on whether the string is stretched or damaged is done by measuring the *brace height* (also called "string height") of the bow. This should be done each time the bow is strung. You might want to acquire a bow square for this purpose but you can also do it with a simple ruler (*see photo*). Bow squares can also help you set your nocking point locator and check its location, too. This is another check on whether your bowstring has changed.

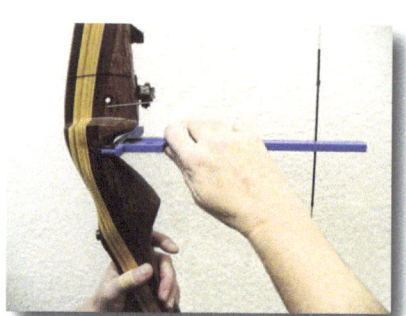

Check your brace height every time you brace your bow. A bow square works well (you can also use a ruler).

Checking Aluminum Arrows If an aluminum arrow gets damaged, it is usually easy to spot (broken nocks, lost arrow points, ripped fletches, etc.). What aren't easy to spot are slight bends, which can be a source of danger as bent arrows may fly very erratically. There are any number of ways to check an arrow to see if it is bent. If you lay the shaft on a flat table (fletches hanging over the edge) a straight arrow should roll fairly easily. Alternatively you can balance an arrow on your palm you can spin it with your fingers (*see photo*) and the arrow shouldn't wobble. Or you can make a "V" out of the fingernails on your off thumb and index finger then spin the shaft and push it so it rides up the groove (*see photo*) and it shouldn't wobble . . . or you can use the same "V" and rest the point in your palm and blow on the fletches to spin the arrow and it shouldn't wobble. (All of these tests take practice. Use a perfectly straight arrow and a slightly bent one for practice. Your AER Coach can demonstrate all of these.)

Notes _____

_____

_____

_____

_____

_____

_____

_____

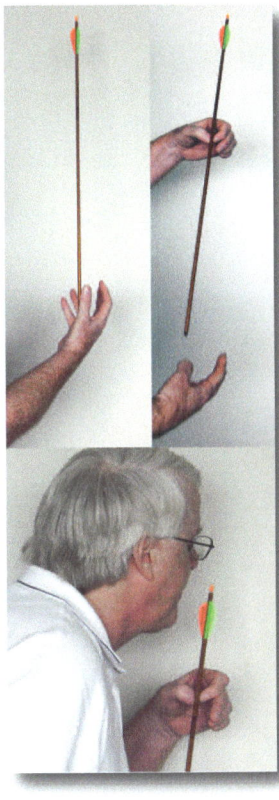

Checking Carbon Arrows If you have chosen to acquire carbon arrows, you are accepting the fact that carbon arrows, while being durable and are almost impossible to bend, may crack. If one of your arrows hits anything other than the target (or hits the target but at a funny angle), it should be inspected. Look it over for cracks. Gently flex it, while rolling it between your fingers, and listen for cracking sounds. If you see or hear a crack, do not shoot that arrow again! Shooting flawed carbon arrows can cause them to shatter upon release! If you break an arrow, be careful about throwing away the pieces as curious children are attracted to arrows and the carbon fibers making up the shaft can be razor sharp! Many people take the pieces home and dispose of them there.

This is the *Signpost* for inspecting your own equipment:

15. Can identify flawed arrows, bow parts .... ☐ Sometimes ☐ Often ☐ Always
    Able to identify arrows with damaged points, nocks or which are bent or cracked, also damaged or worn bowstrings, nock locators, etc.

Grouping Better The ultimate sign of consistency is shooting small sized groups. If the groups aren't in the center, you can move them there by adjusting your sight or POA. But if your groups are not small, all of the arrows won't be in the highest scoring zone of the target. Group size is the universal gauge of consistency in archery. With all of the refinements to your form, execution, and aiming systems you should be able to meet this new criterion. Good shooting! This is the *Signpost* for grouping at the intermediate level:

16. Shoots good groups consistently .... ☐ Sometimes ☐ Often ☐ Always
    Three arrow groups fit into an eight inch circle two ends out of three at 20 yards. Must achieve "Often" to advance to the next Stage.

Stage II Mental Aspects

In the next *Stage* you will focus on how your mind controls your ability to shoot (whether you acknowledge it or not). A shot sequence and the rule of discipline have been introduced and now there are a couple more tools of the mind you can use to good effect.

Talking to Yourself People who talk to themselves out loud are considered a

A fun way to evaluate this *Signpost* (Grouping Better) is to buy some inexpensive 8″ paper plates. Place a small aiming dot (a 2-3″ press-on sticker dot will work) in the center of the plate. Pin these to a target butt and have your archers verify *each end* that results in all three arrows hitting the plate. Doing this two out of three ends or four or more times out of six ends, etc. meets the *Signpost* criterion. Alternatively, you could have them shoot three ends of three arrows and show you at least six arrow holes in the plate at the end. Doing this at least three times in three different sessions (with no lapses) and you get an "Always." Obviously records must be kept. And, younger students may want to decorate/personalize their plates with their names or drawings, but no human likenesses are allowed on a target.

Notes _____

bit odd. Mostly we keep our comments to ourselves by not saying things out loud or muttering to ourselves, especially if the comments are uncomplimentary. Here the discussion is limited to what you say *to* yourself *about* yourself. This is called *self talk*. Self talk, either out loud or in the privacy of your own mind, has an effect and that effect can be good or bad depending on whether the self talk is positive or negative.

If you have ever muttered to yourself such things as "I am such an idiot!" or "Here I go again!" you were experiencing *negative self talk*. This can be motivating in a kind of "pick yourself up by your own bootstraps" kind of way but it is more likely to hurt your performance in archery. It does nothing to change the situation, certainly nothing to make it better.

Positive self talk, on the other hand, can actually help you perform. Here is an example:

Consider that you are having a good time and competing well at an archery event you typically enjoy. And then the skies darken and it begins to rain. Here are two possible responses to the change in the weather:

> *Self Talk Example 1* Oh, no! I hate shooting in the rain! It always lowers my score. There goes my personal best score and I probably won't win, either!
>
> *Self Talk Example 2* Oh, I had better get my rain gear out; I'm glad I came prepared. I probably won't shoot a personal best, but I could still win this thing, especially if the two people ahead of me get bent out of shape because of the rain. Woo hoo!

We are all capable of the disappointment, disgust, and fear associated with Self Talk Example 1. We are all also capable of learning how to achieve Self Talk Example 2 with its apparent happiness (came prepared, might win) and reasonable logic (might win if the two people ahead of me get bent out of shape because of the rain).

The point is that *you can choose how you talk to yourself*. But it is necessary, like all aspects of archery, to practice this. Whenever you think or say something negative about yourself, try rephrasing it as a positive statement. Look for the opportunity to do something better. Here's the self talk *Signpost*:

> Once you introduce "self talk" and "being positive" you really, really have to be careful how you address your students and yourself because they will call you on your lapses, which is good for you, like eating your vegetables.

Notes _____

_____

_____

_____

_____

_____

_____

_____

1. Exhibits positive self talk .... ☐ Sometimes ☐ Often ☐ Always
   Exhibits positive self talk and can take negative references and make them positive. Must achieve "Often" to advance to the next Stage.

Goals This sounds like a boring topic. True, it can be, but only one specific kind of goal is addressed here, a kind of goal that can actually help you become a better archer (and therefore isn't boring!). The goals addressed here are called *process goals*. Process goals are about *how* things happen, not *what* actually happens. If you have a goal of shooting a particular score or making a team, those are what are called *outcome goals*. Either you get the score or you don't; either you make the team or you don't. There is a role for outcome goals . . . but not for now. For now, you are focusing on goals that can actually result in you doing better in some way.

Here is an example of a process goal: "In practice today I will have a strong bow arm for 90% of all shots." A goal like this focuses your attention on making your bow arm stronger. Keeping track of whether you did or didn't have a strong bow arm on each of your shots focuses more of your attention . . . and the results are not necessarily cut and dried. What if it comes out to 89% of your shots you had a strong bow arm. Good enough? (Yes!) What about 92%? What about 13%? There is food for thought here.

Process goals help you focus on what you are doing, not on the results of having done it. If you want to compete on an AER Archery Team, you will have to have at least one process goal based on your shooting plus one deportment goal, too, for each competition. For your first deportment goal at your first archery competition, "Have fun!" is recommended, but if you get distracted talking trash to another competitor at this competition, don't be surprised if your coach tells you that you will have the deportment goal of "I will not talk trash at the tournament" at your next tournament.

Because your form is becoming more and more refined, your process goals can also become more and more refined. Ask your coach for help drafting some for you to use.

A word of caution: having more than 1-2 process goals for any practice session or tournament is a recipe for disaster. You just can't focus on that many things at one time. Work on something. Switch to something else. Come back to the first topic at

As students get more and more serious, it becomes more and more important that there be process goals for each practice session and each competition. This is true for recreational archers striving to get better and mandatory for competitive archers learning how to win.

Notes _____

_____

_____

_____

_____

_____

_____

a later time. Make progress slowly and steadily and you will end up at the top.

This is the *Signpost* regarding process goals for the intermediate level:

2. Helps draft and uses process goals .... ☐ Sometimes ☐ Often ☐ Always
   Can help create process goals and then exhibits using them through self evaluation.

Notes _____

Signposts—Stage III Achieving Mastery
Must have completed requirements of Stage II before beginning.

Congratulations are again in order! You have come a long way and now are ready to pursue the goal of becoming an expert archer. Do you think you are ready? Even if you don't think you are, if you have followed the plan to this point, you are ready!

There are always new things to learn about the physical elements of shooting arrows. You can never know it all, but at this point you know a great deal about yourself and how you shoot arrows. Now things that will improve your performance, which are more about the equipment and the role your mind plays, are addressed.

Advanced Archery Skills

Tuning You may know what it means to give a car a tune-up but tuning your archery equipment is probably a mystery. Tuning the bow-arrow-archer system involves a couple of stages. For simplicity they will be called basic tuning, fine tuning, and microtuning. Here just basic tuning is addressed.

So what is tuning? *Tuning is making adjustments in the bow-arrow system to fit them to the archer better.* No archer is perfect; each makes mistakes (of aiming, of releasing, of . . .). The goal of tuning is to create a bow-arrow setup that minimizes the impact of those mistakes. Consequently the exact same bow-arrow combination will shoot differently in the hands of different archers. Otherwise all archers would need only to shoot what the current world champion or the champion archer who is closest to them in size and style of equipment shoots.

The goal of tuning therefore is a "forgiving" bow-arrow system in the sense that it forgives the archer's mistakes. In "basic" tuning for recurve archers, you tune three things: nocking point height, centershot, and brace height.

Bare Shaft Tuning Here is a basic tuning test (also called the bare shaft planing test). In *bare shaft tuning*, you need to have two arrows with no fletches. If you've already fletched them all or bought them that way, you'll need to strip two of them. (Ask your coach how to do this. Alternatively you can use several wraps of transparent tape to eliminate the steering ability of your arrow's vanes by taping them down to the shaft.) From about 15 yards shoot arrows until you are warmed up and so you can get a good group of three arrows in the center of a target. Then shoot the two

Notes

bare shafts. (You shoot the second to tell if you shot a good shot with the first bare shaft; they should group together!) When the three fletched and two bare arrows form groups, this is what you can learn:

- If the bare shafts strike the target *above* the fletched group, your nocking point is too low.
- If the bare shafts strike the target *below* the fletched group, your nocking point is too high.
- If the bare shafts strike the target to the *left* of the fletched group, your arrow rest is too far from your bow.
- If the bare shafts strike the target to the *right* of the fletched group, your arrow rest is too close to your bow.
- If the bare shafts strike the target anywhere else except as part of the fletched group, you have a combination of adjustments to make.

The left and right bare shaft indications are reversed if you are left-handed. And the farther out the bare shafts are, the bigger the problem. Just a couple of inches of separation between the group of bare shafts and the fletched shafts indicates a pretty good tune.

Making Corrections—Nocking Point Location If your nocking point needs adjusting, you need to adjust it accordingly. This requires tools and/or expertise, so your coach will help you. You do this first!

Making Corrections—Centershot It is strongly recommended that while you are learning to shoot your bow, that you use an inexpensive plastic screw-in arrow rest. If you shoot with a metal arrow rest and cushion plunger (which you may), they are 20-30 times more expensive than the quite adequate screw-in arrow rest and far more complicated to adjust. Centershot adjustments are made by loosening the lock nut on the outside of the bow and screwing the rest closer in or farther out and retightening the nut.

The basic rule when making changes: *make them large (at first)*. If you are sneaking up on a big problem with itty bitty changes, you are going to be at it a long time. If your rest is too far in, make a big change and now it is too far out. Good! You now have outside limits for your adjustments. Split the difference between those two settings, then between that one and one of the others until you get what you want. So,

Tuning is really a complex subject, so the more you can learn about it the better. It is especially important that you, yourself, have done these procedures with your own equipment. We simply are going to refer you to Richard Cockrell's book, *Handbook of Modern Recurve Tuning*, as a starting point and strongly encourage you to read up on this topic. Oh, the Koreans have an attitude summed up by the phrase "teach them to shoot 1300 (out of 1440 in a FITA round, the international standard of "world class"), then tune their bow." Students with technophile personalities view tuning as magic used to increase performance and can spend way more time than it is worth trying to "tune" better scores. This is to be avoided. A well set up bow (see the appropriate Appendix) is all that is needed to shoot very good scores.

We also refer you to the fine (and free!) *Reference Guide for Recurve Archers* Ver. 5, by Murray Elliot, available on the AER website (*www.archeryeducationresources.com*) and elsewhere on the internet. The "Reference Guide" includes tuning information and a little bit of everything else about Olympic-style archery.

Notes _____

_____

when adding or removing "turns" to your arrow rest, start with four or five turns, later you can try, two, or even one twist at a time. But, start with a big change and retest. If there is no effect from the change, maybe that's the wrong "fix."

Making Corrections—Brace Height If trying to fix a "left-right" problem with centershot adjustments doesn't work, it may mean your arrows are too "stiff" or too "weak." If your arrows are too stiff, the bare shafts will hit to the left of the fletched shafts (for right-hand archers, the reverse for left-handers). If your arrows are too weak, the bare shafts will hit to the right of the fletched shafts (for right-hand archers, the reverse for left-handers). If centershot adjustments don't fix the problem or all of the problem, sometimes it is possible to tune in your arrows by changing your brace height. These changes are made like this:

- To make the brace height *higher* add twists to the string to make it shorter (twist in the same direction as the twists already there).
- To make the brace height *lower* remove twists from the string to make it longer (twist in the opposite direction from the twists already there).

Deciding which of these changes you should try can be a little tricky as which you do depends on where your brace height is to start with. If it is too high already, making it higher rarely fixes anything. Similarly, if it is too low already, making it lower doesn't help. So, here is the strategy: try the basic fix . . . and if it doesn't work, try putting everything back they way it was and then making a change the other way.

Here are the basic brace height fixes:

- If your arrows test *too weak* (bare shafts hit right for RH archers) try making the brace height higher (add twists to the string to make it shorter)
- If your arrows test *too strong*/stiff (bare shafts hit left for RH archers) try making the brace height lower (remove twists from the string to make it longer)

The basic rule when making changes is: *make them large (at first)*. If you are sneaking up on a big problem with itty bitty changes, it will take a long time. If you are too low, make a big change and now you are too high. Good! You now have an lower and an upper limit to your adjustments. Split the difference between those two settings until you get what you want.

When adding or removing twists start with eight twists at a time, later you can try four, two, or even one twist at a time. But, start with a big change and retest, if

Notes _____
_____
_____
_____
_____
_____
_____

there is no effect from the change, maybe that's the wrong "fix."

If these changes don't work, then it is likely the arrows are in need of adjustment or replacement.

Making Corrections—Arrow Spine If you make centershot changes and the arrows don't test any better or get worse when you are making a change that should make it better, it is possible that the arrow's spine is incorrect. The spine of an arrow is a gauge of its resilience when being flexed. Some people say it is a measure of the arrow's stiffness. In making changes in arrow spine, you again need to consider your equipment carefully.

- If your arrows hit to the *right* of the target (RH archer), even when the arrow rest is adjusted quite far from the bow, it is likely that the arrows are too weak (low spine).
- If your arrows hit to the *left* of the target (RH archer), even when the arrow rest is adjusted quite far into the bow, it is likely that the arrows are too stiff (high spine).

Stiffening Arrows—If you need a stiffer arrow, you are in luck: arrows are easier to stiffen than to weaken. The simple things you can do to stiffen arrows (in order of the effect) are:

1. Cut them shorter.
2. Use lighter arrow points.

If these don't work, you may have to buy new arrows. (Buying new arrows isn't uncommon for beginners, because as you change draw weight, you need stiffer arrows to handle the increased forces.) The rule on cutting arrows is a little at a time, so cut a half an inch off of a small set of arrows (include the bare shafts) and retest. If you cut them too short, they can only be given away as they will be of no further use to you. Also, too short arrows are a safety hazard!

Weakening Arrows—Weakening arrows is harder because there is no opposite to "cut them shorter." Making them longer will certainly weaken them but you would have to be a magician to do it! Here are some basic things you can do to weaken your arrows:

1. Use heavier arrow points.
2. Switch to feathers or Mylar vanes from plastic vanes (lighter vanes weaken arrows).

Notes

Making Corrections—Draw Weight/Arrow Spine One of the options you have with modern recurve bows is that the draw weight can be easily adjusted over a small range of values. An alternative to adjusting the spine of your arrows, which requires tools and knowledge and time, is to use your bow's draw weight adjustments to make the changes. Here is how it is done:

- If your arrows are *too weak* (low spine), lower the draw weight.
- If your arrows are *too stiff* (high spine), raise the draw weight.

This is done simply by turning the limb bolts of your unbraced bow inward (to raise the draw weight) or outward (to lower the draw weight) and retesting. Read your bow manufacturer's instructions to find out exactly how to do this.

If this adjustment has an effect but after changing things as much as possible it is not enough to fully tune the bow, changing the draw weight farther involves acquiring new limbs. Moving down in draw weight is not generally a good idea because it costs you performance. Moving up in draw weight can also be a problem because, if you increase the draw weight more than just a little at a time, it can seriously distort your archery form. The rule of thumb is to change your draw weight (upwards) only a little at a time (two pounds maximum). If you were planning to go to higher drawing limbs, this may be a good time to do it. The general approach is to see if you can borrow a pair of higher drawing limbs to test. If the change to more draw weight has no effect (you made the limb change and retested and no improvement) then this is probably not the solution to the problem. If the change does make things better, then return your borrowed limbs and acquire your own, then acclimate yourself to your new, higher draw weight. Your coach can assist you in this.

Generally, new arrows are less expensive than new limbs, but you can get bargains on limbs and arrows from other archers who have grown out of their equipment.

This is the *Signpost* for tuning at the intermediate level:

1. Able to tune bow/arrow system (basic) ...... ☐ Sometimes ☐ Often ☐ Always
   Basic tuning involves shooting bare shafts and fletched shafts then deciphering the positions of the two types of arrows. Recurve bows are tuned by making nocking point, centershot, brace height, and/or draw weight adjustments. Arrows are tuned by adjusting their lengths and point and fletch weights.

Notes

Fully Sighting In You may have sighted in just a couple of distances before and by now the range of distances over which you shoot has probably gotten larger, so it is time to get fully sighted in.

Limitations of Target/Moveable Sights This aspect of "sighting in" is simply a matter of using all of the form elements and equipment you have learned so far to get sight settings from your shortest to longest range. Occasionally, though, you will "run out of sight" usually meaning that for your longer distances, the sight aperture is so low it is too close to your arrows. To solve this problem, it is time to switch from a high anchor to a low anchor, if you have not already done so. If you have done that but not switched to a split-finger string grip, it is time to do that.

See the Appendix—The Ins and Outs of Bow Sights for more on this topic.

If these don't work, the next step is to increase your draw weight. If there is draw weight still in your bow, you can screw in your limb bolts (no more than what makes 2# of increased draw—max!) and you will get more cast out of your bow. You need to shoot for several hours at this new weight to get accustomed to it (not all at once!). Realize that whenever you change draw weight, you must sight in again, so make all of the draw weight changes while shooting at the same distance (closer is better than farther) and while making temporary sight aperture position adjustments to keep the arrows on target, then sight in again.

If you can't "make distance" by any of these techniques or you can't increase your draw weight enough right now, there are an number of other things you can try (temporarily) to shoot those distances until you are strong enough for a higher draw weight. For example, your bow sight can often be turned around so that it is inside the bow (and closer to your eye, so your marks will all be clustered closer together) or you can use POA techniques with your bow sight with your sight aperture set at it's highest useable distance setting, for example, aiming at the top of the target (12 o'clock, 1 ring) rather than at the center.

Getting in Focus As you have been learning to shoot, you started by focusing on the target. When you were introduced to "aiming off of the point" you may have switched to focusing your eyes on the arrow point. But which is correct—focusing on the target or the point/aperture? There are arguments that can be made for focusing on the arrow point and arguments that can be made for focusing on the target. (This is true also regarding bow sight apertures.) Rather than discuss the arguments, it is recommended that you try both. Take a very light drawing bow, stand in front of a

Notes

mid-distance target, draw the bow until you are in the "point on target" orientation, then shift your focus to the point/aperture and back to the target, then repeat. Try not to get too fatigued doing this. It is okay to let down, rest for 30 seconds, and then draw again. See if you have a preference for one of the two focal points. If you do, use that one consistently. If you do not, pick one and use that one consistently. After you have shot a while using this technique, check your preference again, it might have changed. (For your information, most Olympic-style archers focus on their bow sight's aperture.)

This is the *Signpost* for sighting in at the intermediate level:

2. Can sight in bow
   for all appropriate distances .... ☐ Sometimes ☐ Often ☐ Always
   This includes the longest distances required by competitive category (even if not competing). Must achieve "Often" to advance to the next Stage.

String Alignment II By now you should be used to noticing the fuzzy image of your string in your full draw sight picture. Now it is time to optimize its position. With a bow sight available, the very best place for your string image is the inside edge of the aperture (the edge closest to the bow) because, well, you have to look at the aperture anyway. Some people just can't do that, so as long as some part of the bow can be easily brought into alignment with the image of the bow string, you are good. Do it the same way, each and every shot and you will become more consistent.

Elite archers often set their bows up by building their preferred string alignment into the setup. The most desirable point, for now, is mentioned here.

This is your *Signpost* for aligning the string at the intermediate level.

3. Uses string alignment comfortably .... ☐ Sometimes ☐ Often ☐ Always
   Aligns string within sight picture consistently to achieve higher accuracy.

Shooting Cool This *Signpost* you have seen before, but as you have made progress you have been shooting longer and longer distances, at least if it is "outdoor" season. (Your coach is taught to encourage that.) This is the *Signpost* for "making distance" at the intermediate level. The goal is to shoot comfortably and well at all competitive distances that you would shoot in competition. Bear in mind that if you do not want to shoot longer distances, you can work with your coach to adjust this *Signpost* (you can't eliminate this one as it is required to reach the next *Stage*).

This is the *Signpost* for shooting all distances comfortably.

Notes _____

_____

_____

_____

_____

_____

_____

4. Can shoot comfortably
at all appropriate distances .... ☐ Sometimes ☐ Often ☐ Always
This includes the longest distances required by competitive category (even if not competing). Must achieve "Often" to advance to the next Stage.

Clickers Every Olympic archer uses a clicker; now you will, too. Clickers help you to control your draw length (make it the same each time you shoot) and also help you to release the string without conscious thought. Clickers are not loaned out so you will have to purchase one and install it on your bow. Your coach will help you with its initial positioning.

Learning the Clicker Start by stripping sight and stabilizer(s) off of your bow and step up to an empty target butt (also called a "blank bale"). Your coach will be directing you and this is how it will go. You will slide an arrow under the clicker and your coach will ask you to draw the arrow while watching the clicker. Your goal is to get to a comfortable full draw position with the clicker still on the arrow but quite near its falling off point. Adjustments will probably have to be made to the position of the clicker.

Then you will draw to full draw (watching the clicker) and then "finish the shot" by extending to the target with your bow arm and rotating your rear elbow toward your back. When the clicker "clicks," you will be doing one of several things (as directed by your coach):
- letting down
- shooting, *or*
- pausing for 1, 2, or 3 seconds and shooting (or letting down)

Your coach will tell you which to do each time. When you first start, at least every other shot will be a "let down." Drawing through the clicker and letting down is called a *clicker check* as you can check whether your back and shoulders feel they are in the right positions at that point and to reinforce that letting down is an option when the clicker "clicks." This is something you will want to do every time you warm up to shoot and then later interspersed with your warm-up shots. (By doing this during warm-ups you are reinforcing that not shooting is an option when the clicker clicks during competition/serious shooting.)

What is being done is your subconscious mind is being trained to assess the

> This *Signpost* can be a real struggle for youths at a particular level of development (especially when they have changed competitive categories (to greater distances) before they were physically ready) and more mature archers with short draw lengths (short draw length means low power). A techno-fix is to buy/acquire lightweight carbon arrows but sometimes even that doesn't work. See *Making Distance* by Steve Ruis in the Coach Resources section of the AER website (www.archeryeducation-resources.com).

> Clickers are considered as being troublesome by many archers and coaches, but they need not be so. Please read *Coach's Opinions* by Steve Ruis in the Coach Resources section of the AER website. This was written imploring coaches to be kinder and gentler but addresses how to teach using a clicker showing you a comparison of the above approach with another fairly common approach.

Notes _____

_____

_____

_____

_____

_____

_____

status of your shot at the point in time that your clicker "clicks" and then either a) finishing the shot (if *every thing is good*) or b) letting down (if *any thing is not good*). Your subconscious mind can do this with lightning speed; your conscious mind would take several minutes to do the same thing! What you do not want is what is called a "conditioned reflex" (a reflex that is trained). A "click-release" trained reflex will cause you a great many poor shots. What you want is "click–check and if okay–release."

This training can be tedious, so it is okay to take a break and shoot without the clicker for a while.

Also, if you are still growing, the position of the clicker will need to be adjusted often. It also needs to be adjusted often if your form isn't fairly solid which is why you have waited until now to learn the clicker.

This is the *Signpost* for using a clicker:

5. Can shoot comfortably using a clicker .... ☐ Sometimes ☐ Often ☐ Always
   Clickers are used by all Olympic-style archers to control draw length and, with training, remove the decision making of when to shoot.

It is okay for archers to skip this *Signpost*. An archer can come back to it at a later time.

Shooting Rhythmically This is a fairly advanced skill and takes quite a bit of time to do, but you may want to attempt this anyway. Most people shoot in a particular rhythm which can be refined by identifying it and using your shot sequence to make it regular.

Finding Your Rhythm This is the hard part. You either need to have someone with a stopwatch help you or you can use a metronome to figure it out. In the stopwatch approach, you have somebody time how many seconds (without you noticing them doing it) it takes from raising your bow to releasing the string. After each shot, you say "yes" if the shot felt good and was in rhythm or "no" if it didn't feel good or was out of rhythm.

After recording the times of many dozens of shots from more than one session, you try to correlate the number of seconds to the quality of the shot. (One way to do this is to enter the number of seconds and the yes's and no's into a two-column spread sheet, sort the rows for time shot and see if the yes's cluster around any particular shot time. For the sake of this discussion let's say that most of the yes's were from 4-6 seconds. Then there are a number of ways to lock in that rhythm (*see below*).

Notes

The metronome approach is to play a metronome and count off your shot, so many "clicks" for each step of the shot sequence. If the metronome is set too fast, you will feel rushed or unable to count fast enough. If it is set too slow, you will feel sluggish and impatient. Eventually you get it set right and then you want to lock in that rhythm.

Locking in Your Rhythm There are a couple of ways to lock in your personal shot rhythm. One way is through feedback. Again, you need somebody with a stopwatch. If your slice of time is 4-6 seconds from raising the bow to loose, your helper practices with you and times each shot. If you shoot quicker than the four seconds, he tells you. If you reach 6 seconds before shooting, he announces "let down" and you must let down the string. The feedback eventually gets you to shoot in your best rhythm. You may need several sessions to do this and you may need to test yourself at intervals to check on your status.

Another method is you may have a snippet of music in your head that is in the same tempo as your shot rhythm (or you may hear it and recognize it then). A great many archers use a sample of a song as part of their shot sequence. It helps them to stay in rhythm.

This is the *Signpost* for shooting rhythmically at the intermediate level:

6. Uses shot sequence to create
   a regular shooting rhythm .... ☐ Sometimes ☐ Often ☐ Always
   Shooting rhythm can be made regular by use of creative shot sequence elements that can only be found by trial and test.

Scoring Now that you have refined form and much practice shooting arrows under your belt, it is time for your first scoring *Signpost*. There is any number of scoring rounds available. You may want to choose one of the common international archery rounds—the FITA Round (144 arrows), a Half-FITA Round (72 arrows), or even the FITA 30m Round (36 arrows) or you might prefer an NFAA field archery round.

Your goal is to score at least as much as 75% of the age group record for that round. Most age group records can be found on the internet and your coach can help you find yours. Good luck and good shooting! (And, yes, this is an "outcome" goal.)

This is the *Signpost* for scoring at the intermediate level:

Of all the things that could be said to underscore the importance of the mental landscape to archers, we simply encourage you to read With Winning in Mind *by Lanny Bassham. If you think "winning" is too crass of a goal, please open up your thinking. Your student's goals are your focus as a coach and the only person who has the power to defeat your archer is him- or herself. Archers compete without any defense from the other archers, the only opposition they have is within themselves. To excel, they must come to know and accept themselves as never before. This is a journey that has more to do with their lives than with archery; archery is just the vehicle.*

Notes _____

_____

_____

_____

_____

_____

_____

7. Can shoot scores of 75% of record level ..... ☐ Sometimes ☐ Often ☐ Always

These can be competition or practice scores shot under competition conditions. Any rounds may be used but must include outdoor rounds. Must achieve "Often" to advance to the next Stage.

Stage III Mental Aspects

You will have to work closely with your coach to see which of these *Signposts* you are willing to attempt. Some will work better than others and some won't work at all . . . for you. You may have to try each of them to see, but start with a discussion with your coach.

Journaling Have you ever had anyone ask "How's archery going?" and you answered "Okay, I guess." This is certainly not a good answer if it is your coach asking the question or, worse, a prominent guest coach who might be able to help you a lot! One of the ways to be aware of what you are doing is to keep a journal. No, not a diary! This is a journal in which you write all of the important things you are doing. Here are some recommendations:

1. Set aside the back of your journal (any small notebook will do) to write down all of the critical numbers about your equipment (your brace height, how many strands in your string, arrow length and size, brand names, fletching sizes, etc.
2. Have a separate place for your practice and competition goals. Always write them down and write an evaluation of how well you met each goal.
3. Have a place to write down the particulars of your "testing" sessions. If you are tuning or testing some new arrows, write down the results. Before you make any change in your setup (brace height, nocking point location, whatever), write down the old value. Write down the numbers of twists put in or taken out of your string. It may seem silly, but if you mess things up, such notes may make it possible for you to make your bow "right" again.
4. Never, ever write anything negative in your journal. (Yes, we know this is a negative statement. It was for emphasis.) Writing things down gives them power, so writing about how you want to do things better and are doing them better is good because it makes progress easier. If you complain in your journal (It was raining . . . I was so miserable . . .) it doesn't help you, it simply focuses your attention on what you were doing wrong. Try to make positive comments like,

---

> You may want to set students loose on the Internet looking for the U.S. age level records of USA Archery (*www.usarchery.org*) on common archery rounds. There are buttons leading to their records but they can be reached directly at *www.usarcheryrecords.org*. For explanations of their age classifications, there is no better source than a table available at *www.texasarchery.org/Documents/Distances/DistanceSummary.htm*.
>
> FITA, the International Archery Federation (Now called "World Archery"), also has a record search engine at their website *www.archery.org* under Results and Records / Best Scores.
>
> Also, check to see if your state organizations post record scores.

Notes _____

_____

_____

_____

_____

_____

"The next time it rains, I am going to practice and see if I can figure out what went wrong . . . I found out that my windbreaker was catching the bowstring causing my arrows to go low-left. I snugged up the sleeve with some rubber bands and shot really well!" These observations can really help and reviewing them later on can show you how you solved problems and made progress.

Here is the *Signpost* for journaling at the intermediate level:

1. Keeps a journal for practice/competition ... ☐ Sometimes ☐ Often ☐ Always
   Journal entries focus on record keeping and finding solutions (not problems) and are positive in nature.

Getting Help from Others As you interact with other archers, you will have the opportunity to learn from them. You are encouraged to engage other archers and talk about archery. If you hear a good idea, you might find it helpful to your improvement. And, as with all other topics, you can also find a lot of misinformation floating around. For example, you can find good information on the Internet, but the warning about misinformation goes double for the Internet. Apparently any fool can post anything.

If you are not sure about something you have read or heard from another archer, discuss it with your coach. If he or she can't help, they likely can point you to someone who can.

A Warning About Advice Many adults like to see beginners, especially kids, starting up in their favorite sport, so if you are young, you will attract all kinds of advice from older archers. When an adult gives advice to a youth and the youth does not immediately accept or test out the advice, they can be perceived as being "standoffish," or "aloof," or "stuck up." (The old expect the young to take their advice.) Here is how you can diffuse any potential criticism. If you are given advice from an older archer ("You know what you ought to do . . .") say to him or her, "Thanks for the advice, I will tell my coach when I see him next week." This satisfies older advice givers apparently because they think you have your very own personal older, wiser person to guide you. But the phrase does work . . . like magic! So, if you are young, you might want to have that phrase in your back pocket when nosey older folks get in your face. (The same is true for female beginners who tend to attract advice from older males.)

This is the *Signpost* for learning from others at the intermediate level:

Don't forget that many of your students won't acquire the *Archer's Guide* so teaching them the "Thanks for the advice, I will tell my coach when I see him/her next week" phrase is worth doing face to face. Of course, this recommendation applies to everything else in this guide, also.

Notes _____

_____

_____

_____

_____

_____

2. Interacts with other archers
   in style to learn .... ☐ Sometimes ☐ Often ☐ Always
   Much can be learned from other archers of the same style. Archers wanting to improve need to seek out useful information and try to apply it to their own game. Must achieve "Often" to advance to the next Stage.

Imagine This It seems as if a shooting sport like archery would have no room for imagination. Archers are solidly embedded in reality! Well, not exactly. You may already know some uses of imagination in other sports and archery is no exception. Most successful archers start out each and every shot by imagining the look, feel, smell, sound, etc. of a perfect shot. This imagery works. It works because you operate mostly subconsciously and a basic aspect of your subconscious mind is it can't tell the difference between reality and something vividly imagined.

The advantage here is that each shot you take is preceded by a perfect, dead center shot and followed by another dead center, perfect shot. It is much easier to do something just after you have done it well and it is very hard to do something right just after you have done it wrong. *Imagery, in the form of imagining perfect shots before shooting them, enables archers to shoot significantly more consistently.*

You will see the same behavior from football kickers as they take practice swings of their legs before they kick field goals (they are imagining the impact of the ball and seeing it tumble through the goalposts). Golfers taking practice swings (they imagine the ball sailing through the air and landing just where they want), and basketball players shooting free throws (they imagine the feel of the ball, the ball's flight, and it settling gently into the net).

This takes practice a) to do it well and b) to make it a habit.

This is the *Signpost* for imagery at the intermediate level:

3. Uses imagery as part of shot sequence .... ☐ Sometimes ☐ Often ☐ Always
   Good shots are imaged/imagined as an early stage in shot sequence (practice and competition). Must achieve "Often" to advance to the next Stage.

Affirmations Affirmations are short statements of personal beliefs that are designed to help you feel better about yourself and your abilities, thus reinforcing those abilities. They may take many forms, but they must always be drafted in:

> *Imagery, in the form of imagining perfect shots before shooting them, enables archers to shoot significantly more consistently.*

Notes

- first person (I . . .)
- positive language, and
- the present tense (now).

They state exactly what you will do in a positive manner. Do not use the words no, never, not, or don't. For example, an affirmation for baseball "I never strike out" is poor as it focuses energy and attention on striking out. It is far better to affirm what you want to happen (focus on the solution, not the problem) like this: "I hit the ball with a high batting average and pretty much where I want it to go."

The classic method involves writing your affirmations on 3x5 cards, but you might want to write them daily in a journal or read them to yourself or aloud, or record affirmations so you can listen to them, or do all of these. Some people post copies of their affirmations where they will see them throughout the day and stop what they are doing to read them each and every time they encounter one. Use your imagery skills as you read or listen; the more senses (sight, smell, touch, etc.) you invoke in the imagery, the more effective it is.

Here are some examples:
- An archer-athlete who gets overly upset when he makes mistakes (which reinforces the mistakes making them easier to be repeated), might make an affirmation "It's normal for me to make mistakes from time to time, as I am still improving."
- If you are affected greatly by the pressure you feel during competitions, you might say, "I appreciate pressure-packed situations because the pressure tells me I am close to winning."

Typically these are archery-related things, but if you have personal issues to deal with, this works on them, too. If you are using 3x5 cards, read each card first thing each morning, and last thing each day. Read them just before each practice and competition, and again immediately afterward. Of course, you may also read them any other time you like (when waiting for a bus, just before a doctor appointment, but not while you are driving a car!).

This is the *Signpost* for using affirmations at the intermediate level:

4. Uses affirmations to achieve goals .... ☐ Sometimes ☐ Often ☐ Always
   Affirmations are used in a prescribed process to achieve goals.

Notes

Shot Thoughts This idea was borrowed from golfers (along with the names for "open" and "closed" stances). Golfers have what are called "swing thoughts." Since a golf swing happens too fast to be thought about consciously, it happens subconsciously. But thoughts in the conscious mind can guide the subconscious. They have to be short thoughts because things are happening fast. So, a golfer might think "relaxed hands" or "balanced followthrough" as they swing. They have similar "thoughts" for their putting routines. If you get a chance to watch golf on TV, watch any golfer. He/she will have a pre-shot and pre-putt routine on display. Golfers, like archers, also use shot sequences.

So, you too may use "shot thoughts" to help your form. This is usually in the context of dealing with a problem. For example, if your bowhand was getting tense as you draw the string, you might think "soft bow hand" to yourself as you draw. Or, if your bow shoulder has begun to creep into the "up" position, you might think "shoulders down" as you raise your bow.

This is the *Signpost* for shot thoughts at the intermediate level:

5. Uses shot thoughts
as part of shot sequence .... ☐ Sometimes ☐ Often ☐ Always

Shot thoughts are used in any step in shot sequence (practice and competition) to address weaknesses or lack of focus.

More on Goals If you feel that goals really work for you, learn more about the goal setting and goal getting process. Here are some important points to consider.
- Let's say you want to win a national championship (an outcome goal). This is too far removed from where you are now to make in a single leap. So, break it down. What kinds of scores do you have to shoot (on what rounds) to win? What was last year's winning score? What is your score on that round now? Create a series of goals for scores on the round, which will tell you about the progress you are making. This is a framework for a plan to achieve your ultimate goal.
- A handy way to describe the desirable characteristics of your goals is the word SMART. *SMART goals* are:
  - Specific

Notes _____

- Measureable
- Attainable/Adjustable/Action-based
- Realistic
- Time-based

If your goals aren't specific, how can you know whether you have met them? If they aren't measurable, what will you use as an indicator of success? If they aren't attainable (I want to jump to the Moon!), what good are they? If you can't adjust them, you can feel trapped and out of control. If they aren't action-based, they won't encourage the actions you need to take to get where you want to go. If they aren't realistic, they will only frustrate you. If they don't have a timeline associated with them (By June, I will . . .), there is no sense of urgency.

There has been much written about goal setting and goal getting and much of it is available on the internet. Try to learn what you can to help with this topic.

This is the *Signpost* for goal setting and getting at the intermediate level:

6. Helps draft and uses process goals .... ☐ Sometimes ☐ Often ☐ Always
   Can help create process goals and then exhibits using them through self evaluation. Must achieve "Often" to advance to the next Stage.

Notes _____
_____
_____
_____
_____
_____
_____
_____
_____
_____
_____
_____
_____

Signposts—Stage IV Owning the Sport
Must have completed requirements of Stage III before beginning.

Wow! You have come a long way. You are now a really accomplished archer. You can shoot high scores and you are in command of your shot. This doesn't mean there isn't more to learn, just that you have come more than 80% of the way. At this point it gets harder to make improvements. This is not a problem, in fact it is normal. When you have done 50% of a task, you have doubled your progress from when you had done 25% of that task. But when you are at the 80% mark, only 20% of the task now remains. Hence the farther along you get, the less far there is to go, and often the harder it is to do, because you have already done the easier tasks. It would be stupid to not do the easiest tasks that give the greatest progress first, no?

In this *Stage* you take over total control of your sport. Coaches are now your partners who work with you on what you want to work on. At this *Stage* you become independent of systems and teachers. You know enough to learn on your own and to seek out new knowledge, test it, and incorporate into your archery. All of these *Stages* can be done in just a few years or it can take longer. How long you have taken to get to this point is not a sign of anything; it just is.

In this last Stage, there are just a few physical skills, and the same list of mental skills as in *Stage III*, but instead of us teaching you everything, some really good references will be supplied for you to explore based on what you think works best for you. You can still consult your AER Coach and other coaches as well. Welcome to the wide world of archery!

Oh, and now the *Signposts* are for you to evaluate and sign off on. As before, your coach is there to help, if you need.

Finishing Your Kit

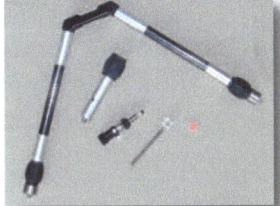

You may want to add a cushion plunger, a metal rest, V-bars, Beiter *Sight Tunnel*, or other goodies.

You may want to invest in a better arrow rest at this point. Most Olympic-style target archers use a more involved arrow rest including a "cushion plunger" and these can cost anywhere from $30-175. Whatever you decide on, set it up according to the manufacturer's instructions.

You may want to upgrade your sight aperture from a simple pin (target/moveable sight) to a loop or square aperture (*e.g.* a Beiter *Sight Tunnel*) or you may want to customize your stabilization system with "V Bars" which stabilize your bow in a

Notes _____

number of ways just a long rod doesn't.

You may also want to purchase a custom bow grip or modify the one you have so it fits your hand better. Expert archers are known to modify their bow's grip using auto body dent filler, tennis racquet wraps, tape, and other substances it make it exactly as they want.

Whatever you might want to do to finish out your setup, now is a good time to do it. Be aware that most archers explore new equipment options continually. Be also aware, though, that if your bow is constantly being changed, you will never learn to shoot it as any change to your bow, arrows, or accessories is the equivalent of getting a new bow. You will have to set the bow up and sight it in again, for example. So, don't fall into the trap of tinkering yourself out of archery.

Changing Gear Olympic-style target archers tend to change accessories on their bows often, looking for better performance. If you are one of these people, do yourself a favor and devise standards to compare the "befores" and "afters" of any such changes. For example, you could use the score on your favorite competitive round. Look up the last three scores for that round in your journal (if you don't have three, shoot them in practice) and take an average. Make the change (new rest, new sight, whatever) . . . but only one thing at a time! Then, after some practice time to get acquainted to your new gewgaw, shoot three more rounds (on different days, not back to back) and average the scores. Any improvement? If not, then maybe spending that money was not a good idea. If yes, then maybe that change was good. The "maybe" is because of what is called the *Hawthorne Effect*: which is any time a change is made that is supposed to make things better, things do get better . . . for a while. This effect is just the "new toy" factor. Any time you have a new something or other, it fascinates you and raises your interest level . . . until you get used to it. The short-term gain in interest and focus can be a source of improvement which disappears later when the change becomes the norm.

> Beware the *Hawthorne Effect*! Any time a change is made that is supposed to make things better, things do get better . . . for a while.

This is about the only way you can tell you are wisely investing your time and money in new equipment, so devise a test before each equipment change (group size, standard round scores, something) and check to see if things really got better or whether you just thought they did.

Students always need help with acquiring new gear. If you are so lucky as to have a quality archery shop in your vicinity, one that has a target archery specialist, you can send your students there. The odds against this being the case are so large, though, that we urge you to get as familiar as you can with target archery gear so you can make informed recommendations. Check out the AER website (*www.archeryeducationresources.com*) forr ecommendations and trainings, but for more advanced equipment, ask the kind folks at Lancaster Archery Supply (*www.lancasterarchery.com*, 800.829.7408) to send you their catalog—also called the "Archer's Wish List"). If you don't have a target archery-minded shop in your locale, you will find Lancaster Archery Supply to be a virtual "one stop shop" for all things target. If you do have a target archery-minded shop in your locale, pay them a visit, strike up a relationship. Shop owners often see the wisdom of encouraging new archers (your students!) with discounts and services. If you are this lucky, don't pass up this opportunity! And, if they don't get your business, they may not be there the next time you need them.

Notes _____

_____

_____

Refining Your Archery Skills

Advanced Tuning Tuning recurve bows takes considerably more time than tuning longbows, and probably a little less than compound bows, but at this point, most of the tuning will be done on the arrows. There is a free arrow tuning resource from the Easton Archery company which is available at the AER website (*www.archeryeducationresources.com*). This guide is for modern arrows (shafts of aluminum, carbon, and carbon-aluminum).

Be sure to review the Appendix—Bow Setup, as a poorly set up bow can defeat any tuning procedure.

Group Tuning Any advanced tuning procedure must include group tuning. Basically, you examine your groups at all distances you shoot. The groups should be round and proportional. Being round means the arrows making the group fit into a circle and would be distributed as much left as right, as much up as down, and be more concentrated toward the center of the group. By proportional, it means the diameters (widths or heights) of the circles should correspond to the distances. If you shoot six arrows in a 10-inch group at 20 yards they should be in a 20-inch circle at 40 yards and a 30-inch circle at 60 yards. If the groups are smaller or larger than they should be at either end of the distance range, there is something wrong with your tune. You can tune for better performance at longer distances but with a sacrifice in performance at shorter, and vice-versa, but generally archers like their equipment to perform equally well over all of the distances they shoot.

> The basic rule of tuning is: *never make more than one change at a time*! If you make two or more changes at one time and there is an improvement, you won't be able to tell which change caused the improvement.

Group tuning can be exhausting as you have to shoot many groups (dozens) to establish a normal group size and you have to do this at a number of distances. Then if you make a tuning change (for example, moving the nocking point locator down just a tiny bit), you have to do it over again. Each change requires a test and the basic rule of tuning is: never make more than one change at a time! If you make two or more changes at one time and there is an improvement, you won't be able to tell which change caused the improvement; maybe Change A caused a big improvement and Change B made it less! There is no way to tell, so one change at a time, then test.

Here is your *Signpost*:

1. Able to tune bow/arrow system (fine) .... ☐ Sometimes ☐ Often ☐ Always
   Starts with careful bow setup, then tuning begins with bare shaft tuning then proceeds to group

Notes _____

tuning. Recurve bows are tuned by making brace height adjustments and occasionally by change string sizes (via numbers of strands, lengths) or changing string materials (Dacron vs. Fastflight). Centershot and nocking point heights are both tuned. Arrows are tuned by adjusting their lengths and point weights and fletching sizes and angles and nock fit. Very fine tuning may be accomplished by changing cushion plunger pressure.

Mastering the Clicker When you were started on a clicker, you were instructed to "watch the point." The reasons for doing so were to decrease your anxiety and also to focus on what you were trying to accomplish. After you have shot many, many arrows, you may find that you do not have to watch the clicker any more. This is actually the long term goal.

Most people start by watching the clicker and switching to watching the sight at full draw position. Then, later, they change to moving the sight aperture very close to where they want it in their sight picture, then switch to the clicker, then switch to watching the sight at full draw position. Finally, they watch the sight throughout the aiming segment of their shot cycle and don't watch the clicker at all. If you try not watching the clicker at all while shooting and your shot rhythm become erratic, go back to watching the clicker. There is no rush. These things happen in time, be patient.

Coaches, you need this book! You would have had another 40 pages of appendices if it were not for the availability of this book! It even is spiral bound, which means it lays flat while you are using it to walk through a procedure. This is a must have "Coach's

Here is your *Signpost*:

2. Uses the clicker fluidly and confidently ...... ☐ Sometimes ☐ Often ☐ Always
   Uses the clicker fluidly and confidently progressing toward the point where the clicker is no longer watched during the draw.

Archery Gear Maintenance There is a great little book with the title *Simple Maintenance for Archery* by Ruth Rowe and Alan Anderson that has step-by-step instructions (with photos) on how to do almost all maintenance on your bow and arrows. It is highly recommend, in fact all archers need a copy of this book. It is inexpensive and can be purchased on AER's website (*www.archeryeducationresources.com*). More specific information focused on Olympic-style archery can also be found on the internet. Try key word searches for anything you want.

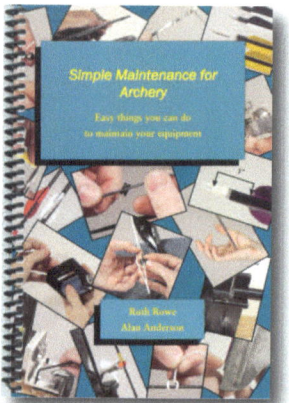

Here is your *Signpost*.

3. Maintains own equipment .... ☐ Sometimes ☐ Often ☐ Always
   Protects equipment from elements, stores equipment properly, and repairs/maintains all archery gear.

Notes _____

_____

_____

_____

_____

_____

_____

This scoring goal is a high but not drastically high goal. Don't be surprised if your better archers sail right on by this Signpost.

Scoring Here is your second scoring goal. Again, it is set relative to what top scores are being shot in your style, age group, etc. At this point you should be looking to shoot these scores in competition rather than in practice. Keeping track of your process goals while you are shooting will probably give you information about what you need to do to improve your scores. Don't expect huge improvements in short time spans, the higher you go, the slower the progress seems! Also realize that any journey, such as your archery, has ups and downs (and plateaus as well). Sometimes one gets stuck and can't go up without going down first! (This is usually a sign of trying too hard.)

Here is your *Signpost*:

4. Can shoot scores of 90% of record level .... ☐ Sometimes ☐ Often ☐ Always
   These can be competition (preferred) or practice scores shot under competition conditions. Any rounds may be used but must include both indoor and outdoor rounds.

Stage IV Mental Aspects

If you are going to explore the mental side of archery further the one book you need to read (and read again) is Lanny Bassham's, *With Winning In Mind* (available on the AER website (*www.archeryeducationresources.com*) and at most online booksellers or ask your local book shop to order it for you). His story borders on the fantastic and his methods are proven. It will open up a great many new concepts and practices.

Here are the *Signposts* for you to sign off on:

1. Keeps a journal for practice/competition .... ☐ Sometimes ☐ Often ☐ Always
   Journal entries focus on record keeping and finding solutions (not problems) and are positive in nature.

2. Interacts with other archers in style to learn .... ☐ Sometimes ☐ Often ☐ Always
   Much can be learned from other archers of the same style. Archers wanting to improve need to seek out useful information and try to apply it to their own game.

3. Uses imagery as part of shot sequence .... ☐ Sometimes ☐ Often ☐ Always
   Good shots are imaged/imagined as an early stage in shot sequence (practice and competition).

Notes _____
_____
_____
_____
_____
_____
_____

4. Uses affirmations to achieve goals .... ☐ Sometimes ☐ Often ☐ Always
   Affirmations are used in a prescribed process to achieve goals.

5. Uses shot thoughts as part of shot sequence ..... ☐ Sometimes ☐ Often ☐ Always
   Shot thoughts are used in any stage in shot sequence (practice and competition) to address weaknesses or lack of focus.

6. Uses shot sequence to create
   regular shooting rhythm .... ☐ Sometimes ☐ Often ☐ Always
   Shooting rhythm can be made regular by use of creative shot sequence elements that can only be found by trial and test.

7. Helps draft and uses process
   and outcome goals .... ☐ Sometimes ☐ Often ☐ Always
   Can help create process and outcome goals and then exhibits using them through self evaluation.

Notes _____

_____

_____

_____

_____

_____

_____

_____

_____

_____

_____

_____

_____

_____

Archery Education Resources
Recreational Archery Curriculum
Compound Track

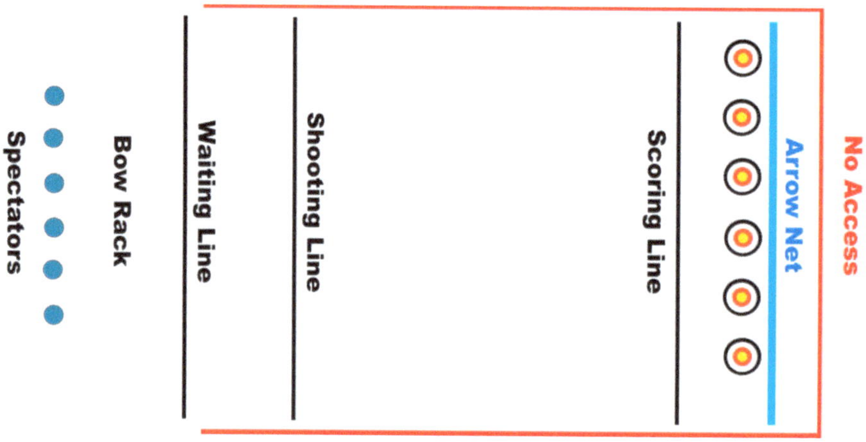

This diagram shows a typical layout for an indoor archery range. Archers are expected to be behind the waiting line when it is not their turn to shoot . . . behaving well.

Archery Education Resources
Recreational Archery Curriculum
Compound Track

Introduction
Shooting arrows with a compound bow is by far the most popular form of archery in the United States. This may be due to the popularity of bowhunting, but compound bows dominate target archery in popularity, too. Compound bows are allowed in almost every competition, except the Olympic Games. While only a few people get to contest archery in major stadiums, archery is contested in smaller sites all over. Our classes are conducted at Parks and Recreation Centers, public school grounds and gymnasiums, and occasionally at permanent archery ranges. And whether the shooting area is set up temporarily or is permanent, it is set up as a target range, because this creates a safe environment in which to practice archery and, after all, compound target archery is contested on target ranges (although compound-style archery is recognized in field archery, too). The first topic in AER archery classes is always orientation and safety. Safety will continue to be a topic as you build safe archery habits, because you don't have to think about a habit, it is just something you do.

Signposts—Stage I Getting Started

Archery Safety
In every *Stage* of every *Track* our most important concern is your safety. Archery is a safe sport because safe behaviors are developed into *habits* and the nice thing about habits is you don't have to think about them, they are just something you do. Consequently all of the *safety Signposts* apply to all of the *Tracks* and all of the *Stages* and all require "Always" ratings for you to proceed forward. But don't fret about this, being safe is just part of having fun!

Good Behavior Is Expected The expectation is that when you are waiting behind the waiting line (*see diagram on the previous page*), that you will do nothing dangerous, nor will you cause any discomfort for other archers. The *Signpost* that

> Usually the idea of good behavior only has to be explained to the 8-12 year-old set, but there are exceptions. If a student has trouble meeting this *Signpost*, ask the sponsor or site staff if he/she has a history of such behavior. Being forewarned is also being forearmed.

Notes _____

_____

_____

_____

_____

_____

_____

you will be evaluated on looks like this:

1. Exhibits good behavior
   when not on shooting line .... ☐ Sometimes ☐ Often ☐ Always
   Other archers and archery equipment treated respectfully while staying behind the waiting line.
   Must achieve "Always" to advance to the next Stage.

The Whistle System The system used to direct a group of archers is called the "Whistle System." Here are the whistle system commands:

The Whistle System

Two Blasts	Archers may come to the shooting line.
One Blast	Archers may place an arrow on their bows and begin shooting.
Three Blasts	Archers may walk to the target to retrieve their arrows.
Five or More Blasts	Emergency letdown! Stop immediately and wait for instructions.

This system is used all over the world at every level of archery (even at the World Championships and the Olympic games), although at competitions an air horn rather than a whistle may be used. A "letdown" from full or partial draw is performed by pointing the arrow at the floor/ground (outdoors) or the target immediately in front of you (indoors) and easing the string back to it's undrawn position. In an "emergency letdown" you also take the arrow off of the bow and place it back in its quiver. The *Signpost* that you will be evaluated on looks like this:

The whistle system was changed in 2008, specifically the "Emergency Letdown" signal was changed from "four or more" blasts to "five or more." Some older materials may not reflect the change and, since it is not a major change, no fuss need be made.

2. Understands and
   follows the whistle system .... ☐ Sometimes ☐ Often ☐ Always
   Knows and obeys all four whistle system commands. *Must achieve "Always" to advance to the next Stage.*

Good Behavior Is Expected Everywhere Just as you are expected to behave in a safe and polite manner when off of the shooting line, the same is true when you are on the shooting line. Trying to distract another archer during a contest is unsportsmanlike and, in general, one doesn't even speak to other archers when "on the line." Here is your *Signpost*:

3. Exhibits good behavior
   when on shooting line .... ☐ Sometimes ☐ Often ☐ Always
   Does not talk to, or interfere with, other archers on the line. *Must achieve "Always" to advance to the next Stage.*

During FITA competitions, if one archer complains about the behavior of another archer, it is taken seriously. A judge can monitor the situation and if the offending archer is judged to have deliberately tried to disadvantage another archer, he/she can be disqualified. For our purpose, this is only good manners. People trash talking on the line in a mean-spirited manner can only lead to a "no fun" situation which conflicts with our second overarching goal.

Notes _____

_____

_____

_____

_____

The Range Safety Rules Must Be Obeyed There are actually quite a few safety rules that apply when you are shooting arrows on a target range. We encourage coaches to post the standard "range rules" so you have an opportunity to read them. Some rules will be given only orally, so you need to listen carefully as there is no tolerance for violations of safety rules. A typical set of range rules is supplied on the next page.

The *Signpost* involved follows. The safety *Signposts* have not been duplicated at each *Stage* as always behaving safely is a requirement to pass out of the first stage. All safety rules will be enforced at each *Stage* of your program.

4. Obeys all safety rules (written/oral) .... ☐ Sometimes ☐ Often ☐ Always
   Even though rules are occasionally violated when they are being learned, there can be no violations for several weeks before an "always" can be given. Must achieve "Always" to advance to the next Stage.

> When you are evaluating *Signposts*, always focus on the *Stage* an archer is in. Here your archer is quite a beginner, so a high level of performance is not expected. What is expected is that the archer places his feet carefully and doesn't move them thereafter. The exact spacing, angle, etc. may vary (a little) and the student could still get an "Often" or "Always." More precision is expected later.

Basic Archery Form

The other major component of *Stage I* is achieving basic good archery form and execution. This is done with the only equipment being a bow and arrows (and an armguard, which is mandatory archery safety equipment).

Taking Your Stance The first part of any archery shot involves placing your feet properly, this is called "taking your stance." The stance everyone starts with is called the "square stance." In this stance your feet are about shoulder width apart with the tips of your shoes lying on a line that leads to the center of the target. (The line isn't there, you have to imagine it.) The line that is there, the shooting line, is supposed to be "straddled," that is you have one foot in front of the line and one foot behind.

Note that this puts you sideways to the target, which is good because that's the best way to shoot arrows. Turning your body either left or right at this stage will interfere with your making good shots, so it is important to not move your feet after you have taken your stance. Here is the associated *Signpost*:

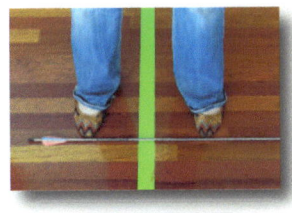

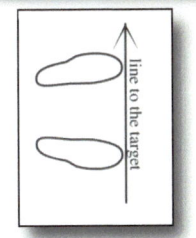

In a square stance the tips of your toes are on a line to the center of the target.

1. Adopts a square stance .... ☐ Sometimes ☐ Often ☐ Always
   Tips of shoes make line to center of target, feet shoulder-width apart, straddling the shooting line.

Standing Well The next step is to have good posture, which is not what your Mom or the military wants from you. You need to stand straight and relaxed. Your

Notes _____

Archery Range Rules

1. Know and obey all range commands.
2. Keep your arrows in your quiver until you are told to shoot.
3. Always wear your arm guard and finger tab.
4. Only use the arrows the instructor gave you and remember what they look like.
5. Always keep your arrows pointed down or toward the target.
6. If you drop an arrow, leave it on the ground until you are told to get your arrows.
7. Always walk at the archery range.

Archery Range Whistle Commands
Two Blasts "Archers to the Shooting Line."
One Blast "Begin Shooting."
Three Blasts "Walk forward and get your arrows."
Five or More Blasts "Stop shooting immediately! Wait for instructions!"

Archery Range Procedures
- Stand behind the waiting line until you hear two (2) whistle blasts or "Archers to the shooting line." Take your bow and straddle the shooting line.
- Keep your arrows in your quiver until you hear one (1) whistle blast.
- After you have shot all of your arrows, step back from the shooting line, set your bow on the rack, and wait behind the waiting line.
- After everyone is done shooting and is behind the waiting line, the instructor will blow the whistle three (3) times, then walk forward to the target line.

Pulling Your Arrows
- Two archers at a time from each target may go forward from the target line to pull their arrows.
- Stand to the side of the target and make sure that no one is standing behind your arrows.
- Pull your arrows out, one at a time, and put them into your quiver.
- After you have pulled all of your arrows, return to the waiting line.

Notes _____
_____
_____
_____
_____
_____
_____
_____

Younger archers tend to elevate their shoulders, neck, and head when they draw the bow. Watch for this. Encourage them to keep their upper body "down." Reason: elevating the chest and shoulders restricts the ability of the back muscles to come into play while drawing the bow (as they are involved in the elevating).

knees are neither bent nor locked back. Your chest is not puffed out, it is relaxed downward. Here is the associated *Signpost*:

2. Exhibits good archery posture .... ☐ Sometimes ☐ Often ☐ Always
   Stands relaxed and straight up and down, doesn't lean left or right, forward or backward. Knees straight but not locked.

Keeping Your Shoulders Down A particular part of archery posture that has its own Signpost involves your shoulders. Your shoulders are to be "down." If you don't know what this means ask your coach about the "Shoulders Up, Shoulders Down Drill." We are not telling you why this is done this way; if you are curious, ask your coach. (In general, we are organizing your skeleton and muscles to work together most effectively.) The *Signpost* here is:

3. Keeps shoulders low .... ☐ Sometimes ☐ Often ☐ Always
   Shoulders are in the "down" position throughout shot.

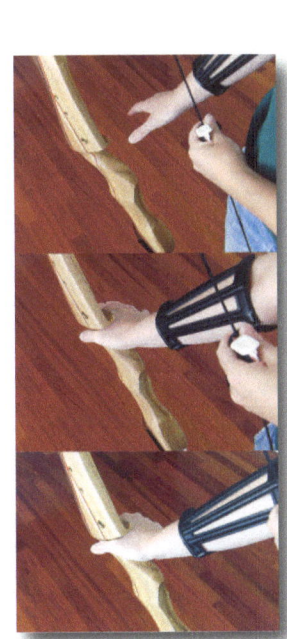

Setting Your Bow Hand One of the spots beginner's struggle is in placing their bow hand onto the bow. The spot on the bow where this happens is called the "grip," and it looks much the same as the grip on a pistol, but you neither hold it like a pistol nor do you "grip" or squeeze the bow. You don't want to squeeze the grip area of the bow because doing that doesn't help you draw the bow; in fact squeezing the bow detracts from your ability to pull the bowstring. (It makes you stiff and weak!) Holding a bow like a pistol puts the back of the hand parallel with the bow, which causes the archer's elbow to turn inward (sideways), very close to the path the bowstring takes when it is "loosed." So close, in fact, that it is easy for the string to whack your elbow that way (your armguard won't protect it as it is protecting your forearm, not your elbow)!

To set your bowhand correctly, you start with your hand relaxed, flat, and with your palm facing the floor/ground. You slide your hand (between thumb and first finger) into the "throat" (deepest part) of the grip. Then you bend your wrist down onto the bow and relax your fingers (they do not wrap around the bow). The knuckles of your bow hand are now at about a 45 angle to the ground, which is one way for you to check to see that you've got it right (see photo). The bow actually sits on the pad of your thumb and doesn't touch the other half of your hand. When you do

It is not "normal" to raise a bow while keeping the shoulders "down." One has to exert some effort to keep them down. This is a primary reason why students are to do the steps of the shot sequence as separate steps. (Note—They aren't introduced to shot sequences until *Stage II*, but you are guiding them that way all along.) During the "Raise the Bow" step, one makes a conscious effort to keep the shoulders "down." This is very hard to learn if one is simultaneously drawing the bow. Make sure students don't "draw on the way up" . . . until they can draw with their shoulders "down" as a matter of habit. Introduce the *AER Shoulders Up, Shoulders Down Drill* here if you haven't already done so.

Notes _____

_____

_____

_____

this you will find that your elbow has rotated away from the path of the bowstring and out of harm's way.

There are a few people who are very, very flexible and who can adopt this bow hand still have their elbow sideways. These archers need to learn how to rotate their elbows out of the way. Here is a test to see if you are one of these people: take a bow and set your bow hand properly, then hold the bow out as if you were going to shoot (don't use an arrow as you won't be shooting). Then bend the elbow of your bow arm. The bow should swing around and come up against your chest (*see photo right*). If it does, you are good to go. If the bow swings up in an arc toward your head, ask your coach about the *AER Elbow Rotation Drill*. Rotating your elbow will become one of the steps you will need to do to safely shoot arrows. Please, whacking your elbow is not a nice way to learn this! Do the test and find out whether you are doing it right or not.

Here's your *Signpost*:

4. Exhibits good bow hand .... ☐ Sometimes ☐ Often ☐ Always
   Bow hand is relaxed, in proper position with bow sitting on pad of thumb, fingers curled slightly and relaxed.

Positioning Your Head Another posture element that gets its own *Signpost* is head position. Since you are standing sideways to the target, you must turn your head to look over your shoulder to see the target. This is correct archery posture. On the other hand, tilting your head at all makes everything more difficult. Student-archers often do this in an attempt to "look down the arrow" as a way to aim. This technique does not work for a number of reasons, the primary one being that as soon as the arrow comes off of the bow, it falls, therefore it cannot hit the point sighted at. At very close distances, like where we begin shooting arrows, the amount the arrow falls is very small leading to the impression that "this works" but, as you move back from the target, the arrow will impact lower and lower compared to the aiming point. The idea of using the arrow to aim with is not a bad idea as you will see later, but the technique of looking down the shaft plainly does not work. Here is your *Signpost*:

5. Exhibits good head position through shot ..... ☐ Sometimes ☐ Often ☐ Always
   Head is turned toward target erect, neither tilted nor dipped.

BAD

GOOD

The bow hand is a major problem area for students. It can be compounded by the use of wooden-handled recurve bows or large compound bows, which have thick grip areas which in turn make it hard for smaller students to get a proper bow hand on them. Lack of a good bow hand is a major cause of bruised bow arms. Show students the elbow bending test as a way of emphasizing that they can check themselves from time to time.

Tilted heads can be made erect with a finger. Use just one finger to reposition your archer's head properly. Once they have found out what the correct position is (and have resisted the urge to look down the arrow) they will be able to replicate it fairly easily.

Notes _____

_____

_____

_____

_____

Beginners need to know how to start (finger and elbow placement), how to pull (using their back muscles to rotate their draw shoulder with some torso rotation thrown in), and where they are going (to their firm anchor position). At the same time they are supposed to maintain their good archery posture! So, this is quite a complex task. In general, the more complex the task, the more time it takes to master, so you should not be too quick to give "Oftens" and "Always" here.

Drawing the String There are people who are very cautious and do things carefully and slowly. Others, more exuberant in nature, rush everything. Archery is done somewhere in the middle. If you are slow and cautious, it might take you ten seconds to draw the bow. This is too slow—your muscles are getting tired even as you pull and the longer it takes, the more tired you will be when the pull required gets greater toward the end of the draw. Energetic folks tend to yank the string back; you can recognize them because their arrows tend to fall off of their arrow rest when they pull without caution. It should take only 1-2 seconds to draw the string. This is not rushed, nor is it slow. It is smooth and strong. In the beginning you may take longer than this, 2-3 seconds, because you are still learning to get the bowstring all the way back to where it belongs. This is okay, but the goal is to draw the string in a smooth, strong, and controlled fashion.

This is done with the draw elbow level with the draw hand or higher.

Here is the *Signpost* for drawing the string:

6. Draws the bow smoothly and in rhythm ..... ☐ Sometimes ☐ Often ☐ Always
   Bow string is drawn smoothly and quickly without hurrying, draw elbow is high.

Finding Your Anchor Position An "anchor" position in archery refers to the position of your drawing hand with regard to your body. Over the years there have been many anchors, from behind the ear to down at the chest, but for consistent accuracy, the anchor position must bring the bow string in front of your aiming eye. You will be taught two anchors—a high anchor first and a low, or Olympic-style, anchor later.

The high anchor is found by pressing your draw hand against your face such that the tip of your index finger is positioned in the corner of your mouth and your top finger wraps around your cheek bone (*see photo*). If you have difficulty finding this position, your coach will help you find it, first without a bow and then with a bow. This is the *Signpost* for finding your anchor position:

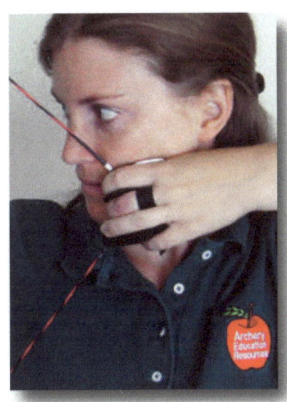

7. Exhibits a reasonably tight anchor .... ☐ Sometimes ☐ Often ☐ Always
   Anchor position is consistent with draw hand pressed against face (high anchor) bringing the string in front of the aiming eye.

Many students, young and old, are hesitant to have something unknown (like a bowstring and the end of an arrow) right next to their eyes or face (or glasses). Others it doesn't bother. So, it may take some patience with the sensitive ones, which is entirely their due. And once they are convinced it won't hurt them, they become fine with it.

The biggest bugaboo is having the thumb of the draw hand "up" which equates to "in the way." The thumb must be held "down" so it ends up under the jaw at anchor. Then it can be relaxed. Having the thumb in any "up" position blocks the hand from achieving a tight anchor. Having the pad of the draw hand thumb on the little fingernail positions both thumb and little finger correctly. After anchor has been found, these can be relaxed.

Notes _____
_____
_____
_____

Following Through Bowlers follow through, golfers follow through, baseball batters follow through, and . . . archers follow through. The archery "followthrough" form element is simply to maintain your body position after each arrow is shot for at least one second. A key part of this, because your bow hand is relaxed, is that your bow will rock gently in your hand after the bow string is released. This rocking is an indicator that tells you how well you executed the release of the string and held your followthrough position by how regular it is. (Does it happen the same way each time?) This is the *Signpost* for following through:

8. Exhibits good followthrough .... ☐ Sometimes ☐ Often ☐ Always
   After the string is released, bow arm stays up and draw hand moves backward along face.

Getting in Line This *Signpost* holds the key for consistent accuracy. In order for everything to work in this style, your draw elbow has to be in line with your arrow at full draw (*see photos*). It is that simple. Most beginners end with their draw elbows too low and sticking out away from them. As you progress your elbow needs to get "in line" as this alignment with the arrow allows your fingers to slip from the string in the most relaxed manner. (Tense draw fingers can cause arrows to fly sideways!) The sooner you can get into this position, the sooner everything else comes together to make great shots.

A key element in archery is achieving good form as quickly as possible because you do not want to practice doing it wrong! At some time or other in school one of your teachers had you rewrite each of your misspelled words on an assignment ten times. This is a fairly good rule of thumb: if you practice something *incorrectly*, it will take ten times the work doing it *correctly* to fix the incorrect execution. So, if you shoot arrows 10 times incorrectly, it takes 100 correct shots to make doing it correctly somewhat of a habit (1000 incorrect shots requires 10,000 correct ones!). So, never settle for doing something "any old way." If it is not right, start over.

This is the *Signpost* for achieving good alignment:

9. Exhibits good alignment .... ☐ Sometimes ☐ Often ☐ Always
   At full draw, draw elbow lines up with the arrow line extended backward.

"Grouping" Your Shots When anyone first begins shooting arrows, we celebrate all "bull's eyes." But as time goes on, the goal is not just hitting the target's

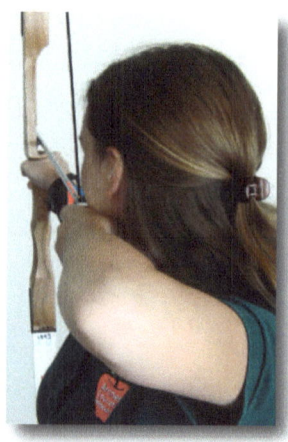

Good alignment (top) is essential for consistency; poor alignment (below) causes "plucked" releases (bottom) and poor consistency.

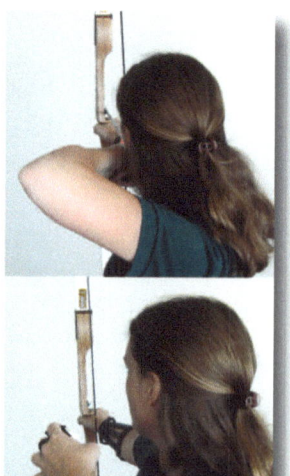

If the bow hand is relaxed the bow will "bow" (as in to "take a bow") and it takes about 1-2 seconds for it to do so, so one of the cues you can use is *Hold your form until the bow 'bows.'* This is a good indicator of how long to hold their followthroughs as the amount of time is constant (as opposed to "until the arrow hits the target") and it encourages good form. The same will be true when stabilizers are introduced, but the top limb will "bow" forward instead of backward as it will now.

Line, line, line! Alignment is the key to good form and accuracy. If the draw elbow is behind the arrow, the forces in the bow and archer's body are arrayed properly and the draw wrist and hand can be relaxed and the fingers can come off the string as a unit. If there is a "kink" in the alignment, there is no relaxation and no smooth release. A ragged release causes the string to swing wildly (you can see this in slow-motion video) and arrows to fly all over the place. The importance of line cannot be emphasized too much—to coaches. Athletes should not be thinking about "line" as it is too abstract; their cues/shot thoughts are "reach to the target" (bow arm) and "swing elbow backward" (draw arm), both of which contribute to good line.

> You can encourage students to keep track of their groups by asking them "How big are your groups, normally?" They often will not include "flyers" (arrows that don't group) at the beginning, which is okay . . . in the beginning. Archers typically use phrases like "I am holding the red" (all arrows in the red and gold (7-10 rings) or "I usually hold the five ring" (all arrows in the blue, red, gold or 5-10 rings. Most people specify the yardage, too, but that comes later. As time goes on, more and more attention will be paid to the size of the groups. Right now attention is being paid to the act of grouping arrows and less so to their location. The key point is: if they can group their arrows they can move the group into the center with aiming techniques. If they can't group (a sign of inconsistent form), then aiming doesn't matter, so reasonable "grouping" must precede learning to aim.

center, it is hitting it consistently, which is why the concept of "grouping" is introduced here. Shooting arrows that all land in (roughly) one place is even more important than hitting those bull's eyes, because if you can shoot arrows so they land all in the same place you can move those arrows to a new place using an aiming technique. (Most people prefer the center as a landing location.) But, if you can't "group" your arrows and you get a bull's eye, the next arrow will be somewhere else and each subsequent arrow in yet another location.

So, how do you get "good groups?" Grouping is an outcome of consistency; grouping is the outcome of doing the same thing, the same way, over and over. There is a very old saying: "Repetition is the Mother of Learning." This is true in archery, but repetition without good form and execution is worse than not practicing! You must strive to "do it right" over and over.

Be aware, though, that there is not a lot of "trying" involved. (Actually "trying too hard" blocks making progress in archery.) The target gives you feedback: either the arrows are in nice, tight groups, or they are not. If you are reasonably careful about how you shoot, even moderate amounts of practice will result in good groups in very little time.

Here is your first target-oriented *Signpost*:

10. Shoots good groups consistently .... ☐ Sometimes ☐ Often ☐ Always

   Three arrow groups fit into an eight inch circle two ends out of three at 10 yards. Must achieve "Often" to advance to the next Stage.

Aiming "Off the Point" Back when we addressed where an archer needs to put his or her head, the wrong idea of aiming by looking down the arrow shaft was mentioned. The idea of using the arrow was good but the wrong part (the shaft) was being used. An accurate aiming system, that needs no additional equipment attached to the bow, is the technique of *aiming off the point* (the arrow point).

Because we shoot arrows up into the air so they can arc down into the target (due to the large effect gravity has on relatively slow flying arrows), we hold the rear end of the arrow down under our aiming eye so that the arrow shaft points upward. If you are executing shots with good alignment, a soft bow hand, and a decent followthrough, your arrows will rarely miss left or right of a vertical centerline on the target. (We use a clock face for orientation on circular targets. The very top of the tar-

> The answer to the question, "I am going to use a bow sight, why do I have to learn this?" is obviously, "You don't have to." But, this is fun. It teaches part of the aiming technique needed to use a bow sight well, and it doesn't require all of the fiddling needed when setting up a bow sight to use. One possible tongue-in-cheek rejoinder is "It's boring to shoot just one way!"

Notes _____

_____

_____

_____

_____

get is 12 o'clock, the bottom is 6 o'clock, the left edge 9 o'clock, and the right edge is 3 o'clock (*see diagram*). We can then specify any location on the target by naming the ring and the time, *e.g.* 6:30 in the red or 11 o'clock in the 3-ring. So, if you meet the requirements mentioned, your arrows will be in a narrow band from 12 o'clock to 6 o'clock and rarely left or right of that band. You will have solved the "windage problem" which is "How do I aim left and right?"

The other question: "How do I aim up and down?" is called the "elevation problem" and is more difficult to solve. You can do it by shooting many hundreds of arrows at each of a great many different distances and let your brain do the math, or you can use an aiming technique like "aiming off the point."

Here is how it works. Imagine that you are about to release the string on a perfect shot, one in which the arrow will strike the target dead center. Now imagine what you are seeing through your aiming eye just before the arrow is shot. This is called your "sight picture." Because you are focused on the target, the target is about the only thing you will notice, but in your field of view is part of the bow and also part of the arrow. The point of the arrow in your sight picture is in some position relative to the image of the target, *e.g.* blue ring at 6 o'clock. (If you haven't mastered all of the previous steps or if your bow and arrows aren't perfectly matched (and this typically is the case with borrowed or program equipment) you may be to one side or the other of that 12 o'clock—6 o'clock line; in any case, it is somewhere on or near the target). You release the arrow and it goes right into the center. Ah, but you want to do it again, don't you? Are their any clues as to how to get your body and bow back into that perfect full draw position time after time? The answer is "the position of the arrow point in your sight picture." *If your foot positions, posture, and shot execution are exactly the same and the arrow point is at the exact same place in your sight picture, the arrow will land in the same location.* This is aiming off the point.

There is one distance at which if you put the point onto the center of the target in your sight picture, the arrow goes into the center. This is called "point blank

Notes _____

This point of aim diagram is from a pamphlet printed in 1932. The technique was invented in the mid-1800s.

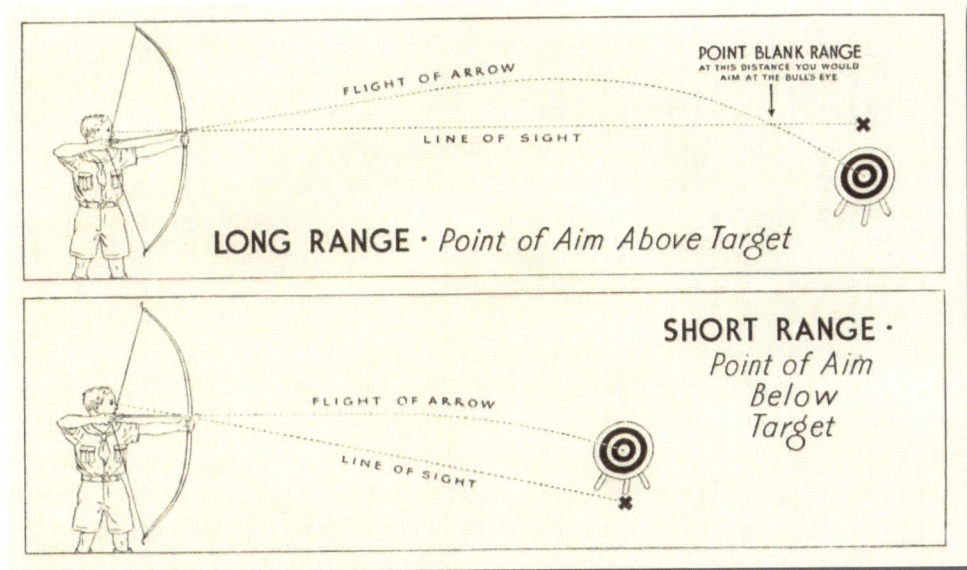

range." Archers now usually refer to it as being at their "point on target" distance or their "point on" for short. At closer distances than the point-on-target-distance, the point of aim is lower than the center and at longer distances than the point-on-target-distance, the point of aim is higher on the target. At very short distances, the POA (point of aim) may be on the ground or floor and for much longer distances it may be up on the wall or the hill, or trees on top of the hill (*see the diagram*)!

This is the *Signpost* for aiming off of the point:

11. Uses arrow point to aim with .... ☐ Sometimes ☐ Often ☐ Always
    Must be able to find and use a point of aim for at least one distance (7-15 yards).

Notes _____

Signposts—Stage II Getting Better
Must have completed requirements of Stage I before beginning.

Congratulations! By making it out of *Stage I* you are now quite a good archer. You know how to stand, fit an arrow to the string, raise up the bow, draw it smoothly, release the shot cleanly and followthrough . . . and your arrows go mostly into the center of the target at shorter distances. You can stop at this point and enjoy archery for the rest of your life this way. But, after you have acknowledged that you have come a long way, you might feel like there is more to learn . . . and there is. If you want to keep going then you are going to learn *intermediate archery form* and in order for you to do so you must acquire your own equipment.

The equipment you need is the same equipment you have been using: bow, arrows, and armguard but there is more you will have to get as you go (tab, bow sight, stabilizer(s), specialized arrow rests, mechanical release aids). The reason you need your own equipment is the equipment needs to be fitted to you. For example, now that your draw length has become regular, you don't need extra-long arrows (used by beginners for safety). If you intend on buying your own gear, ask your AER Archery Coach if he/she does "Bow Fittings." This is a service in the form of a private lesson that measures you up for the equipment style you favor, so that you will know exactly what to buy as well as where you can shop and what you can reasonably expect to pay.

If you are borrowing equipment, the same criteria apply, so consult your coach as to what exactly you need to acquire.

The big change (a very big change) is that you have probably learned *Stage I* form on a "zero letoff" compound bow (*e.g. Genesis* bow) or even on a recurve bow. If you are acquiring a compound bow to tailor to your own needs, it will probably have "letoff." Letoff is what makes compound bows so popular. When you draw a compound bow with letoff here is what happens: as you pull it gets harder and harder to pull until you get about two thirds of the way back and then it gets easier, and easier, and easier! At full draw, you are typically holding one third to one quarter of the "peak" (highest) draw weight you experienced. For example, a compound bow with a 40# draw with 80% letoff leaves you with only 8# to hold at full draw. What this means is that at full draw, you are under much less stress than you are with

Now You Need Your Own ...

bow

arrows

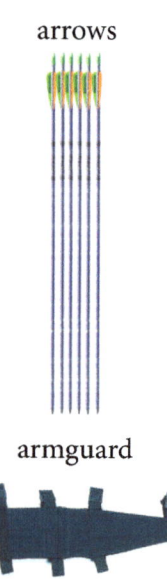

armguard

Notes

a recurve bow or a longbow and you are therefore more comfortable, so you can take more time to aim. The comfort at full draw and having time to aim are the primary causes of the popularity of compound bows. Adjustments to your form will be made to utilize this feature of compound bows.

When you have your own equipment, the first thing you are going to want to do is set it up correctly. The first step is to place a nocking point locator (like on your class bow) on the string, then you will need to set the position of your arrow rest. (We recommend an inexpensive, screw-in plastic arrow rest for now.) The next step after that is to adjust the bow's draw length to match your draw length (exactly). Then you can start shooting your way through this next *Stage*.

Intermediate Archery Form

Modifying Your Stance Everybody starts with a square stance but everybody is also different from everybody else. Sometimes a different stance can help you shoot better. Stances are classified as "square" (or "even"), which you have learned already, or as being "open" or "closed." An open stance has the front foot swung around and or back from the square position. A closed stance has the rear foot swung around and back from the square stance. What we recommend is that you try these stances for a class or two to see if they make an improvement in your comfort or accuracy. It takes a class or two or longer attempt because making any change is difficult.

A basic AER learning principle is: *anytime you change something, your archery gets worse before it gets better*. Because archery is a repetition sport, you have had many repetitions of your archery shot making it comfortable and "normal." Whenever you make a change, it feels uncomfortable and "not normal" which automatically makes you worse! It takes a fair number of repetitions to overcome this effect and make the new way seem at least reasonable. And you can't evaluate whether the change was good or bad until you have taken many shots. If the "result" of the change is your archery gets worse and then gets better than when you started, it is a good change. If it gets worse and never gets back to where you were before the change, it is a bad change. But without a fair chance, you will never make any changes. Don't be an archer who says, "I tried that for ten minutes and it wasn't as good!" Nothing in archery will be better after only ten minutes of trying. (Of course, if something creates pain, we recommend you stop doing it immediately!).

See the Appendix—*On Stances* for more detail. Be aware that because the square stance is taught to beginners, many seem to think it is the "baby stance." Nothing could be further from the truth. The square stance can be used by one and all for a great many purposes and for a great many styles, which is why it is taught first. If student doesn't want to experiment with a new stance, this *Signpost* may be skipped until later or altogether.

A basic AER learning principle is: *any time you change something, your archery gets worse before it gets better.*

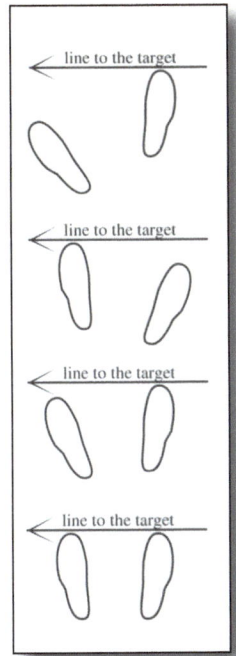

Stances (from bottom to top) can be "square," or "open," or "closed," or "wide open" or done other ways (not shown).

Notes _____

_____

_____

_____

_____

If you try, say, an open stance and it doesn't work for you, don't go straight to a closed stance and try that. Return to your "normal" square stance for several lessons and get back to the feel of "normal" before you try the closed stance (or anything else).

Generally, an open stance is the most popular stance with compound archers (although popularity is not a guarantee of anything as every individual is unique) and a closed stance makes it easier to get into line. So, if you are struggling with getting or keeping good line, try the close stance. If you want to look like all of the other archers, try the open stance.

But realize, you do not have to change your stance! In fact, unless you have certain evidence that a difference stance works better for you, changing is not recommended. But if you don't try the other options you will never know if there is a better archery stance out there for you.

The prime criterion to evaluate form changes is "Can it be done the same way, each and every shot?" This is your Signpost if you modify your stance:

1. Adopts a personal stance consistently .... ☐ Sometimes ☐ Often ☐ Always
   If open or closed stance is adopted, must adopt that stance consistently.

Modifying Your Posture A refinement of the form you have learned so far is the *hip tuck* or "hip tilt." If you rotate your hips slightly (bottom of your hips is rotated forward), your back becomes flat (*see photos*) and your center of gravity drops slightly. The flat back allows your back muscles (instrumental in drawing the bowstring) freer reign and the lower center of gravity makes you more stable (less tendency to sway back and forth as you shoot). While this is a small change, so are all of the others as you build better form, but the sum of many small changes can be a big improvement in score! Here is the *Signpost* for your refined archery posture:

2. Exhibits good archery posture .... ☐ Sometimes ☐ Often ☐ Always
   Stands relaxed and straight up and down, doesn't lean left or right, forward or backward. Knees straight but not locked. Shoulders down. Small of back flat.

Using a Finger Tab Bows used in beginner classes are very light drawing. As you gain experience the amount of draw weight you can handle goes up. But as the draw weight goes up, so does the tension on the bowstring along with the pressure

Without the hip tuck, the archer's back is hollow; with it, it is flat.

Photo Courtesy of Tom Lee

If you are not familiar with the hip tuck, try this: stand straight up in front of a vertically hung mirror and then let your body flow "down." (We tend to hold ourselves "up" a little due to mom's or the military's posture exhortations. Then tilt your pelvis as described while looking straight forward in the mirror. You will see yourself drop a slight bit more. This is a lowering of your center of gravity which makes you slightly more stable and, more importantly, causes your lower back to line up with your upper back (with no "hollow" in your lower back—see photos). You can see this standing sideways to the mirror as you do the hip tuck. This "flat back" gives you a more rounded back which, in turn, gives your back muscles more range of motion to draw the bow. A stiff, military "chest out" posture uses much of the back muscles' range of motion to puff out the chest and does nothing to help an archer in his/her task, so it is to be avoided.

Notes _____

_____

_____

_____

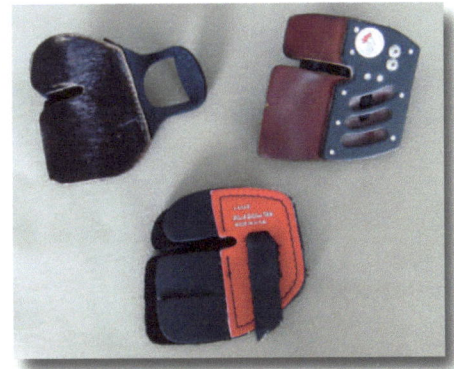

it creates on your fingers during the draw. At very high draw weights, this pressure, can damage the nerves in your fingers. Long before that would happen the discomfort of shooting leads to some form of finger protection. The vast majority of target archers use a finger tab for this purpose. In addition to protecting your draw fingers, tabs also provide a slick surface for the string to slide from.

It makes no sense to stint when buying a tab because they do not cost much. The most expensive tabs cost almost $30, but a very good tab (the *Black Widow* tab made by the Wilson Brothers) typically can be had for around $10, if not under $10. If you are a very serious archer, you may want to buy two, not because they wear out fast but they are small enough to get lost and you want to have a backup tab. If you alternate days using them, the two tabs will be near identical in their performance (both will be "broken in" to the same extent). There are many styles of tabs, even from a single manufacturer, so consult with your coach or read the catalogs or online information carefully.

At the same time you break in a new tab, you will probably want to try a "split-finger" placement on the bowstring. This usually happens when you begin to shoot longer distances (outdoors). Placing one finger above the arrow (the other two below) instead of all three below the arrow and using the same anchor position, effectively lowers the back end of the arrow the width of your top finger. This is actually a great deal. The effect is to point the arrow upward more and thus greater "cast" or distance can be had. The *Black Widow* tab has leather flaps between the top two fingers that protect your fingers from developing calluses and reduce "finger pinch," that is pinching the arrow between your top two fingers. The reason you were started "three fingers under" was that beginners tend to tense their hands when they draw, which if you use a "split-finger" position from the start a) causes the fingers to pinch the arrow and b) causes the string and the arrow to rotate away from (and fall off of!) the bow. This is very frustrating for beginning archers. The "three fingers under" approach eliminates this source of frustration and once beginning archers learn to relax their draw hands while drawing, a change to split finger is possible.

Having said this, if you intend to walk the string (*see Signpost #5 in Stage IV*

Finger tabs can be sources of problems but also sources of information. Tabs need to be fitted (the tab's material must wrap around the top and bottom fingers somewhat as the string wraps around them—only trim off unnecessary material) and worn snuggly. The draw fingers still need to be held in a fixed position (typically touching one another and the arrow), but without tension. As tabs wear, the indentations (from the pressure of the string) and wear patterns on the tab can tell you how that tab is being used. For example, if the indentation from the string is narrow, this indicates the tab being placed consistently on the string; if wide, maybe the archer is a little careless at this. The position of the indentation shows you where the string is regarding the fingers (you have to see where the archer wears his tab, of course) and the depth of the indentation shows you where the pressure is greatest and least. See *The Magic Release* by Don Rabska in the Coach Resources section of the AER website for an excellent article about the finger release.

We have gone to some length to explain to archers desiring to use a release aid why we are keeping them on a tab while they learn. For insistent students, you may have to make an accommodation and move forward the release training *Signposts*. Use your judgment of the maturity of the student to guide you.

below), there is absolutely no need to try a split-finger approach. But many people want to learn all they can, so try it anyway. It is your choice.

If you intend to eventually shoot your bow with a mechanical release aid, you may be wondering why we still have your fingers on the bowstring. The reason to do this is to make sure your archery form is quite solid before we introduce the release aid. There is quite a bit of technique involved in shooting a release aid correctly, and if you are trying to focus on it and several elements in your shooting form as well, it is easy to develop some really poor habits that are hard to break. This approach works. And, some people do shoot compound bows with a finger release. How do you know you are not one of them if you don't try it?

This is the *Signpost* for using a finger tab:

3. Uses an archery tab correctly .... ☐ Sometimes ☐ Often ☐ Always
   Can put on a fitted archery tab and use it properly as a guide to placing fingers on string. Later archer may switch to release aid but only after all other accessories have been incorporated and are used comfortably. Before release aid is used on bow, an arrow rest change may be required.

Modern Bowhand Technique Compound bow grips come in a number of styles. There are even companies that make custom grips to fit the best-selling bows. And many expert archers modify their bow's grip using auto body dent filler, tennis racquet wraps, tape, and other substances it make it exactly as they want. Rather than complicate matters unnecessarily, fine tuning of the grip of your bow will be left until later. There is only one exception to this recommendation: if the (removable) grip supplied with your bow really doesn't fit your hand or is quite uncomfortable, take it off. You can then wrap the grip area with "tennis racquet tape" to make a softer surface to place your hand. (Note—You do not want a sticky or non-slip surface there; you want your hand to slide into place.)

This is the *Signpost* for your new bow hand position:

4. Exhibits good bow hand .... ☐ Sometimes ☐ Often ☐ Always
   Bow hand is relaxed, with bow sitting on pad of thumb, fingers curled slightly and relaxed.

Drawing Smoothly There is a little you have to change to bring your draw up to intermediate archer standards, if you have worked to get a quick smooth draw in the previous *Stage*, especially if your bow now has letoff. Because of the letoff, the

There is no part of archery that is more "personal" than the grip area of the archer's bow. Maybe this is because everyone's bow hands are different, but it is also a critical area for a shot. After the string is loosed, the arrow is still on the string and the bow still in the bow hand (the only remaining point of contact!) for about 20 milliseconds. This doesn't seem like much time, but if the bow is placed improperly in the bow hand or if the bow hand is not relaxed, there are forces being exerted on the grip that are acting when the string is let go. (The official term is "pre-loaded bow hand torque.") So, this is one area of the bow that archers will cus-tomize. This issue is de-emphasized early in the program by emphasizing that "the wrist drops down placing the pad of the thumb onto the grip"(thus conforming to its shape) and that the bow hand is very relaxed, both of which will serve later, no matter how an archer personalizes his or her equipment.

The key factor that coaches have to keep in mind with compound archers is the sheer mass of the bows—they are heavy and this affects everything, including the grip.

The draw is *the* major movement, with everything else being either smaller or involving less tension creation. In order for an archer to be relaxed (a requirement for performance) the draw must be smooth and strong, under control. Yanking on the string is a sign of fatigue (or cluelessness). Shaking while drawing or at full draw is a sign of being "overbowed" (too much draw weight) which pretty much kills any chance of achieving good form. Archers should be able to draw their bows smoothly and seemingly effortlessly with the bow held straight up and down (arrow level, pointed at target). Any other draw (higher, lower, draw elbow too low, etc.) is dangerous in the event of a premature loose of the string. If archers struggle to draw, they need less draw weight—this is an absolute.

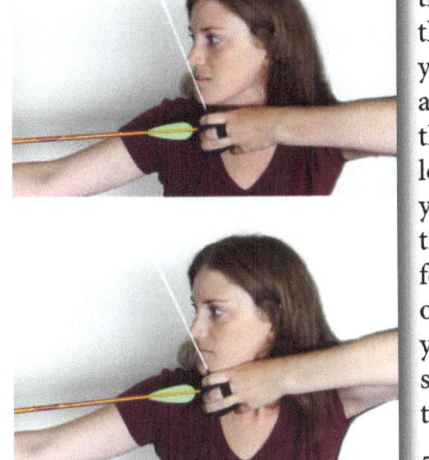

bow's draw weight increases much faster at the beginning of the draw that you have experienced, so you have to pull harder, at first. Then when the bow reaches its "peak weight" you have to "slow down" your pull so you arrive at full draw in as relaxed a state as you can. You will see other archers jerk the bow back all of the way. This is not an advantage, in fact there are several drawbacks to doing the draw that way. What you are looking for is a smooth, strong, draw with rhythm. If you have changed your finger position (to "split-finger") and changed your bowhand positioning and have more draw weight to handle, then it will take some time for all of those elements to become comfortable. Then, with a little focus on your draw, you can get back to the smooth, controlled, but quick draw you had using a light-drawing program bow. This *Signpost* is worded the same as before because the goal is the same, but reaching the goal will take some time and effort as things have changed quite a bit:

5. Draws the bow smoothly and in rhythm ☐ Sometimes ☐ Often ☐ Always

Bow string is drawn smoothly and quickly without hurrying, draw elbow is high.

Anchors Away? It was mentioned in *Stage I* that there are other anchors and that you would be learning two. It is time to learn a *low* anchor. This typically happens as you move to longer distances (as with the split-finger string grip). Moving your anchor position from alongside your face to under your jaw lowers the back end of the arrow far more than any other change you are making. It creates much greater "cast" (distance shot) because of this.

To execute the "low or Olympic-style anchor" use a light-drawing practice bow at first (even without arrows; just draw, anchor, and then let down the string—then repeat until comfortable). What you will find is that your head position has to be modified slightly. You must raise your chin a fraction of an inch. If you do not, your chin can block off your new hand position. The bow is drawn to slightly (1-2 inches, max) below the chin, then you "find your anchor" by raising your hand up until it presses against the bottom edge of your jaw (*see the photos*). Some people draw until the bowstring touches the corner of their chin before they raise their draw hand and they say that, in this manner they know whether they have drawn the string

What many beginners struggle with is that the anchor position requires the draw hand to be pressed firmly against the cheek (high anchor) or against the under jaw (low anchor). Hovering/floating the anchor hand is a major source of poor group sizes. The goal is to get the bowstring right in front of the aiming eye and "pressing the flesh" is a requirement for this and for the stability of the position. Head position cannot be affected by this. Note that this does not apply to compound archers shooting mechanical release aids. The anchor position of a release aid is closer to a "touch point" than it is a firm anchor (due to the peep sight being the thing that keeps its position from shot it shot (as the bow goes up, the anchor point goes down (slight-ly), etc.). Be very leery of applying technique from one kind of bow to others that are significantly different (recurve bows and longbows are much alike, but compound bows (due to low string tension at full draw) can be quite different.

Also, many compound archers who shoot "fingers" prefer to shoot with a "dead release." See *Is the Dead Release Really Dead?* by Steve Ruis in Coach Resources on the AER website.

Notes _____

the correct distance. You do not want the bowstring any farther back (along the edge of your jaw) as the string will then drag on the skin of your face and worse, cause the arrow to fly offline!

Obviously, if this lower anchor gives you greater distance, it is less useful at short distance. Adult Olympic-style archers do not shoot anything shorter than 30 meters (about 33 yards) outdoors but field archers shoot arrows as close as at ten yards or less, so field archers will often use the high anchor for short shots and the low anchor for the long ones. So, it is best to practice both. (If you are not interested in field archery, you can just shoot the low anchor.)

This is the *Signpost* for evaluating your new low anchor:

6. Exhibits Tight Anchor .... ☐ Sometimes ☐ Often ☐ Always
   Anchor position is consistent with draw hand pressed against jaw (low anchor) bringing the string in front of the aiming eye (low anchor optional for those intending to shoot a release aid).

Stabilizing the Shot It is time to add a stabilizer to your bow. We are starting with a single "long rod" stabilizer as they are prominent in many compound bow shooting styles, but if you wish you may opt for a short stabilizer. (Short stabilizers conform with hunting practices which form the basis for several compound bow shooting styles.)

When you add a long stabilizer, it changes the feel of the bow greatly. Beginners must exercise extra care as you are not used to having that long thing sticking out in front and it is all too easy to hit people with it by swinging your bow around too quickly.

Start getting used to it by drawing your bow on a target (at short distance) and then letting down. Repeat this several times before trying a shot. We start you at short distance because adding the stabilizer changes the impact points of your arrows, in other words all of your points of aim will have to be relearned. Now shoot some arrows, gradually getting back to the longer distances you were shooting at before the stabilizer was introduced.

Stabilizers are allowed in all common compound bow shooting styles and because they make your aim and shot steadier, they are an advantage. You can, of course, choose not to shoot with one if you really don't like it. After you have gotten used to the long rod, if you don't like it, try a shorter

Some take readily to a stabilizer, others do not. Adding a stabilizer affects where the arrow hits the target and this change may create the impression "This thing is no good." For those who get this impression you can try some blank bale shooting—eyes closed—short range. This actually emphasizes the objectionable "feel" of the stabilizer, which can result in it being accepted quicker because what is being blocked out is the influence of the target and the inevitable judging of the shot by where it lands. Alternatively, you can try introducing the sling (below) and then go back to trying a stabilizer. Sometimes the lack of acceptance can be related to a feeling that the student is going to drop their bow (being made even more awkward by the stabilizer) and be embarrassed.

Notes _____

_____

_____

_____

stabilizer. If you find one you like and it was borrowed, you will need to acquire your own.

This is the *Signpost* for shooting with a stabilizer:

7. Shoots comfortably with a stabilizer .... ☐ Sometimes ☐ Often ☐ Always
    A stabilizer makes a bow easier to hold steady at full draw and through release.

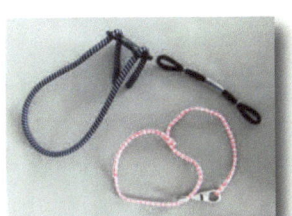

Bow slings (top left) attach to the bow and you put your hand through the loop before gripping the bow; finger slings (top right) connect bow thumb and first finger; wrist slings (bottom) go around the wrist, around the bow and hook back to the loop.

Adding a Sling Most people shoot with some kind of "sling." It might be a finger sling, or a wrist sling, or a bow sling. Most compound archers like the simplicity of a bow sling (*see photo*). All you need do is slip your hand through the loop of the bow sling before setting your bow hand.

What the sling does is make it okay for you to have a relaxed bow hand throughout the entire shot. Even though we are taught this is the correct way to shoot, sometimes subconsciously/unknowingly we are concerned about dropping the bow (like on a downhill shot) and will involuntarily squeeze the grip. This tension is undesirable.

To get used to a bow sling (or finger sling or wrist sling) put the sling on (or slip your hand through the bow sling) and then hold your bow out at arm's length and let go of it! When you do this, the bow will be caught by the sling! This may be a little dramatic, but you have just made the point to your subconscious mind that you cannot drop your bow if you are using your sling. Now, it can relax it's vigilance regarding that happening.

You must used your sling for each and every shot you take from now on, no exceptions! You are creating a new habit.

This is the *Signpost* for shooting with a sling:

8. Shoots comfortably with a sling .... ☐ Sometimes ☐ Often ☐ Always
    Uses a finger/wrist sling comfortably and easily.

Still Following Through There is a little you need to modify in your followthrough. The difference is that with a long rod stabilizer, your bow will tend to gently rock forward upon releasing the shot, instead of rocking backward as it did before. But the same rationale applies: the followthrough gives feedback about the latter stages of the shot by its consistency.

We have also included this *Signpost* because it is easy to let the followthrough

A sling is not absolutely necessary but the vast majority of compound archers use them. If an archer's bow hand position is weak, they may be holding onto the bow, resulting in the feeling that they do not need a sling . . . which is an argument for working more on their bow-hand position, not for whether to use a sling. An exercise to teach proper bow hand position is to kneel in front of an archer (and toward the bow side) as they shoot over your shoulder without a sling. (There is a question of trust here—or there should be!) Everything done properly results in the bow flying out of the archer's hand (which you are there to catch, of course)! They should be able to do this three shots in a row. Note that this is an advanced exercise and should not be done casually.

In the Appendix—*Making Your Own Gear* we show you how to make inexpensive wrist slings you can give away, use for a fundraiser, whatever. Check it out.

Also, do have your archers "drop their bows" (see immediately above) from time to time to reinforce to their subconscious minds that they do not have to "grab the bow" when an arrow is shot.

Notes _____

work it's way back into the release. For example, one bad habit is called "dropping your bow arm." This happens to compound bow archers often because the bows are so heavy, but whether the cause is due to the weight of the bow or not, the flaw is to allow the bow to drop down immediately after the shot. The problem with this is: shoot drop, shoot drop, shoot drop can easily become: shoot drop, shoot drop, drop shoot (ooops)! So, an archer does well at the time of releasing the string to be thinking about doing the followthrough correctly.

This is the *Signpost* for following through:

9. Exhibits good followthrough .... ☐ Sometimes ☐ Often ☐ Always
   After the string is released, bow arm stays up as the bow jumps straight out into bow sling, then "bows," and draw hand moves backward along face.

Lining Up Alignment is, like the followthrough, something that you cannot just set and forget. Focus on it needs to be continual. You can check your own alignment with a mirror (an inexpensive closet door mirror propped against a wall will do) or you can ask your coach or even another knowledgeable archer to check it for you from time to time. The goal is to always have your elbow exactly in line with the arrow.

This is the *Signpost* for getting into good line:

10. Exhibits good alignment .... ☐ Sometimes ☐ Often ☐ Always
    At full draw, draw elbow lines up with but is not behind the arrow line extended backward.

Step-by-Step The key to consistent accuracy is to get accurate and then get consistent. Getting accurate with bow and arrow involves getting good form and good execution. Getting consistent is largely a mental task of being focused on doing things the same way each time. Being focused means not letting your mind drift. The question is: "How can I do this?" The answer is "With a strong mental program."

The start of the mental game in archery begins with what is called a *shot sequence* or a "shot routine." This is simply a list of the things you do to make a good archery shot. At first a basic set of steps is learned, then as time goes on you will modify the sequence by changing steps or even adding or removing steps until it is your personal shot sequence.

Learning a basic shot sequence is the goal of this *Signpost*, but keep in mind

Unlike Olympic-style archers whose alignment goal is to get their draw elbow's *behind* arrow line, compound archers need to be exactly *in line*, with their draw elbows being neither inside nor outside that line. For those destined for a release aid, the bow string actually touches their face. If the draw elbow is wrapped around, so is the bowstring and when released it will drag on the chin. For those with a finger release, the lack of tension at full draw (a 60# bow has only 20# or less of holding weight) there is less urgency to loose the string. Even a "dead release" is possible. If you are interested in the latter, read *Is the Dead Release Really Dead?* by Steve Ruis in the Coach Resources section of the AER website.

Following through can be practiced while dry-firing the bow(!). The archer has to be on the shooting line, but with no arrow in her bow. The bow is held in the position it would be while aiming, except that the draw is 1-2 inches (max!). The string is loosed and the bow makes its bow. Another way to do this that is more realistic is to attach a loop of string to the nocking point. The size of the loop is draw length – brace height). Then the archer puts her fingers through the loop and assumes full draw position (which results in 1-2 inches of draw—if not, shorten the loop). The string is loosed and the followthrough ensues.

A great many elite compound archers "cut off" their followthroughs, that is before the bow "bows," they pull the bow inward toward their bodies. They can do this because they know the feel of a good shot and they don't want to waste energy holding a heavy bow at arm's length for no compelling reason. This is not to be emulated by beginning to intermediate archers. It has to be earned through a great many good followthroughs executed, just like those elite archers did.

"Dropping the bow arm" must be looked for all of the time in compound archers as it can show up without any seeming cause. Be vigilant. Every wrong shot takes many good ones to clear away its influence.

that a shot sequence is just a tool. The ultimate goal is to learn to use it to guarantee consistency. Here are what a shot sequence is to be used for:
- practice of the sequence ensures all of the steps are done (and in the right order).
- the sequence provides a common set of terms for discussions with your coach.
- each step of the sequence has physical and mental checks to occupy your mind.
  - the sequence can be used to diagnose problems in your shot.
  - The sequence is the foundation upon which your mental program will be built.

> **The Rule of Discipline**
> *If anything, anything at all—mental or physical—intrudes from a prior step or from your environment, you must let down and start over.*

The last point is a little vague, but here is the rule that makes it work: *if anything, anything at all—mental or physical—intrudes from a prior step or from your environment, you must let down and start over.* So, for example, if you are about to draw the bow but your feet/stance feels funny, you must let down. Without this discipline, it will be very hard to improve at all. Shooting a bad shot requires ten good shots to wash away it's influence. Not shooting a shot that feels wrong (in any way) actually will help you shoot good shots in the long run!

A Basic Shot Sequence On the next three pages a basic shot sequence is provided for you to use shooting any kind of bow. You will personalize it later.

This is the *Signpost* for learning the basic shot sequence:

11. Knows and can demonstrate
    steps in shot sequence .... ☐ Sometimes ☐ Often ☐ Always
    Using a light-drawing bow or stretch band, can demonstrate steps in whatever shot sequence has been adopted

Having your entire class doing the basic sequence either with *mimetics* (play acting) or with stretch bands while shouting out the names of the steps is not a bad idea at all. With younger students, be aware that they may want to snap other students when they loose they stretch bands. This is not to be tolerated—ever. Alternatively, you can walk around with a clipboard/binder and ask individual students to "stand and deliver" a shot sequence performance. There are *AER Basic Shot Sequence* handouts available for downloading in the Coach Resources section of the AER website. Students with the *Archer's Guide* have the photos to learn from.

Notes _____

_____

_____

_____

Take Your Stance

Place your feet shoulder width apart, with your toes on line to target (a square stance), legs are straight (neither bent nor locked back at knees), shoulders are down, chest is down, head is balanced on top of spine and turned toward target; everything is relaxed.

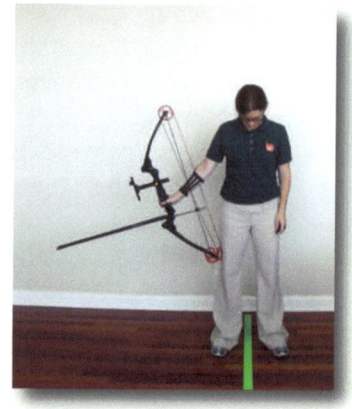

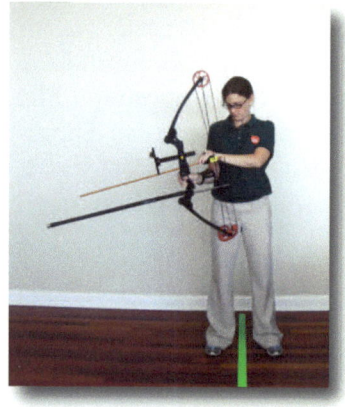

Nock an Arrow

Check to *hear* the arrow snap onto the string, *see* that arrow is on arrow rest, and *see* that the index vane is pointing away from the bow.

Set Your Hands

(*Draw Hand*) Fingers wrap around string in a "deep hook" (slightly behind first joint of fingers) and *not* on the fingertips; thumb reaches down to touch little finger tip. 1-2″ of draw keeps hands from moving to different positions. (*Bow Hand*) Palm flat to ground is slid into the grip's throat, them the wrist is bent until the bow sits upon the pad of the thumb. Other fingers are relaxed (curled); see that bowhand knuckles make 45° angle to ground.

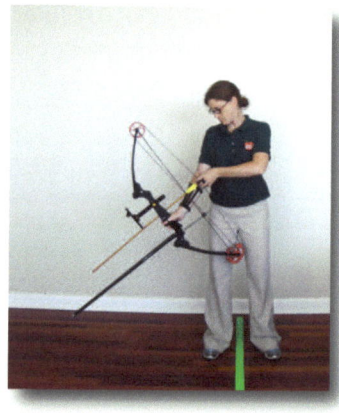

Notes _____

Raise the Bow
Maintaining slight draw of string, the bow is raised to a height at which draw hand is between chin and eye level, bow hand brings sight aperture to top of target or arrow point to top of target. Draw elbow must be as high or higher than draw hand.

Draw the String
Maintaining high draw elbow, the string is drawn to just under the chin. All muscles except shoulder and back muscles need to be as relaxed as possible with no extra tension. Both shoulders need to be kept in "down" position

Find Your Anchor
Move your draw hand to its anchor position (here the high anchor is being used). Draw hand must be firmly pressed against bone. String must be visible in aiming eye. Increase the tense feeling between shoulder blades by moving the draw elbow around toward the back.

Notes _____

_____

_____

_____

_____

_____

Aim
Move the bowsight aperture/arrow point to where it is desired and increase the tense feeling between shoulder blades by moving the draw elbow around toward the back. Relax. Check to see aperture/arrow point are steady (not necessarily still). Once learned, aiming is natural and easy. (Later you will first check string alignment and adjust.)

Release the String
Continure to increase the tense feeling between your shoulder blades by moving your draw elbow around toward the back as the fingers of the draw hand are relaxed. Stop holding the string. This is not so much an activity as it is the stopping of the effort to keep the fingers curled.

Follow Through
Allow the bow to rock forward (if long stabilizer used) or back (if no stabilizer is used) while maintaining the position of the bow arm and both shoulders until the shot is completed. Due to the squeezing of the shoulder blades together, the draw hand's fingertips should finish moving when just below the ear.

Notes _____
_____
_____
_____
_____
_____
_____
_____

Using A Bow Sight It has taken this long to introduce a bow sight because until a beginning archer has fairly steady form, the focus on aiming that is inherent in the use of a bow sight can detract from learning good form. Here we will focus on target/moveable sights. If you prefer to use a pin sight, we start you with a single pin if the sight allows (the other pins are either removed temporarily or slid down out of the sight picture). After the sight is properly bolted onto your bow and set up you can begin "sighting in."

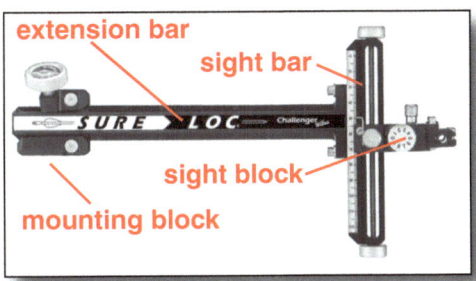

A Target Sight

Sighting In *Sighting in* is the process of discovering which sight aperture positions correspond to which target distances, and is started at close range. This is a distance at which you have a good point of aim (*e.g.* 10 yards/meters or so). You begin by shooting by point of aim (POA) while ignoring the bow sight's aperture/pin, then after several successful shots in a row, notice the position of the sight aperture in your sight picture just before you shoot. The aperture is then moved until when sighting POA correctly, the aperture is centered on the target in your field of vision. The two sight pictures now represent the same "aim" and either should result in arrows landing in the center of the target. As you become accustomed to using the sight's aperture to aim with, you can then move back incrementally (no more than five yards at a time) and shoot without moving the aperture. Note the change in the point of impact (as you move back the arrow impacts lower). Before adjusting the aperture for this new distance, be sure to write down the aperture position for the previous distance, either as a scale reading or by marking it's position on a blank piece of tape affixed to the sight.

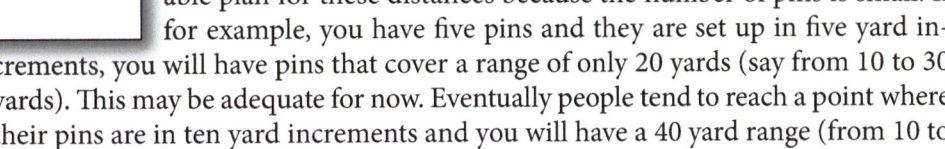

A Pin Sight

If you are using a pin sight, you will introduce a new pin for each new distance. Your coach will have to help you establish a reasonable plan for these distances because the number of pins is small. If for example, you have five pins and they are set up in five yard increments, you will have pins that cover a range of only 20 yards (say from 10 to 30 yards). This may be adequate for now. Eventually people tend to reach a point where their pins are in ten yard increments and you will have a 40 yard range (from 10 to 50 or 20 to 60 yards).

Once you have your "pin stack" sighted in, try out some intermediate yardages,

See the Appendix—*The Ins and Outs of Bow Sights* for a more detailed treatment of bow sights.

Notes _____

like 25 yards. If you have a pin for 20 yards and one for 30 yards, try lining up the point exactly half way in between with the center of the target. It should be quite close. Getting at distances that are different from those of the pin settings requires a bit of imagination. For 26 yards, for example, the 20 and 30 yard pins should be slightly higher in your sight picture than for 25 yards (specifically 6/10s of the way down from your 20 yard pin to your 30 yard pin. For 27 yards it is slightly higher, for 28 yards higher still, and for 29 yards your 30 yard pin is just below target center. This is called interpolation, and if you can do it (most people required just some practice) you will have pin positions for every one yard of distance you are shooting from top to bottom!

There is more to using a pin sight, including how to handle distances beyond your highest yardage pin, how to handle distances shorter than your lowest yardage pin, and refined techniques, but those come later.

Meters or Yards? Should you "sight in" in meters or yards? The answer depends on the types of rounds you shoot. If the rounds specify distances in meters (typical for international competition) then meters is more convenient. If the rounds specify distances in yards (typical for U.S. field archery competitions, for example) then yards is more convenient. If you want to shoot both, pick one or the other and then here's a simple conversion table (make all of the distance conversions before hand and write them down because doing math while shooting arrows is not a good idea):

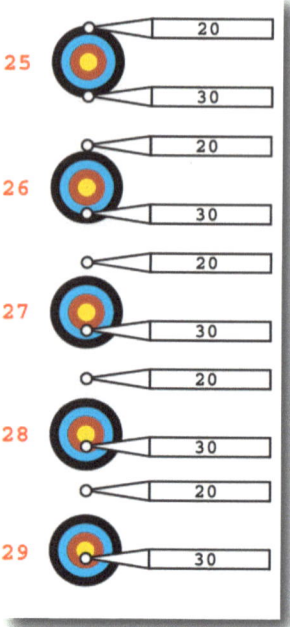

By bracketing pins around the center of a target (using a little imagination), all of the distances between pins can be shot accurately (see text).

Yards ▶	Meters	Meters ▶	Yards
10	9.14	10	10.94
20	18.29	20	21.87
30	27.43	30	32.95
40	36.58	40	43.75
50	45.72	50	54.92
60	54.86	60	65.90
70	64.01	70	76.88
80	73.15	80	87.49
90	82.30	90	98.85

Notes

If you want to do the calculations yourself:

$$1 \text{ yard} = 0.9144 \text{ meters}$$
$$1 \text{ meter} = 1.0936 \text{ yards}$$

This is the *Signpost* for beginning to use a bow sight:

12. Uses bow sight to aim with .... ☐ Sometimes ☐ Often ☐ Always
    Using a simple target/moveable bow sight can aim bow.

String Alignment There is another use for fixing the positions of things in your sight picture; it is called *string alignment*. This technique enables you to fine tune the windage (left-right) of a shot. In your sight picture all along there has been part of your bow, part of your arrow, and . . . part of the bowstring. Most people pay no attention to the bowstring because it is so close to your aiming eye that it is very fuzzy (it is out of focus). But if you do pay attention to it, it enables you to keep your head and your bow in the same relationship to one another. And if you are keeping your head straight up and down (no tilt!), you will be keeping your bow straight up and down, too.

You may have seen pictures of traditional hunters tilting their bows quite a bit. This is called *canting the bow*, and when you are aiming off of the point there is very little effect on your shot, but if you are using a bow sight on a bow there is a big effect! In target archery, for the greatest accuracy you want the bow to be at the same angle each and every shot. Straight up and down is an angle you can find reliably (as gravity is your guide), which is something hard to say for other angles.

Aligning the string is simply lining up the fuzzy string image with something on the bow, such as the inside edge of the sight aperture or the arrow. Many people don't want to use the arrow because the string gets in the way of seeing the point, but you get the idea. If you practice lining up the string after you get to full draw each arrow you shoot, it will become a habit and less and less time will need to be devoted to it.

Start with a light drawing bow (10#), get to your full draw position, and look for the string in your sight picture. Play with it, see if you can get it to line up at various points on the bow or your bow hand. Don't stay at full draw so long you get fatigued. Let down, rest for 30 seconds, and start over. After you get used to seeing the bowstring in your sight picture, try some shots at a close in target with your bow. Be

Be aware that there are compound styles that do not use bow sights and for which knowing and being able to use string alignment is valuable. Also, with a 10# bow, you can draw and anchor facing a student to show them the position of the bowstring in front of your eye (no arrow!). Make sure you can see the string in your sight picture, that you are looking along the inside edge of the string (the edge closest to you), and that you are lined up with the string over the arrow rest. Warn students before doing this as it can be disconcerting.

Notes _____

consistent in your placement of the string in your sight picture.

This is the *Signpost* for aligning the string:

13. Can identify string in sight picture
and align string with bow .... ☐ Sometimes ☐ Often ☐ Always
Able to identify position of bowstring in sight picture at full draw and adjust accordingly.

Using a Release Aid For those of you intending all along to use a release aid, you are probably saying "Finally!" The reasons for waiting until this point have already been made, so we can get right to the topic.

If you think waiting until now to try a release aid was hard, it now gets harder because you must put down your bow. You don't have to stop shooting, but to train on a release aid, you will start with a rope loop and not a bow.

Types of Release Aids There are many types of release aids and many variations on each type. We do not supply release aids for you to try, so you will need to have a release aid to attempt this *Signpost*. There are two general classifications of release aids: "hand held" and "wrist strap" releases (for want of better names). Target archers tend to prefer hand held releases by a substantial margin but, of course, you may use either kind. There are also two major kinds of release aid: triggerless and triggered releases. We strongly recommend you begin your training with a triggerless release, for two reasons: they are easier to learn good technique and they are far less expensive.

Other Considerations A release aid must fit your hand. If it is too big, or too small, or too thick, or fits your wrist too loosely or can't be adjusted to fit your hand, etc. you will struggle using it. Release aids are not inexpensive pieces of archery equipment and you will do well to get professional help at a quality archery shop when considering which to purchase. If they sell you a release aid that does not fit, you can exchange it for one which

There are hundreds of release aids to choose from, but to be effective, it must fit your hand/wrist.

Coaches, if you are unfamiliar with release aids, borrow one and make yourself a rope loop (also called a "rope bow"). Don't let the students have all of the fun. There are a number of articles in support of this task in the Coach Resources section of the AER website (*www.archeryeducationresources.com*).

Notes _____

_____

_____

_____

_____

does. If you buy one off of the Internet and it doesn't fit, well, we hope you can sell it to someone it does fit as we will not waste your time or our time trying to train you to use a release aid that will not work well.

Beginning Release Training The first thing you will need is a length of 3/16″ rope (such as nylon clothesline) you can make into a loop long enough to represent your draw length. Your coach will help to adjust the length of the loop to be just right. The loop fits over your bow hand (in the same position as your bow would be) and the release aid connects to the loop and is pulled back until it stops next to your face (so your hand is in its full draw location). To find your beginning draw hand position, adopt your full draw position (no bow) and twist your wrist as far as it will go in both directions. Then find a position about half way in between the two extreme positions of rotation (*see photos*). This should be near the most comfortable position for your arm, hand, and wrist.

Bring your draw hand/release up to a touch point on your face (typically somewhere near where your jawbone turns from being up and down to being horizontal). This is a starting point for your practice. (Remember that the anchor position has to result in the bow string being in front of your aiming eye; that is still a goal.) Be aware that, unlike with a finger release where the anchor is in the same position each time, the spot the release hand rests varies from distance to distance (ever so slightly). What stays in the same place on each shot will be the peep sight (not yet introduced) and when the front of the bow is raised (long shot) the release has to be lowered (a bit); when the front of the bow is lowered (short shot) the release has to be raised (a bit). There is nothing you have to do to make these changes as they will happen automatically, but we do not want you to think your hand has to be in the exact same position for every distance. Having made that claim, it is important that your full draw position be as consistent as you can make it, and we are not saying you can place your hand anywhere you want.

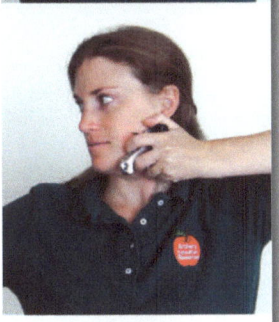

Training Once you have the rope loop the correct size, and the correct positions for the release against your face (and in your hand), you train by pulling gently (using your back muscles) against the rope, then activating your release aid. Since there are so many different kinds of release aids, your coach will have to assist you in the proper technique here.

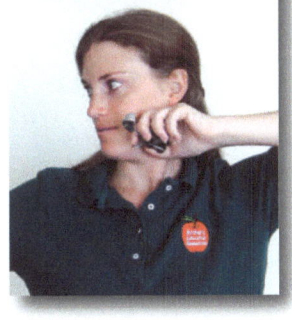

A proper execution of the release will result in the rope loop flying away from

Notes

your hand in a straight line. If the loop flies off at an angle or just flops on the floor, try again. You need to pull straight back, in proper full draw position, and execute the release properly. Once you can demonstrate you can do this consistently, you will be allowed to try with your bow, an arrow, and a blank target butt . . . with your eyes closed. (Of course, you can still shoot arrows without the release aid.) Good luck and have fun!

This is the first *Signpost* for using a release aid:

14. Practices using a release aid .... ☐ Sometimes ☐ Often ☐ Always
    Release aids are typically taught using a triggerless release aid and a rope loop. Practice may require weeks before bow is reintroduced.

Equipment Inspection No matter how good your equipment is, it does suffer wear and tear. It is necessary for you to inspect your equipment often, even between shots!

*See the Appendix—
Equipment Maintenance
and Repair.*

If, for instance, you hear a slight cracking or creaking noise from your bow, don't keep shooting it. Compound bows are generally very reliable, but failures of limbs and even risers are known. If you hear or see something "funny" here is how to test your bow. On a folded towel or soft carpet, lay the bow down so you can pull the string while holding the bow down with your foot (*see photo*). This way, if the bow fails, the pieces will fly into the floor instead of into you! Draw the bow smoothly and listen for any sounds the bow makes. If you hear any kind of cracking sound, let down and take your bow to a good archery shop to see if it can be repaired. If you hear no sound, the bow is probably sound. It can't hurt to get the bow checked by a reliable bow mechanic at a local archery shop, though.

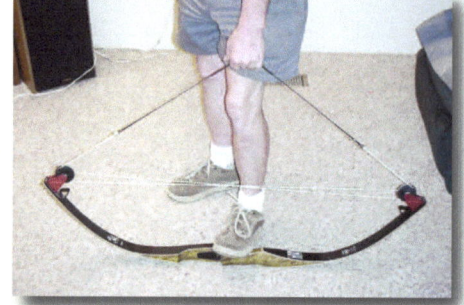

Inspecting Strings Compound bowstrings and cables tend to be durable but if, upon inspection, either has broken stands sticking out, they obviously need to be replaced. Strings and cables can be replaced separately, but if you have two identical cables on your bow, it is a good idea to replace both at the same time. Consult a quality compound bow technician at a good archery shop for this service.

Don't just pull a suspicious bow using normal form—do a safety pull test instead as is being shown with this old compound bow.

Checking Brace Height A check on whether the string or the cables have

Notes _____
_____
_____
_____
_____
_____
_____

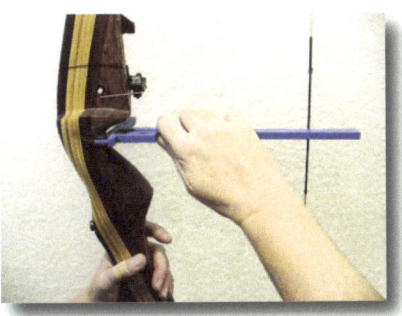

Checking your brace height can tell you if your cables or string have stretched. This is done the same way as with a recurve bow (as shown).

Marking the eccentrics so you can tell if they change positions is a good idea.

stretched or are damaged is measuring the brace height of the bow. You might want to acquire a bow square for this purpose but you can also do it with a simple ruler (*see photo*). Bow squares can also help you set your nocking point locator and check its location as well as other measurements, too. This is another check on whether your bowstring or cables have changed. An alternative method is to make marks on both of your bow's eccentrics that line up with the limbs (*see photo*). If either of those marks changes position, something is out of adjustment.

Checking Aluminum Arrows If an aluminum arrow gets damaged, it is usually easy to spot (broken nocks, lost arrow points, ripped fletches, etc.). What aren't easy to spot are slight bends, which can be a source of danger as bent arrows may fly very erratically. There are any number of ways to check an arrow to see if it is bent. If you lay the shaft on a flat table (fletches hanging over the edge) a straight arrow should roll fairly easily. Alternatively you can balance an arrow on your palm you can spin it with your fingers (see photo) and the arrow shouldn't wobble. Or you can make a "V" out of the fingernails on your off thumb and index finger then spin the shaft and push it so it rides up the groove (see photo) and it shouldn't wobble . . . or you can use the same "V" and rest the point in your palm and blow on the fletches to spin the arrow and it shouldn't wobble. (All of these tests take practice (*see photos next page*). Use a perfectly straight arrow and a slightly bent one for practice. Your AER Coach can demonstrate all of these.)

Checking Carbon Arrows If you have chosen to acquire carbon arrows, you are accepting the fact that carbon arrows, while being durable and are almost impossible to bend, may crack. If one of your arrows hits anything other than the target (or hits the target but at a funny angle), it should be inspected. Look it over for cracks. Gently flex it, while rolling it between your fingers, and listen for cracking sounds. If you see or hear a crack, do not shoot that arrow again! Shooting flawed carbon arrows can cause them to shatter upon release! If you break an arrow, be careful about throwing away the pieces as curious children are attracted to arrows and the carbon fibers making up the shaft can be razor sharp! Many people take the pieces home and dispose of them there.

This is the *Signpost* for inspecting your own equipment:

Notes _____
_____
_____
_____
_____
_____
_____

15. Can identify flawed arrows, bow parts ...... ☐ Sometimes ☐ Often ☐ Always
    Able to identify arrows with damaged points, nocks or which are bent, also damaged or worn bowstrings, cables, nock locators, etc.

Grouping Better The ultimate sign of consistency is shooting small sized groups. If the groups aren't in the center, you can move them there by adjusting your sight or POA. But if your groups are not small, all of the arrows won't be in the highest scoring zone of the target. Group size is the universal gauge of consistency in archery. With all of the refinements to your form, execution, and aiming systems you should be able to meet this new criterion. Good shooting! This is the Signpost for grouping at the intermediate level:

16. Shoots good groups consistently .... ☐ Sometimes ☐ Often ☐ Always
    Three arrow groups fit into an eight inch circle two ends out of three at 20 yards. Must achieve "Often" to advance to the next Stage.

Stage II Mental Aspects

In the next *Stage* you will focus on how your mind controls your ability to shoot (whether you acknowledge it or not). A shot sequence and the rule of discipline have been introduced. For now there are a couple of more tools of the mind you can use to good effect.

Talking to Yourself People who talk to themselves out loud are consider a bit odd. Mostly we keep our comments to ourselves by not saying things out loud or muttering to ourselves, especially if the comments are uncomplimentary. Here the discussion is limited to what you say *to* yourself *about* yourself. This is called *self talk*. Self talk, either out loud or in the privacy of your own mind, has an effect and that effect can be good or bad depending on whether the self talk is positive or negative.

If you have ever muttered to yourself such things as "I am such an idiot!" or "Here I go again!" you were experiencing *negative self talk*. This can be motivating in a kind of "pick yourself up by your own bootstraps" kind of way but it is more likely to hurt your performance in archery. It does nothing to change the situation, certainly nothing to make it better. *Positive self talk*, on the other hand, can actually help you perform. Here is an example:

A fun way to evaluate this *Signpost* is to buy some inexpensive 8″ paper plates. Place a small aiming dot (2-3″ press-on sticker dots work well) in the center of the plate. Pin these to a target butt and have your archers verify each end that results in all three arrows hitting the plate. Doing this two out of three ends or four or more times out of six ends, etc. meets the *Signpost* criterion. Alternatively, you could have them shoot three ends of three arrows and show you at least six arrow holes in the plate at the end. Doing this at least three times in three different sessions (with no lapses) and you get an "Always." Obviously records must be kept. And, younger students may want to decorate/ personalize their plates with their names or drawings, but no human likenesses are allowed on a target.

Notes _____

_____

_____

Consider that you are having a good time and competing well at an archery event you typically enjoy. And then the skies darken and it begins to rain. Here are two possible responses to the change in the weather:

Self Talk Example 1 Oh, no! I hate shooting in the rain! It always lowers my score. There goes my personal best score and I probably won't win, either!

Self Talk Example 2 Oh, I had better get my rain gear out; I'm glad I came prepared. I probably won't shoot a personal best, but I could still win this thing, especially if the two people ahead of me get bent out of shape because of the rain. Woo hoo!

> **Once you introduce "self talk" and "being positive" you really, really have to be careful how you address your students and yourself because they will call you on your lapses, which is good for you, like eating your vegetables.**

We are all capable of the disappointment, disgust, and fear associated with Self Talk Example 1. We are all also capable of learning how to achieve Self Talk Example 2 with its apparent happiness (came prepared, might win) and reasonable logic (might win if the two people ahead of me get bent out of shape because of the rain).

The point is that *you can choose how you talk to yourself*. But it is necessary, like all aspects of archery, to practice this. Whenever you think or say something negative about yourself, try rephrasing it as a positive statement. Look for the opportunity to do something better. Here's the self talk *Signpost*:

1. Exhibits positive self talk .... ☐ Sometimes ☐ Often ☐ Always
   Exhibits positive self talk and can take negative references and make them positive. Must achieve "Often" to advance to the next Stage.

Goals This sounds like a boring topic. True, it can be, but only one specific kind of goal is addressed here, a kind of goal that can actually help you become a better archer (and therefore isn't boring!). The goals addressed here are called *process goals*. Process goals are about *how* things happen, not *what* actually happens. If you have a goal of shooting a particular score or making a team, those are what are called *outcome goals*. Either you get the score or you don't; either you make the team or you don't. There is a role for outcome goals . . . but not for now. For now, you are focusing on goals that can actually result in you doing better in some way.

Here is an example of a process goal: "In practice today I will have a strong bow

Notes

arm for 90% of all shots." A goal like this focuses your attention on making your bow arm stronger. Keeping track of whether you did or didn't have a strong bow arm on each of your shots focuses more of your attention . . . and the results are not necessarily cut and dried. What if it comes out to 89% of your shots you had a strong bow arm. Good enough? (Yes) What about 92%? What about 13%? There is food for thought here.

Process goals help you focus on what you are doing, not on the results of having done it. If you want to compete on an AER Archery Team, you will have to have at least one process goal based on your shooting plus one deportment goal, too, for each competition. For your first deportment goal at your first archery competition, "Have fun!" is recommended, but if you get distracted talking trash to another competitor at this competition, don't be surprised if your coach tells you that you will have the deportment goal of "I will not talk trash at the tournament" at your next tournament.

Because your form is becoming more and more refined, your process goals can also become more and more refined. Ask your coach for help drafting some for you to use.

A word of caution: having more than 1-2 process goals for any practice session or tournament is a recipe for disaster. You just can't focus on that many things at one time. Work on something. Switch to something else. Come back to the first topic at a later time. Make progress slowly and steadily and you will end up at the top.

This is the *Signpost* regarding process goals for the intermediate level:

2. Helps draft and uses process goals .... ☐ Sometimes ☐ Often ☐ Always
   Can help create process goals and then exhibits using them through self evaluation.

> As students get more and more serious, it becomes more and more important that there be process goals for each practice session and each competition. This is true for recreational archers striving to get better and mandatory for competitive archers learning how to win.

Notes _____

Signposts—Stage III Achieving Mastery
Must have completed requirements of Stage II before beginning.

Congratulations are again in order! You have come a long way and now are ready to pursue the goal of becoming an expert archer. Do you think you are ready? Even if you don't think you are, if you have followed the plan to this point, you are ready!

There are always new things to learn about the physical elements of shooting arrows. You can never know it all, but at this point you know a great deal about yourself and how you shoot arrows. Now things that will improve your performance which are more about the equipment and the role your mind plays are addressed.

Advanced Archery Skills
Peeping Through the String Now that you are adept at drawing, anchoring, and releasing the string with a release aid (or you still shoot "fingers" but your compound bow style allows a peep sight), it is time to install the peep sight. You coach will help you. The best starting position is to measure the distance from the corner of your mouth to your eye and install your peep sight in the string that many inches above your nocking point. Then draw with your bow sight aperture set for the middle distance you shoot at a target at that distance. Then keep repositioning the peep sight until it falls right in front of your eye when you draw on that target. When a proper position is found, the peep is then secured in place.

Practicing with the Peep in Place Start at a short distance at first, then move to longer distances as you get used to using the peep. The procedure, once you can see through the peep, is to place the aperture where you want it to be in your sight picture. Then you need to do some or all of the following:
- If you are using a telescopic aperture, you must line up the peep opening with the circular housing (they need to be concentric—*see photo at left*)
- If your sight's aperture has a bubble level, you must check to see if the bubble is centered and adjust the bow if not.
- If you are using a pin sight, you need to arrange your sight picture so the tip of the pin being used is exactly the center of the peep's circle (*see photo next page*).

Students will need help installing, positioning, and locking in their peep sights before issues of using them can even be addressed. *Simple Maintenance for Archery* by Ruth Rowe and Alan Anderson is a wonderful source of help for installing peep sights. Setting the peep's initial position is described here. A source of problems not covered is orientation. Due to bow strings being twisted (and made inconsistently) a peep that faces backward while at brace might rotate and face sideways at full draw. To fix this problem, the peep can be reinserted so that when it rotates it will be in the correct orientation. Alternatively, one can take individual bowstring strands and move them from one side of the peep to the other. This may pull the peep into an orientation that will result in it being properly positioned at full draw. This can be very vexing for an archer if they are not able to see through the peep!

If your archer shoots a release aid, an easy solution to the peep rotation problem is to install a "D Loop." Instructions for doing so are in *Simple Maintenance for Archery* and numerous other places. See *Why You Should Shoot a D-Loop* by George Chapman (in Coach Resources on the AER website) for the many reasons they are a benefit and the simplest instructions for installing them. The key here is that if the D Loop is installed so it points the same direction as the peep sight hole, it will pull the string and peep into alignment during the draw.

Some pin sights have circular housings to help you line them up with the circular opening in the peep itself. For these sights, you do not put the pin being used in the center, you line up the peep opening with the housing. If you have this kind of pin sight, you have to sight in doing this!

Finally your attention goes back to the relationship between the sight aperture and the target.

There is more to learn about peep sights: how big of an opening do you need (it depends), how to optimize its position for different types of competition, etc., but these will come later. This is the *Signpost* for using a peep sight with your bow sight:

1. Can use peep sight correctly .... ☐ Sometimes ☐ Often ☐ Always
   Once set up, a peep sight improves accuracy by being a dependable rear sight. Must be aligned with aperture housing or pin. Bubble level is checked and adjusted when peep is aligned.

Mastering Your Release Aid You will find out that people who shoot release aids like to try different types of them (they are always looking for a "better" way). What we address here is you being in command of your release aid. If you decide to switch to another style of release or even to another manufacturer's version of the release you now use, we urge you to go back to the rope loop to train on the new release. Many, many archers have tried a new release aid right on their bow and they have knocked themselves silly when the release "let go" of the string at mid draw and their release came back and smacked them in the face. Don't have this happen to you!

Getting Fluid The goal for the operation of the release aid is to execute your shot without conscious thought of triggering the release and having the release "let go" of the string on its own schedule, in it's own way while you are focused on keeping your aperture where you want it on the target in your sight picture. This is called a "subconscious release." By repeatedly executing shots this way, you will acquire a very easy release technique and become more accurate at the same time. There are some archers who can press on a trigger willingly and consciously to get their shots off, but there are only a few who can do it well, so that is not recommended.

Signs that your release technique is good are: that you don't think about the release during the shot, that your shots go off in good rhythm, and that occasionally the release doesn't "go off" in a reasonable time (a definition of "too long" is you starting to wonder why the release hasn't "gone off") and you must let down and

Blank bale shooting is a good way to get one's shot timing back when changes are being made. All of the steps can be addressed without the distraction of a target face, and shooting up close means one doesn't have to walk as far to retrieve one's arrows.

If your pin sight has a circular pin guard, line up that guard with the peep's hole. If not. you have to be sure the end of whichever pin you are using is centered in the peep's hole.

Notes _____

you don't know why.

Note that once you have installed a peep sight and there are more things to do at full draw (check this, line up that), that your shot timing may be different (probably somewhat longer). This is normal and it may take some time to get used to.

2. Can use release aid fluidly .... ☐ Sometimes ☐ Often ☐ Always

Archer may adopt release aid but only after all other accessories have been incorporated and are used comfortably. Before release aid is used on bow, considerable practice must occur, and an arrow rest change may be required.

Fully Sighting In You may have sighted in just a couple of distances before and by now the range of distances over which you shoot has probably gotten larger, so it is time to get fully sighted in.

Limitations of Target/Moveable Sights This aspect of "sighting in" is simply a matter of using all of the form elements and equipment you have learned so far to get sight settings from your shortest to longest range. Occasionally, though, you will "run out of sight" usually meaning that for your longer distances, the sight aperture is so low it is too close to your arrows. To solve this problem, if you are using a finger release, it is time to switch from a high anchor to a low anchor. If you are using a release aid, you need to find the highest peep sight position (in the bowstring) for which you can find a reasonable touch point anchor position.

If these don't work, the next stage is to increase your draw weight. If there is draw weight still in your bow, you can screw in your limb bolts (one turn at a time) and you will get more cast out of your bow. You need to shoot for several hours at this new weight to get accustomed to it (not all at once!). Then you can turn in the limb bolts another turn. Realize that whenever you change a limb bolt, you must sight in again, so make all of the draw weight changes while shooting at the same distance (closer is better than farther) and while making temporary sight aperture position adjustments to keep the arrows on target, then sight in again.

Pin Sights You may already have distances for all of the pins in your pin sight stack already, but if the distances you can shoot have gotten longer you may want to sight in those pins again to bring those longer distances into the stack.

Now you get to learn how to shoot the distances outside of your pins. The shorter distances are rather simple. Let us say that your shortest distance pin is for

See the Appendix—
The Ins and Outs of Bow
Sights **for more on this topic.**

Notes _____

_____

_____

_____

_____

_____

a 20 yard target distance. For fifteen yards, you can probably just put the 20 yard pin on the bottom edge of the center scoring ring and you are good. For ten yards, a little lower. It only takes a little practice because this is just the point of aim (POA) sighting technique using the lowest distance pin as a reference!

For distances past your longest pin (it is always a terrible surprise to show up at a competition and find out your pin stack doesn't cover all of the shooting distances) you are going to stack your pins. Let us say, that your highest yardage pin is set for 50 yards, but you have a 60 yard target. You need to aim 10 yards higher with your lowest pin, but you don't have a POA. Yes, you do! As a reasonable approximation, you can but your 50 yard pin on target center. The 40 yard pin (just above the 50 yard pin) is now pointing to a POA that is ten yards farther! (Well, not exactly, but it is reasonably close.) Look at where that forty yard pin is and create a description (3 ring, 12 o'clock) or find an arrow hole or flaw in the butt, or leaf on a bush behind the butt, etc. that you can use as a point of aim. Then put your 50 yard pin on that point of aim and release. As always, you can make adjustments based on how your first few arrows land, but at least you will have a good chance of scoring those first arrows well.

Getting in Focus As you have been learning to shoot, you started by focusing on the target. When we introduced "aiming off of the point" you may have switched to focusing your eyes on the arrow point. But, which is correct? There are arguments that can be made for focusing on the arrow point or the sight aperture and arguments that can be made for focusing on the target. Rather than discuss the arguments, we recommend you try both. Take a very light drawing bow (or if your holding weight at full draw is low enough to allow you to hold it for 20 seconds, you can use it), stand in front of a target, draw the bow until you are in the point or aperture on target orientation, then shift your focus to the point/aperture and back to the target, then repeat. Try not to get too fatigued doing this. It is okay to let down, rest for 30 seconds, and then draw again. See if you have a preference for one of the two focal points. If you do, use that one consistently. If you do not, pick one and use that one consistently. After you have shot a while using this technique, check your preference again, it might have changed. (For later, most compound archers who use target sights

For distances beyond your farthest pin, you can "stack" pins to approximate those distances. In this example, to reach a 60 yard target, the 50 yard pin is placed on center (*top*) and the position of the 40 yard pin is then used as a POA for the fifty yard pin (*bottom*).

Notes

focus on the target.)

This is the *Signpost* for sighting in at the intermediate level:

3. Can sight in bow
for all appropriate distances .... ☐ Sometimes ☐ Often ☐ Always
This includes the longest distances required by competitive category (even if not competing). For those using pin sights, must be able to shoot distances above and below their pin stack distances. Must achieve "Often" to advance to the next Stage.

Shooting Cool This *Signpost* you have seen before, but as you have made progress you have been shooting longer and longer distances, at least if it is "outdoor" season. (Your coach is taught to encourage that.) This is the *Signpost* for "making distance" at the intermediate level. The goal is to shoot comfortably and well at all competitive distances that you would shoot in competition. Bear in mind that if you do not want to shoot longer distances, you can work with your coach to adjust this *Signpost* (you can't eliminate this one as it is required to reach the next *Stage*).

This is the *Signpost* for shooting all distances comfortably.

4. Can shoot comfortably
at all appropriate distances .... ☐ Sometimes ☐ Often ☐ Always
This includes the longest distances required by competitive category (even if not competing). Must achieve "Often" to advance to the next Stage.

Tuning You probably know what it means to give a car a tune-up but tuning your archery equipment is probably a mystery. Tuning the bow-arrow-archer system involves a couple of stages. For simplicity we will call them basic tuning, fine tuning, and microtuning. Here we address ourselves to basic tuning.

So what is tuning? Tuning is making adjustments in the bow-arrow system to fit them to the archer better. No archer is perfect; each makes mistakes (of aiming, of releasing, of . . .). The goal of tuning is to create a bow-arrow setup that minimizes the impact of those mistakes. Consequently the exact same bow-arrow combination will shoot differently in the hands of different archers. Otherwise all archers need only shoot what Dave Cousins or any other top professional compound archer or the archer who is closest to them in size and style of equipment shoots.

The goal of tuning therefore is a "forgiving" bow-arrow system in the sense that

This *Signpost* can be a real struggle for youths in a particular level of development (especially when they have changed competitive categories (to greater distances) before they were physically ready) and more mature archers with short draw lengths (short draw length means low power). A techno-fix is to buy/acquire lightweight carbon arrows but sometimes even that doesn't work. See *Making Distance* by Steve Ruis in the Coach Resources section of the AER website.

Having said this, most compound archers don't experience these problems because their bows (pound for pound of draw weight) pack much more energy than do recurve bows and longbows. But occasionally students do struggle. One asset they have is the easy adjustability of the draw weight of a compound bow (typically at least 10-15# of adjustment). When buying a compound bow, it is a very good idea to have the archer's initial draw weight be at the bottom of the range of available draw weights. It is more likely a student will go up in draw weight with experience than go down. If there is no more draw weight to be had in the bow, some of the other techniques can be tried, or even the extreme of "new bow time."

Notes _____

it forgives the archer's mistakes. In "basic" tuning for compound archers, we tune two things: nocking point height and centershot.

Bare Shaft Tuning Here is a very basic tuning test (also called the bare shaft planing test) that works better for finger releases than for release aid releases, but it does work. In bare shaft testing, you need to have two arrows with no fletches. If you've already fletched all of your arrows, you'll need to strip two of them (Ask your coach how to do this. Alternatively you can use several wraps of transparent tape to eliminate the steering ability of your arrow's vanes by taping them down to the shaft). From about 10-15 yards shoot fletched arrows until you are warmed up and so you can get a good group of at least three arrows in the center of a target. Then shoot the two bare shafts. (You shoot the second to tell if you shot a good shot with the first bare shaft; they should each group!) Here is what you can learn:

- If the bare shafts strike the target *above* the fletched group, your nocking point is too low.
- If the bare shafts strike the target *below* the fletched group, your nocking point is too high.
- If the bare shafts strike the target to the *left* of the fletched group, your arrow rest is too far from your bow.
- If the bare shafts strike the target to the *right* of the fletched group, your arrow rest is too close to your bow.
- If the bare shafts strike the target anywhere else except as part of the fletched group, you have a combination of adjustments to make.

The left and right bare shaft indications are reversed if you are left-handed. And the farther out the arrows are, the bigger the problem. Just a couple of inches of separation between the group of bare shafts and the fletched shafts indicates a pretty good tune.

Making Corrections—Nocking Point Location If your nocking point needs adjusting, you need to adjust it accordingly. This requires tools and/or expertise, so your coach will help you. You do this first!

Making Corrections—Centershot We strongly recommend that while you are learning to shoot a compound bow, that you use an inexpensive plastic screw-in arrow rest, especially if you are going to shoot with fingers on the string. If you shoot

Tuning is really a complex subject, so the more you can learn about it the better. It is especially important that you, yourself, have done these procedures with your own equipment. We simply are going to refer you to *Tuning Your Compound Bow*, 4th Ed. by Larry Wise, as a starting point and strongly encourage you to read up on this topic. Oh, the Koreans have an attitude summed up by the phrase "teach them to shoot 1300 (out of 1440 in a FITA round, the international standard of "world class"), then tune their bow." Students with technophile personalities view tuning as some magic ways to increase performance and can spend way more time than it is worth trying to "tune" better scores. This is to be avoided. A well set up bow (see the Appendix—*Bow Setup*) is all that is needed to shoot very good scores.

Notes _____

_____

_____

with a release aid, you will want an arrow rest specifically designed for them (but are 10-20 times more expensive than the quite adequate plastic screw-in arrow rest (*see photo*). Centershot adjustments are made by loosening the lock nut on the outside of the bow and screwing the rest closer in or farther out and retightening the nut.

The basic rule when making changes: make them large (at first). If you are sneaking up on a big problem with itty bitty changes, you are going to be at it a long time. If your rest is too far in, make a big change and now it is too far out. Good! You now have outside limits to your adjustments. Split the difference between those two settings, then between that one and one of the others until you get what you want. So, when adding or removing "turns" to your arrow rest, start with four or five turns, later you can try, two, or even one twist at a time. But, start with a big change and retest If there is no effect from the change, maybe that's the wrong "fix."

Making Corrections—Arrow Spine If you make centershot changes and the arrows don't test any better or get worse when you are making a change that should make it better, it is possible that the arrows spine is incorrect. The spine of an arrow is a gauge of its resilience when being flexed, some people say it is a measure of the arrows stiffness. In making changes in arrow spine, you again need to consider your equipment carefully.

- If your arrows hit to the *right* of the target (RH archer), even when the arrow rest is adjusted quite far from the bow, it is likely that the arrows are too weak (low spine).
- If your arrows hit to the *left* of the target (RH archer), even when the arrow rest is adjusted quite far into the bow, it is likely that the arrows are too stiff (high spine).

Stiffening Arrows—If you need a stiffer arrow, you are in luck: arrows are easier to stiffen than to weaken. The simple things you can do to stiffen arrows (in order of the effect) are:

1. Cut them shorter.
2. Use lighter arrow points.

If these don't work, you may have to buy new arrows. Buying new arrows isn't uncommon for beginners, because as you change draw weight, you need stiffer arrows to handle the forces. The rule on cutting arrows is a little at a time, so cut a half an inch off of a small set of arrows (include the bare shafts) and retest. If you cut

Notes

them too short, they can only be given away as they will be of no further use to you. (Also, too short arrows are a safety hazard!)

Weakening Arrows—Weakening arrows is harder because there is no opposite to "cut them shorter." Making them longer will certainly weaken them but you would have to be a magician to do it! Here are basic some things you can do to weaken your arrows:

1. Use heavier arrow points.
2. Switch to Mylar vanes from plastic vanes (lighter vanes weaken arrows).

Making Corrections—Draw Weight One of the advantages of compound bows is that the draw weight can be easily adjusted over a wide range of values. An alternative to adjusting the spine of your arrows, which requires tools and knowledge and time, is to use your bow's draw weight adjustments to make the changes. Here is how it is done:

- If your arrows are *too weak* (low spine), lower the draw weight.
- If your arrows are *too stiff* (high spine), raise the draw weight.

This is done simply by turning the limb bolts inward (to raise the draw weight) or outward (to lower the draw weight) and retest. This comes with a warning, though. If the arrows are far from being matched to your bow, large changes in draw weight will be necessary. If you increase the draw weight more than just a little at a time, it can seriously distort your archery form. The rule of thumb is to change your draw weight (upwards) only a little at a time. We suggest no more than one half to one turn on the limb bolts at a time and if the bow feels quite hard to pull after doing so, take some of the turns off and go up only one half turn at a time. Shooting for several sessions is required between each adjustment, so this can be quite time consuming. So the general approach is to see if making a draw weight adjustment has any effect (make a change and retest) if it does make things better, then acclimate yourself to your new, higher draw weight, then after a while add a little more draw weight and retest. Be very careful to never exceed the number of full turns limb bolts can be backed out according to the manufacturer's specifications—this could be dangerous! When you have finished adjusting your draw weight, you must "sight in" again. You coach can assist you in this.

This is the *Signpost* for tuning at the intermediate level:

Notes _____
_____
_____
_____
_____
_____
_____

5. Able to tune bow/arrow system (basic) ..... ☐ Sometimes ☐ Often ☐ Always
   Basic tuning involves shooting bare shafts and fletched shafts then deciphering the positions of the two types of arrows. Compound bows are tuned by making centershot and nocking point height adjustments. Arrows are tuned by adjusting their lengths and point and vane weights.

It is okay for archers to skip this Signpost. An archer can come back to it at a later time.

Shooting Rhythmically This is a fairly advanced skill and takes quite a bit of time to do, but you may want to attempt this anyway. Most people shoot in a particular rhythm which can be refined by identifying it and using your shot sequence to make it regular.

Finding Your Rhythm This is the hard part. You either need to have someone with a stopwatch help you or you can use a metronome to figure it out. In the stopwatch approach, you have somebody time how many seconds (without you noticing them doing it) it takes from raising your bow to releasing the string. After each shot, you say "yes" if the shot felt good and was in rhythm or "no" if it didn't feel good or was out of rhythm.

After recording the times of many dozens of shots from more than one session, you try to correlate the number of seconds to the quality of the shot. (One way to do this is to enter the number of seconds and the yes's and no's into a two-column spread sheet, sort the rows for time shot and see if the yes's cluster around any particular shot time. For the sake of this discussion let's say that most of the yes's were from 4-6 seconds. Then there are a number of ways to lock in that rhythm (see below).

The metronome approach is to play a metronome and count off your shot, so many "clicks" for each step of the shot sequence. If the metronome is set too fast, you will feel rushed or unable to count fast enough. If it is set too slow, you will feel sluggish and impatient. Eventually you get it set right and then you want to lock in that rhythm.

Locking in Your Rhythm There are a couple of ways to lock in your personal shot rhythm. One way is through feedback. Again, you need somebody with a stop watch. If your slice of time is 4-6 seconds from raising to bow to loose, your helper practices with you and times each shot. If you shoot quicker than the four seconds, he tells you. If you reach 6 seconds before shooting, he announces "let down" and you must let down the string. The feedback eventually gets you to shoot in your best

Notes _____
_____
_____
_____
_____
_____
_____

rhythm. You may need several sessions to do this and you may need to test yourself at intervals to check on your status.

Another method is you may have a snippet of music in your head that is in the same tempo as your shot rhythm (or you may hear it and recognize it then). A great many archers use a sample of a song as part of their shot sequence. It helps them to stay in rhythm.

This is the *Signpost* for shooting rhythmically at the intermediate level:

6. Uses shot sequence to create
   a regular shooting rhythm .... ☐ Sometimes ☐ Often ☐ Always
   Shooting rhythm can be made regular by use of creative shot sequence elements which can only be found by trial and test.

Scoring Now that you have refined form and much practice shooting arrows under your belt, it is time for your first scoring *Signpost*. There are any number of scoring rounds available. You may want to choose one of the common international archery rounds—the FITA Round (144 arrows), a Half-FITA Round (72 arrows), or even the FITA 30m Round (36 arrows) or you might prefer an NFAA field archery round.

Your goal is to score at least as much as 75% of the age group record for that round. Most age group records can be found on the internet and your coach can help you find yours. Good luck and good shooting! (And, yes, this is an "outcome" goal.)

This is the *Signpost* for scoring at the intermediate level:

7. Can shoot scores of 75% of record level .... ☐ Sometimes ☐ Often ☐ Always
   These can be competition or practice scores shot under competition conditions. Any rounds may be used but must include outdoor rounds. Must achieve "Often" to advance to the next Stage.

Stage III Mental Aspects

You will have to work closely with your coach to see which of these *Signposts* you are willing to attempt. Some will work better than others and some won't work at all . . . for you. You may have to try each of them to see, but start with a discussion with your coach.

You may want to set students loose on the internet looking for U.S. age level records of USA Archery (*www.usarchery.org*) on the common international rounds. There are buttons leading to their records but they can be reached directly at www.us-archeryrecords.org. For explanations of their age classifications, there is no better source than a table available at *www.texasarchery.org/Documents/Distances/DistanceSummary.htm*.

FITA, the International Archery Federation, also has a record search engine at their website *www.archery.org* under "Results" and then "Records/ Best Scores."

The NFAA doesn't make national records easily available, but many of the NFAA's state organizations do with their records. On the NFAA's website, click on "Archery Links" to find your state organization. They may have posted records. For example, the California organization (*www.cbhsaa.net/index.htm*) has a button for "State Records" right on their home page. If your state doesn't have posted records, use a neighboring state, or use California's as it was the birthplace of the NFAA.

Notes _____

Of all the things that could be said to underscore the importance of the mental landscape to archers, we simply encourage you to read With Winning in Mind *by Lanny Bassham. If you think "winning" is too crass of a goal, please open up your thinking. Your student's goals are your focus as a coach and the only person who has the power to defeat your archer . . . is himself or herself. Archers compete without any defense from the other archers, the only opposition they have is within themselves. To excel, they must come to know and accept themselves as never before. This is a journey that has more to do with their lives than with archery; archery is just the vehicle.*

Journaling Have you ever had anyone ask "How's archery going?" and you answered "Okay, I guess." This is certainly not a good answer if it is your coach asking the question or, worse, a prominent guest coach who might be able to help you a lot! One of the ways to be aware of what you are doing is to keep a journal. No, not a diary! This is a journal in which you write all of the important things you are doing. Here are some recommendations:

1. Set aside the back of your journal (any small notebook will do) to write down all of the critical numbers about your equipment (your brace height, how many strands in your string, arrow length and size, brand names, fletching sizes, etc.
2. Have a separate place for your practice and competition goals. Always write them down and write an evaluation of how well you met each goal.
3. Have a place to write down the particulars of your "testing" sessions. If you are tuning or testing some new arrows, write down the results. Before you make any change in your setup (brace height, nocking point location, whatever), write down the old value. Write down the numbers of twists put in or taken out of your string. It may seem silly, but if you mess things up, such notes may make it possible for you to make your bow "right" again.
4. Never, ever write anything negative in your journal. (yes, we know this is a negative statement. It is for emphasis.) Writing things down gives them power, so writing about how you want to do things better and are doing them better is good because it makes progress easier. If you complain in your journal (It was raining . . . I was so miserable . . .) it doesn't help you, it simply focuses your attention on what you were doing wrong. Try to make positive comments like, "The next time it rains, I am going to practice and see if I can figure out what went wrong . . . I found out that my windbreaker was catching the bowstring causing my arrows to go low-left. I snugged up the sleeve with some rubber bands and shot really well!" These observations can really help and reviewing them later can show you how you solved problems and made progress.

Here is the *Signpost* for journaling at the intermediate level:

1. Keeps a journal for practice/competition . ☐ Sometimes ☐ Often ☐ Always
Journal entries focus on record keeping and finding solutions (not problems) and are positive in nature.

Notes _____

Getting Help from Others As you interact with other archers, you will have the opportunity to learn from them. You are encouraged to engage other archers and talk about archery. If you hear a good idea, you might find it helpful to your improvement. And, as with all other topics, you can also find a lot of misinformation floating around. For example, you can find good information on the internet, but the warning about misinformation goes double for the internet. Apparently any fool can post anything.

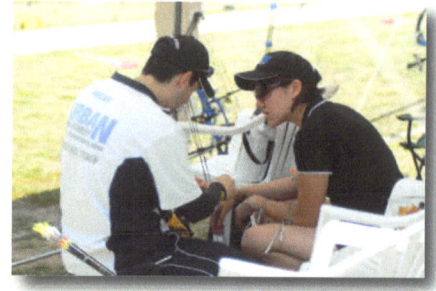

If you are not sure about something you have read or heard from another archer, discuss it with your coach. If he or she can't help, they likely can point you to someone who can.

A Warning About Advice Many adults like to see beginners, especially kids, starting up in their favorite sport, so if you are young, you will attract all kinds of advice from older archers. When an adult gives advice to a youth and the youth does not immediately accept or test out the advice, they can be perceived as being "standoffish," or "aloof," or "stuck up." (The old expect the young to take their advice.) Here is how you can diffuse any potential criticism. If you are given advice from an older archer ("You know what you ought to do . . .) say to him or her, "Thanks for the advice, I will tell my coach when I see him next week." This satisfies older advice givers apparently because they think you have your very own personal older, wiser person to guide you. But the phrase does work . . . like magic! So, if you are young, you might want to have that phrase in your back pocket when nosey older folks get in your face. (The same is true for female beginners who tend to attract advice from older males.)

This is the *Signpost* for learning from others at the intermediate level:

2. Interacts with other archers
   in style to learn .... ☐ Sometimes ☐ Often ☐ Always
   Much can be learned from other archers of the same style. Archers wanting to improve need to seek out useful information and try to apply it to their own game. Must achieve "Often" to advance to the next Stage.

Imagine This It seems as if a shooting sport like archery would have no room for imagination. Archers are solidly embedded in reality! Well, not exactly. You may

Don't forget that many of your students won't acquire this *Archer's Guide* so teaching them the "Thanks for the advice, I will tell my coach when I see him next week" phrase is worth doing face to face. Of course, this recommendation applies to everything else in this guide also.

Notes _____

_____

_____

_____

_____

_____

already know some uses of imagination in other sports and archery is no exception. Most successful archers start out each and every shot by imagining the look, feel, smell, sound, etc. of a perfect shot. This imagery works. It works because you operate mostly subconsciously and a basic aspect of your subconscious mind is it can't tell the difference between reality and something vividly imagined.

The advantage here is that each shot you take is preceded by a perfect, dead center shot and followed by another dead center, perfect shot. It is much easier to do something just after you have done it well and it is very hard to do something right just after you have done it wrong. *Imagery, in the form of imagining perfect shots before shooting them, enables archers to shoot significantly more consistently.*

You will see the same behavior from football kickers as they take practice swings of their legs before they kick field goals (they are imagining the impact of the ball and seeing it tumble through the goalposts). Golfers taking practice swings (they imagine the ball sailing through the air and landing just where they want), and basketballers shooting free throws (they imagine the feel of the ball, the ball's flight, and it settling gently into the net).

This takes practice a) to do it well and b) to make it a habit.

This is the *Signpost* for imagery at the intermediate level:

3. Uses imagery as part of shot sequence ...... ☐ Sometimes ☐ Often ☐ Always
    Good shots are imaged/imagined as an early stage in shot sequence (practice and competition).
    Must achieve "Often" to advance to the next Stage.

Affirmations Affirmations are short statements of personal beliefs that are designed to help you feel better about yourself and your abilities, thus reinforcing those abilities. They may take many forms, but they must always be drafted in:
- first person (I . . .)
- positive language, and
- the present tense (now).

They state exactly what you will do in a positive manner. Do not use the words no, never, not, or don't. For example, an affirmation for baseball "I never strike out" is poor as it focuses energy and attention on striking out. It is far better to affirm what you want to happen (focus on the solution, not the problem) like this: "I hit the ball with a high batting average and pretty much where I want it to go."

Notes

The classic method involves writing your affirmations on 3x5 cards, but you might want to write them daily in a journal or read them to yourself or aloud, or record affirmations so you can listen to them, or do all of these. Some people post copies of their affirmations where they will see them throughout the day and stop what they are doing to read them each and every time they encounter one. Use your imagery skills as you read or listen; the more senses (sight, smell, touch, etc.) you invoke in the imagery, the more effective it is.

Here are some examples:
- An archer-athlete who gets overly upset when he makes mistakes (which reinforces the mistakes making them easier to be repeated), might make an affirmation "It's normal for me to make mistakes from time to time, as I am still improving."
- If you are affected greatly by the pressure you feel during competitions, you might say, "I appreciate pressure-packed situations because the pressure tells me I am close to winning."

Typically these are archery-related things, but if you have personal issues to deal with, this works on them, too. If you are using 3x5 cards, read each card first thing each morning, and last thing each day. Read them just before each practice and competition, and again immediately afterward. Of course, you may also read them any other time you like (when waiting for a bus, just before a doctor appointment, but not while you are driving a car!).

This is the *Signpost* for using affirmations at the intermediate level:

4. Uses affirmations to achieve goals .... ☐ Sometimes ☐ Often ☐ Always
   Affirmations are used in a prescribed process to achieve goals.

Shot Thoughts This idea was borrowed from golfers (along with the names for "open" and "closed" stances). Golfers have what are called "swing thoughts." Since a golf swing happens too fast to be thought about consciously, it happens subconsciously. But thoughts in the conscious mind can guide the subconscious. They have to be short thoughts because things are happening fast. So, a golfer might think "relaxed hands" or "balanced followthrough" as they swing. They have similar "thoughts" for their putting routines. If you get a chance to watch golf on TV, watch any golfer. He/she will have a pre-shot and pre-putt routine on display. Golfers, like

Notes _____

archers, also use shot sequences.

So, you too may use "shot thoughts" to help your form. This is usually in the context of dealing with a problem. For example, if your bowhand was getting tense as you draw the string, you might think "soft bow hand" to yourself as you draw. Or, if your bow shoulder has begun to creep into the "up" position, you might think "shoulders down" as you raise your bow.

This is the *Signpost* for shot thoughts at the intermediate level:

5. Uses shot thoughts
   as part of shot sequence .... ☐ Sometimes ☐ Often ☐ Always
   Shot thoughts are used in any step in shot sequence (practice and competition) to address weaknesses or lack of focus.

More on Goals If you feel that goals really work for you, learn more about the goal setting and goal getting process. Here are some important points to consider.

- Let's say you want to win a national championship (an outcome goal). This is too far removed from where you are now to make in a single leap. So, break it down. What kinds of scores do you have to shoot (on what rounds) to win? What was last year's winning score? What is your score on that round now? Create a series of goals for scores on the round, which will tell you about the progress you are making. This is a framework for a plan to achieve your ultimate goal.
- A handy way to describe the desirable characteristics of your goals is the word SMART. *SMART goals* are:
  - Specific
  - Measureable
  - Attainable/Adjustable/Action-based
  - Realistic
  - Time-based

    If your goals aren't specific, how can you know whether you have met them? If they aren't measurable, what will you use as an indicator of success? If they aren't attainable (I want to jump to the Moon!), what good are they? If you can't adjust them, you can feel trapped and out of control. If they aren't action-based, they won't encourage the actions you need to take to get where

Notes

you want to go. If they aren't realistic, they will only frustrate you. If they don't have a timeline associated with them (By June, I will . . .), there is no sense of urgency.

There has been much written about goal setting and goal getting and much of it is available on the Internet. Try to learn what you can to help with this topic.

This is the *Signpost* for goal setting and getting at the intermediate level:

6. Helps draft and uses process goals .... ☐ Sometimes ☐ Often ☐ Always
   Can help create process goals and then exhibits using them through self evaluation. Must achieve "Often" to advance to the next Stage.

Notes _____

Signposts—Stage IV Owning the Sport

Must have completed requirements of Stage III before beginning.

Now you may want to complete your setup with (*from top*) a launcher rest, a telescopic aperture (a "scope"), a custom grip, and/or a quick disconnect for your stabilizer.

Wow! You have come a long way. You are now a really accomplished archer. You can shoot high scores and you are in command of your shot. This doesn't mean there isn't more to learn, just that you have come more than 80% of the way. At this point it gets harder to make improvements. This is not a problem, in fact it is normal. When you have done 50% of a task, you have doubled your progress from when you had done 25% of that task. But when you are at the 80% mark, only 20% of the task now remains. Hence the farther along you get, the less far there is to go, and often the harder it is to do, because you have already done the easier tasks. It would be stupid to not do the easier tasks that give the greatest progress first, no?

In this *Stage* you take over total control of your sport. Coaches are now your partners who work with you on what you want to work on. At this *Stage* you become independent of systems and teachers. You know enough to learn on your own and to seek out new knowledge, test it, and incorporate into your archery. All of these *Stages* can be done in just a few years or it can take longer. How long you have taken to get to this point is not a sign of anything; it just is.

In this last *Stage*, there are just a few physical skills, and the same list of mental skills as in *Stage III*, but instead of us teaching you everything, some really good references will be supplied for you to explore based on what you think works best for you. You can still consult your AER Coach and other coaches as well. Welcome to the wide world of archery!

Oh, and now the *Signposts* are for you to evaluate and sign off on. As before, your coach is there to help, if you need.

Refining Your Archery Skills

Finishing Your Kit If you have decided to shoot with a release aid, you may want to invest in a better arrow rest at this point. Most compound target archers use a "launcher style" arrow rest and these can cost anywhere from $30-100. Set it up according to the manufacturer's instructions.

You may want to upgrade your sight aperture from a simple pin (on a target/moveable sight) to a telescopic aperture (start with low "power" 2-4X). You may

Notes _____
_____
_____
_____
_____
_____

want to customize your stabilization system with a "quick disconnect adapter" which allows you to mount your stabilizer in a half twist, instead of screwing it into place each time.

You may also want to purchase a custom bow grip or modify the one you have so it fits your hand better. Expert archers are known to modify their bow's grip using auto body dent filler, tape, tennis grip wraps, and other substances it make it exactly as they want.

Whatever you might want to do to finish out your setup, now would be a good time to do it.

Be aware that compound archers tend to be more mechanically minded and often change out accessories on their bows looking for better performance. If you are one of these people, do yourself a favor and devise a standard to compare the "befores" and "afters" of any such changes. For example, you could use the score on your favorite competitive round. Look up the last three scores for that round (if you don't have three, shoot them!) and take an average. Make the change (new rest, new sight, whatever . . . but only one thing at a time!). Then, after some practice time to get acquainted to your new gewgaw, shoot three more rounds (on different days, not back to back) and average the scores. Any improvement? If not, then maybe spending that money was not a good idea. If yes, then maybe that change was good. We say maybe, because of what is called the *Hawthorne Effect*: which is any time a change is made that is supposed to make things better, things do get better . . . for a while. This effect is just the "new toy" factor. Any time you have a new something or other, it fascinates you and raises your interest level, until you get used to it. The short term focus can be a source of improvement which disappears later when the change becomes the norm.

> Beware the *Hawthorne Effect*! Any time a change is made that is supposed to make things better, things do get better . . . for a while.

This is about the only way you can tell you are investing wisely in your money, so devise a test before each equipment change (group size, standard round scores, something) and check to see if things really got better or whether you just thought they did.

Advanced Tuning Tuning compound bows is more time consuming than tuning either longbows or recurve bows, but at this point, most of the tuning is done on the arrows. There is a free arrow tuning resource from the Easton Archery com-

Students always need help with acquiring new gear. If you are so lucky as to have a quality archery shop in your vicinity, one that has a target archery specialist, you can send your students there. The odds against this being the case are so large, though, that we urge you to get as familiar as you can with target archery gear so you can make informed recommendations. Check out the AER website (www.archeryeducationresources.com) for recomendations and trainings, but for more advanced equipment, ask the kind folks at *Lancaster Archery Supply* (www.lancasterarchery.com, 800.829.7408) to send you their catalog—also called the "Archer's Wish List"). If you don't have a target archery-minded shop in your locale, you will find Lancaster Archery Supply to be a virtual "one stop shop" for all things target. If you do have a target archery-minded shop in your locale, pay them a visit, strike up a relationship. Shop owners often see the wisdom of encouraging new archers (your students!) with discounts and services. If you are this lucky, don't pass on this opportunity! And, if they don't get your business, they may not be there the next time you need them.

Notes _____

> The basic rule of tuning is: *never make more than one change at a time*! If you make two or more changes at one time and there is an improvement, you won't be able to tell which change caused the improvement.

pany which is available at the AER website or at various places on the internet. This guide is for modern arrows (shafts of aluminum, carbon, and carbon-aluminum).

Group Tuning Any advanced tuning procedure must include group tuning. Basically, you examine your groups at all distances you shoot. The groups should be round and proportional. Being round means the arrows making the group would fit in a circle and would be distributed as much left as right, as much up as down, and be more concentrated toward the center of the group. By proportional, it means the diameters (widths or heights) of the circles should correspond to the distances. If you shoot six arrows in a 10 inch group at 20 yards they should be in a 20 inch circle at 40 yards and a 30 inch circle at 60 yards. If the groups are smaller or larger than they should be at either end of the distance range, there is something wrong with your tune. You can tune for better performance at longer distances but with a sacrifice in performance at shorter, and vice-versa, but generally archers like their equipment to perform equally well over all of the distances they shoot.

Group tuning can be exhausting as you have to shoot many groups (dozens) to establish a normal group size and you have to do this at a number of distances. Then if you make a tuning change (for example, moving the nocking point locator down just a tiny bit), you have to do it over again. Each change requires a test and the basic rule of tuning is: never make more than one change at a time! If you make two or more changes at one time and there is an improvement, you won't be able to tell which change caused the improvement; maybe Change A caused a big improvement and Change B made it less! There is no way to tell, so one change at a time, then test.

Here is your *Signpost*:

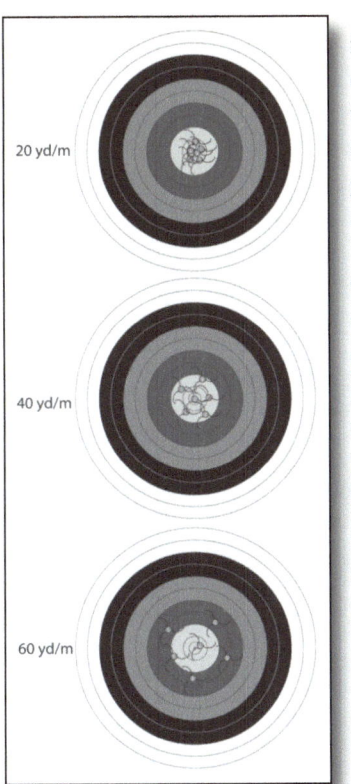

1. Able to tune bow/arrow system (fine) ☐ Sometimes ☐ Often ☐ Always
   Starts with careful bow setup, then tuning begins with bare shaft tuning then proceeds to group tuning. Compound bows are tuned by making centershot and nocking point height adjustments. Arrows are tuned by adjusting their lengths and point weights and fletching sizes/angles and nock fit. Very fine tuning may be accomplished by changing rest pressure and micro centershot and nocking point adjustments when group tuning.

Be sure to review *Bow Setup* in the Appendices, as a poorly set up bow can defeat any tuning procedure.

Notes _____

Archery Gear Maintenance There is a great little book with the title *Simple Maintenance for Archery* by Ruth Rowe and Alan Anderson that has step-by-step instructions (with photos) on how to do almost all maintenance on your bow and arrows. It is highly recommend, in fact, all archers need a copy of this book. It is inexpensive and can be purchased on AER's website (*www.archeryeducationresources.com*). More information focused on compound archery can also be found on the internet, but caveat emptor, there is no requirement that people know what they are talking about before they post things on the internet! Try key word searches for anything you want.

2. Maintains own equipment .... ☐ Sometimes ☐ Often ☐ Always
   Protects equipment from elements, stores equipment properly, and repairs/maintains all archery gear.

Coaches, you need this book! We would have had to have another 40 pages of appendices if it were not for the availability of this book! It even is spiral bound which means it lays flat while you are using it to walk through a procedure. This is a must have "Coach's Friend."

Scoring Here is your second scoring goal. Again, it is set relative to what top scores are being shot in your category. At this point you should be looking to shoot these scores in competition rather than in practice. Keeping track of your process goals while you are shooting will probably give you information about what you need to do to improve your scores. Don't expect huge improvements in short time spans, the higher you go, the slower the progress seems! Also realize that any journey, such as your archery, has ups and downs (and plateaus as well). Sometimes we get stuck and can't go up without going down first! (This is usually a sign of trying too hard.)

Here is your *Signpost*:

3. Can shoot scores of 90% of record level .... ☐ Sometimes ☐ Often ☐ Always
   These can be competition or practice scores shot under competition conditions. Any rounds may be used but must include both indoor and outdoor rounds.

Getting the Point If you have rejected shooting with a bow sight, it is time to make sure that you can use the point of aim (POA) method over all of the distances you shoot. String alignment is important for compound barebow archers, so special care must be taken with it, especially at the longer distances.

This is your *Signpost* for "sighting in" off the point:

4. Uses arrow point to aim with .... ☐ Sometimes ☐ Often ☐ Always
   Must be able to find and use a point of aim at all reachable distances (for compound archer shooting "fingers" style).

This scoring goal is a high but not drastically high goal. Don't be surprised if your gifted archers sail right on by this *Signpost*.

Notes _____

_____

_____

_____

_____

_____

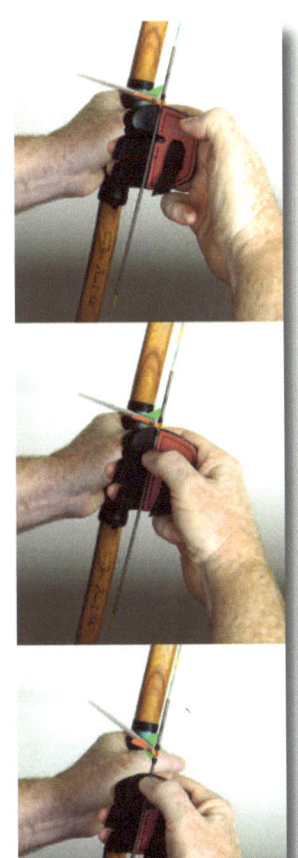

To "crawl" down the string, set the tab up against the arrow, count down how many stitches or serving wraps and insert thumbnail, then move tab to that position.

Walking the String An alternative to the basic point of aim (POA) method described above is *stringwalking*. In this aiming technique you still position the arrow point in your sight picture, but you place it in the same place every time (typically the target's center). This, of course, would work at your point blank range/point on target distance, but what about all of the other distances? The others are dealt with by "walking" the string. Physically you move your tab and draw fingers down the string away from the arrow. Every fraction of an inch you move down moves the arrow nock higher compared to your anchor position. You then draw to your normal anchor position and shoot. Raising the back end of the arrow point and keeping the point of the arrow at the same elevation (on your line of sight to the target) causes the arrow to strike the target lower. (In effect, you are pointing the arrow more or less "downhill.") There is a correspondence between how much lower on the target and how far down the string and . . . there is a correspondence with lower on the target and bull's eyes at shorter distances. In other words, the distance you move down the string (called a crawl as in "you have to crawl before you can walk" or string walk) correlates exactly to the shooting distance. From your "point on target" distance inward, there is a crawl that corresponds to that distance. And like the point of aim method, once you know the crawls for 20 and 30 yards, the crawl for 25 yards is half way in between, etc.

Setting Your Crawls The accompanying photos show how a crawl is set. This must be done deliberately and carefully because even small mistakes make for large differences in outcome. To figure out how far down to go, people use two systems: tab stitches and serving wraps. Many finger tabs have a line of stitching that parallels the bowstring. By placing the tab up against the arrow, the stitches can be used to determine the crawls (a "point on" of forty yards is a zero crawl (by definition), and if 20 yards is eight stitches down, 30 yards is four stitches, etc. For those who like to count serving wraps instead, they serve the center of their bowstrings with "monofilament" serving material (essentially fishing line). This is harder than braided serving thread and you can run your thumbnail down such a served bowstring and it will click, one click for each wrap of the string. Typically one wrap corresponds to a yard or a fraction of a yard.

Beyond Your Point On Crawls work for distances closer in than your point on target distance. To reach distances beyond your point on, you need to increase the

Coaches, if you haven't "walked the string" yet, you are missing a lot of fun. Get a light drawing bow and go try it!

Notes

"point on" distance . . . by changing anchors. You already have a point on target distance for your high anchor that will be used for shorter distances, and a point on target distance for your low anchor that will be used for longer distances. The crawls for both distances will be similar in that a crawl that gives you a bull's eye for five yards closer than your high anchor "point on" distance will be very close to a bull's eye for a distance five yards closer than your low anchor "point on" distance. Hopefully, the two ranges of distances overlap. If not, there are additional techniques to employ but this is enough for now: two anchor positions (high and low) resulting in two point on target distances and two (very similar) sets of crawls for distances shorter than those. Be sure to take notes on these things as they are easy to forget!

If you like this, adding a long stabilizer to your compound bow and then walking the string to aim is exactly the NFAA's Barebow shooting style.

This is the *Signpost* for walking the string:

5. Can walk the string to aim .... ☐ Sometimes ☐ Often ☐ Always
   Able to identify moderate crawls and execute shots with them (for compound archer shooting "fingers" style).

Stage IV Mental Aspects

If you are going to explore the mental side of archery further the one book you need to read (and read again) is Lanny Bassham's, *With Winning In Mind* (available on the AER website (*www.archeryeducationresources.com*) and at most online booksellers or ask your local book shop to order it for you). His story borders on the fantastic and his methods are proven. It will open up a great many new concepts and practices.

Here are the *Signposts* for you to sign off on:

1. Keeps a journal for practice/competition ...... ☐ Sometimes ☐ Often ☐ Always
   Journal entries focus on record keeping and finding solutions (not problems) and are positive in nature.

2. Interacts with other archers in style to learn .. ☐ Sometimes ☐ Often ☐ Always
   Much can be learned from other archers of the same style. Archers wanting to improve need to seek out useful information and try to apply it to their own game.

Notes _____

_____

_____

_____

_____

_____

_____

_____

3. Uses imagery as part of shot sequence ...... ☐ Sometimes ☐ Often ☐ Always
   Good shots are imaged/imagined as an early stage in shot sequence (practice and competition).

4. Uses affirmations to achieve goals .... ☐ Sometimes ☐ Often ☐ Always
   Affirmations are used in a prescribed process to achieve goals.

5. Uses shot thoughts as part of shot sequence ... ☐ Sometimes ☐ Often ☐ Always
   Shot thoughts are used in any stage in shot sequence (practice and competition) to address weaknesses or lack of focus.

6. Uses shot sequence to create
   regular shooting rhythm .... ☐ Sometimes ☐ Often ☐ Always
   Shooting rhythm can be made regular by use of creative shot sequence elements which can only be found by trial and test.

7. Helps draft and uses process
   and outcome goals .... ☐ Sometimes ☐ Often ☐ Always
   Can help create process and outcome goals and then exhibits using them through self evaluation

Notes _____

Archery Education Resources
Recreational Archery Curriculum
Traditional Track

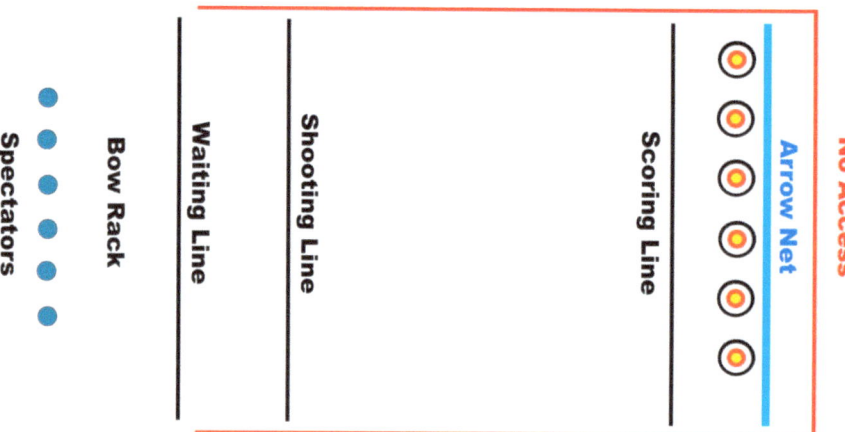

This diagram shows a typical layout for an indoor archery range. Archers are expected to be behind the waiting line when it is not their turn to shoot . . . behaving well.

Archery Education Resources
Comprehensive Archery Curriculum
Traditional Track

Introduction
While traditional archery is often practiced out in the woods, our classes are conducted at Parks and Recreation Centers, public school grounds and gymnasiums, and occasionally at permanent archery ranges. And whether the shooting area is set up temporarily or is permanent, it is set up as a target range, because this creates a safe environment to practice archery in. The first topic in AER archery classes is always orientation and safety. Safety will continue to be a topic as we help you build safe archery habits, because you don't have to think about a habit, it is just something you do.

Signposts—Stage I Getting Started

Archery Safety

Good Behavior Is Expected The expectation is that when you are waiting behind the waiting line (*see diagram on revious page*), that you will do nothing dangerous, nor will you cause any discomfort for other archers. The *Signpost* that you will be evaluated on looks like this:

Usually the idea of good behavior only has to be explained to the 8-12 year-old set, but there are exceptions. If a student has trouble meeting this *Signpost*, ask the sponsor or site staff if he/she has a history of such behavior. Being forewarned is also being forearmed.

1. Exhibits good behavior
   when not on shooting line .... ☐ Sometimes ☐ Often ☐ Always
   Other archers and archery equipment treated respectfully while staying behind the waiting line.

The Whistle System The system used to direct a group of archers is called the "Whistle System." Here are the whistle system commands:

The Whistle System

Two Blasts	Archers may come to the shooting line.
One Blast	Archers may place an arrow on the bow and begin shooting.
Three Blasts	Archers may walk to the target to retrieve their arrows.
Five or More Blasts	Emergency letdown! Stop immediately, wait for instructions.

Coaches are expected to teach all of the safety aspects covered in the *AER Beginning Archery Class Instructor Guide*. Adherence to the safety rules surrounding pulling arrows—the most dangerous aspect of archery—is paramount. You need to have a zero-tolerance attitude toward safety violations. *Signpost* evaluations of "Often" should be delayed several lessons for any infraction.

Notes _____

_____

_____

_____

_____

This system is used all over the world at every level of archery (even the World Championships and the Olympic games), although at competitions an air horn rather than a whistle may be used. A "letdown" from full or partial draw is performed by pointing the arrow at the floor/ground immediately in front of you and easing the string back to it's neutral position. In an "emergency letdown" you also take the arrow off of the bow and place it back in its quiver. The *Signpost* that you will be evaluated on looks like this:

2. Understands and
   follows the whistle system .... ☐ Sometimes ☐ Often ☐ Always

   Knows and obeys all four whistle system commands. *Must achieve "Always" to advance to the next Stage.*

Good Behavior Is Expected Everywhere Just as you are expected to behave in a safe and polite manner when off of the shooting line, the same is true when you are on the shooting line. Trying to distract another archer during a contest is unsportsmanlike. In general, one doesn't speak to other archers when "on the line." Here is your Signpost:

3. Exhibits good behavior
   when on shooting line .... ☐ Sometimes ☐ Often ☐ Always

   Does not talk to, or interfere with, other archers on the line. *Must achieve "Always" to advance to the next Stage.*

The Range Safety Rules Must Be Obeyed There are actually quite a few safety rules that apply when you are shooting arrows on a target range. We encourage coaches to post the standard "range rules" so you have an opportunity to read them. Some rules will be given only orally, so you need to listen carefully as there is no tolerance for violations of safety rules. Here is a typical set of range rules.

The *Signpost* involved follows. We have not duplicated the safety Signposts at each stage as behaving safely is a requirement to pass out of the first stage. All safety rules will be enforced at each stage of your program.

4. Obeys all safety rules (written/oral) .... ☐ Sometimes ☐ Often ☐ Always

   Even though rules are occasionally violated when they are being learned, there can be no violations for several weeks before an "always" can be given. *Must achieve "Always" to advance to the next Stage.*

The whistle system was changed in 2008, specifically the "Emergency Letdown" signal was changed from "four or more" blasts to "five or more." Some older materials may not reflect the change and, since it is not a major change, no fuss need be made.

During FITA competitions, if one archer complains about the behavior of another archer, it is taken seriously. A judge can monitor the situation and if the offending archer is judged to have deliberately tried to disadvantage another archer, he/she can be disqualified. For our purpose, this is only good manners. People trash talking on the line in a mean-spirited manner can only lead to a "no fun" situation which conflicts with our second

You are empowered to add to the Range Rules (for your classes)! If you are having a particular problem, write a new rule to deal with it. Remember to be positive and to state the behavior allowed, not the behavior forbidden, e.g. "Arrows always point to the target" rather than "never point an arrow at a person." Later you can remove the rule or keep it if it has particular utility. An ideal set of rules doesn't exist, but whatever they are they should be short, and positive, etc.

Notes _____

_____

_____

_____

_____

Archery Range Rules

1. Know and obey all range commands.
2. Keep your arrows in your quiver until you are told to shoot.
3. Always wear your arm guard and finger tab.
4. Only use the arrows the instructor gave you and remember what they look like.
5. Always keep your arrows pointed down or toward the target.
6. If you drop an arrow, leave it on the ground until you are told to get your arrows.
7. Always walk at the archery range.

Archery Range Whistle Commands
Two Blasts "Archers to the Shooting Line."
One Blast "Begin Shooting."
Three Blasts "Walk forward and get your arrows."
Five or More Blasts "Stop shooting immediately! Wait for instructions!"

Archery Range Procedures
- Stand behind the waiting line until you hear two (2) whistle blasts or "Archers to the shooting line." Take your bow and straddle the shooting line.
- Keep your arrows in your quiver until you hear one (1) whistle blast.
- After you have shot all of your arrows, step back from the shooting line, set your bow on the rack, and wait behind the waiting line.
- After everyone is done shooting and is behind the waiting line, the instructor will blow the whistle three (3) times, then walk forward to the target line.

Pulling Your Arrows
- Two archers at a time from each target may go forward from the target line to pull their arrows.
- Stand to the side of the target and make sure that no one is standing behind your arrows.
- Pull your arrows out, one at a time, and put them into your quiver.
- After you have pulled all of your arrows, return to the waiting line.

Notes

Basic Archery Form

The other major component of *Stage I* is achieving basic good archery form and execution. This is done with the only equipment being a bow and arrows (and an armguard, which is mandatory archery safety equipment).

Taking Your Stance The first part of any archery shot involves placing your feet properly; this is called "taking your stance." The stance everyone starts with is called the "square stance." In this stance your feet are about shoulder width apart with the tips of your shoes lying on a line that leads to the center of the target. (The line isn't there, you have to imagine it.) The line that is there, the shooting line, is supposed to be "straddled," that is you have one foot in front of the line and one foot behind.

Note that this puts you sideways to the target, which is good because that's the best way to shoot arrows. Turning your body either left or right at this stage will interfere with you making good shots, so it is important to not move your feet after you have taken your stance.

Here is the associated *Signpost*:

1. Adopts a square stance .... ☐ Sometimes ☐ Often ☐ Always
   Tips of shoes make line to center of target, feet shoulder-width apart, straddling the shooting line.

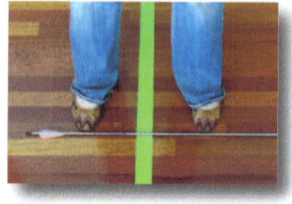

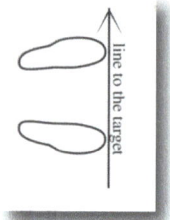

In a square stance the tips of your toes are on a line to the center of the target.

Standing Well The next step is to have good posture, which is not what your Mom or the military wants from you. You need to stand straight and relaxed. Your knees are neither bent nor locked back. Your chest is not puffed out, it is relaxed downward. Here is the associated *Signpost*:

2. Exhibits good archery posture .... ☐ Sometimes ☐ Often ☐ Always
   Stands relaxed and straight up and down, doesn't lean left or right, forward or backward. Knees straight but not locked.

Keeping Your Shoulders Down A particular part of archery posture that has its own Signpost involves your shoulders. Your shoulders are to be "down." If you don't know what this means ask your coach about the *Shoulders Up, Shoulders Down Drill*. We are not telling you why this is done this way; if you are curious, ask your coach. (In general, we are organizing your skeleton and muscles to work together most effectively.) The *Signpost* here is:

When you are evaluating *Signposts*, always focus on the *Stage* an archer is in. Here your archer is quite a beginner, so we are not looking for a high level of performance. What we expect is that the archer places his feet carefully and doesn't move them thereafter. The exact spacing, angle, etc. may vary (a little) and the student could still get an "Often" or "Always." later we will expect more precision.

Younger archers tend to elevate their shoulders, neck, and head when they draw the bow. Watch for this. Encourage them to keep their upper body "down." Reason: elevating the chest and shoulders restricts the ability of the back muscles to come into play while drawing the bow (as they are involved in the elevating).

It is not "normal" to raise a bow while keeping the shoulders "down." One has to exert some effort to keep them down. This is a primary reason why they are to do the steps of the shot sequence as separate steps. (Note—They aren't introduced to shot sequences until *Stage II*, but you are guiding them that way all along.) During the "Raise the Bow" step, one makes a conscious effort to keep the shoulders "down." This is very hard to learn if one is simultaneously drawing the bow. Make sure students don't "draw on the way up" . . . until they can draw with their shoulders "down" as a matter of habit. Introduce the *AER Shoulders Up, Shoulders Down Drill* here if you haven't already done so.

Notes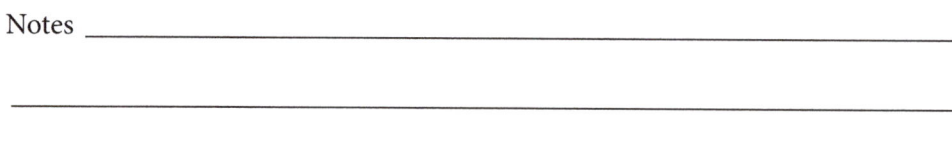

3. Keeps shoulders low .... ☐ Sometimes ☐ Often ☐ Always
   Shoulders are in the "down" position throughout shot.

Setting Your Bow Hand One of the spots beginner's struggle is in placing their bow hand onto the bow. The spot on the bow where this happens is called the "grip," and it looks much the same as the grip on a pistol, but you neither hold it like a pistol nor do you "grip" or squeeze the bow. We don't want to squeeze the grip area of the bow because doing that doesn't help us draw the bow; in fact squeezing the bow detracts from the ability to pull the bowstring. (It makes you stiff and weak!) Holding a bow like a pistol puts the back of the hand parallel with the bow, which causes the archer's elbow to turn inward (sideways), very close to the path the bowstring takes when it is "loosed." So close, in fact, that it is easy for the string to whack your elbow that way and your armguard won't protect it as it is protecting your forearm, not your elbow!

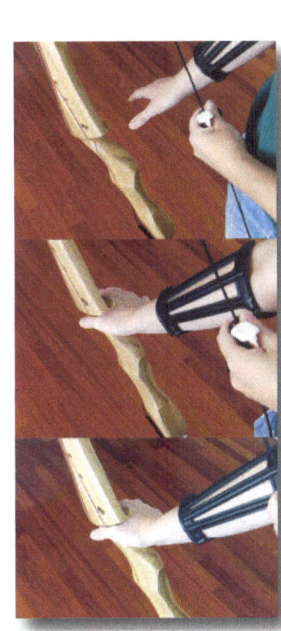

To set your bowhand correctly, you start with your hand flat and your palm facing the floor/ground. You slide your hand (between thumb and first finger) into the "throat" (deepest part) of the grip. Then you bend your wrist down onto the bow and relax your fingers (they do not wrap around the bow). The knuckles of your bow hand are now at about a 45° angle to the ground, which is one way for you to check to see that you've got it right (*see photos next page*). The bow actually sits on the pad of your thumb and doesn't touch the other half of your hand. When you do this you will find that your elbow has rotated away from the path of the bowstring and out of harm's way.

There are a few people (who are very, very flexible) who can adopt this bow hand and still have their elbow sideways. They need to be taught how to rotate their elbows out of the way. Here is a test to see if you are one of those people: take a bow and set your bow hand properly, then hold the bow out as if you were going to shoot (don't use an arrow as you won't be shooting). Then bend the elbow of your draw arm. The bow should swing around and come up against your chest (*see photo next page*). If it does, you are good to go. If the bow swings up in an arc toward your head, ask your coach about the *Elbow Rotation Drill*. Rotating your elbow will become one of the steps you will need to do to safely shoot arrows. Please, whacking your elbow is not a nice way to learn this! Do the test and find out whether you are

The bow hand is a major problem area for students. It can be compounded by the use of wooden-handled recurve bows, which have thick grip areas which makes it hard for smaller students to get a proper bow hand on. Some longbows encourage a "pistol grip" and have to be addressed carefully. Lack of a good bow hand is also a major cause of bruised bow arms. Show students the elbow bending test as a way of emphasizing that they too can check themselves from time to time.

Notes _____

doing it right or not.

Here's your *Signpost*:

4. Exhibits good bow hand .... ☐ Sometimes ☐ Often ☐ Always
   Bow hand is relaxed, in proper position with bow sitting on pad of thumb, fingers curled slightly and relaxed.

Positioning Your Head Another posture element that gets its own *Signpost* is head position. Since you are standing sideways to the target, you must turn your head to look over your shoulder to see the target. This is correct archery posture. Tilting your head at all makes everything more difficult. (You may be surprised as to why this is so.) Student-archers often do this in an attempt to "look down the arrow" as a way to aim. This technique does not work for a number of reasons, the primary one being that the second the arrow comes off of the bow, it falls, therefore it cannot hit the point sighted down. At very close distances, like where we begin shooting arrows, the amount the arrow falls is very small leading to the impression that "this works" but, as you move back from the target, the arrow will impact lower and lower compared to the aiming point. The idea of using the arrow to aim with is not a bad idea as you will see later, but the technique of looking down the shaft plainly does not work. Here is your *Signpost*:

5. Exhibits good head position through shot ..... ☐ Sometimes ☐ Often ☐ Always
   Head is turned toward target erect, neither tilted nor dipped.

Drawing the String There are people who are very cautious and do things carefully and slowly. Others, more exuberant in nature, rush everything. Archery is done somewhere in the middle. If you are slow and cautious, it might take you ten seconds to draw the bow. This is too slow—your muscles are getting tired even as you pull and the longer it takes, the more tired you will be when the pull required gets greater toward the end of the draw. Energetic folks tend to yank the string back; you can recognize them because their arrows tend to fall off of their arrow rest when they pull without caution. It should take only 1-2 seconds to draw the string. This is not rushed, nor is it slow. It is smooth and strong. In the beginning you may take longer than this, 2-3 seconds, because you are still learning to get the bowstring all the way back to where it belongs. This is okay, but the goal is to draw the string in a

BAD

GOOD

Tilted heads can be made erect with a finger. Use just one finger to reposition your archer's head properly. Once they have found out what the correct position is (and have resisted the urge to look down the arrow) they will be able to replicate it fairly easily.

Beginners need to know how to start the draw (finger and elbow placement), how to pull (using their back muscles to rotate their draw shoulder with some torso rotation thrown in), and where they are going (their firm anchor position). At the same time they are supposed to maintain their good archery posture! So, this is quite a complex task. In general, the more complex the task, the more time it takes to master, so you should not be too willing to give "Oftens" and "Always" here.

smooth, strong, and controlled fashion.

This is done with the draw elbow level with the draw hand or higher.

Here is the *Signpost* for drawing the string:

6. Draws the bow smoothly and in rhythm ..... ☐ Sometimes ☐ Often ☐ Always
   Bow string is drawn smoothly and quickly without hurrying, draw elbow is high.

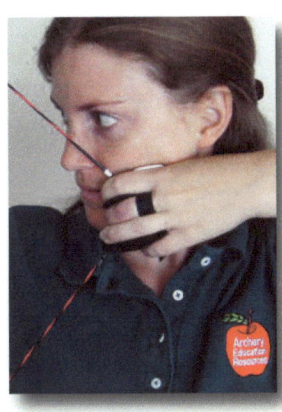

Finding Your Anchor Position An "anchor" position in archery refers to the position of your drawing hand with regard to your body. Over the years there have been many anchors, from behind the ear to down at the chest, but for consistent accuracy, the anchor position must bring the bow string in front of your aiming eye. You will be taught two anchors—a high anchor first and a low, or Olympic-style, anchor later.

The high anchor is found by pressing your draw hand against your face such that the tip of your index finger is positioned in the corner of your mouth and your top finger wraps around your cheek bone (*see photo*). If you have difficulty finding this position, your coach will help you find it, first without a bow and then with a bow. This is the *Signpost* for finding your anchor position:

7. Exhibits a reasonably tight anchor .... ☐ Sometimes ☐ Often ☐ Always
   Anchor position is consistent with draw hand pressed against face (high anchor) bringing the string in front of the aiming eye.

Following Through Bowlers follow through, golfers follow through, baseball batters follow through, and . . . archers follow through. The archery "followthrough" form element is simply to maintain your body position after each arrow is shot for at least one second. A key part of this, because your bow hand is relaxed, is that your bow will rock gently in your hand after the bow string is released. This rocking is an indicator that tells you how well you executed the release of the string and held your followthrough position by how regular it is. (Does it happen the same way each time?) This is the *Signpost* for following through:

8. Exhibits good followthrough .... ☐ Sometimes ☐ Often ☐ Always
   After the string is released, bow arm stays up and draw hand moves backward along face.

Getting in Line This *Signpost* holds the key for consistent accuracy. In order

Many students, young and old, are hesitant to have something unknown (like a bowstring and the end of an arrow) right next to their eyes or face. Others it doesn't bother. So, it may take some patience with the "sensitive" ones, which is entirely their due. And once they are convinced it won't hurt them, they become fine with it.

The biggest bugaboo is having the thumb of the draw hand "up" which equates to "in the way." The thumb must be held "down" so it ends up under the jaw at anchor. Then it can be relaxed. having the thumb in any "up" position blocks the hand from achieving a tight anchor.

If the bow hand is relaxed the bow will "bow" (as in to "take a bow") and it takes about 1-2 seconds for it to do so, so one of the cues you can use is "hold your form until the bow 'bows.'" This is a good indicator of how long to hold their followthroughs as the amount of time is constant (as opposed to "until the arrow hits the target" in which it is not) and it encourages good form. This will obviously not happen if your longbow archer is using a strong grip. In which case, the bow arm, with bow, just needs to stay up "for a count of two seconds" after the shot.

for everything to work in this style, your draw elbow has to be in line with your arrow (*see photo*). It is that simple. (There are some fine points to be addressed . . . later.) Most beginners start with their draw elbows too low and sticking out away from them. As you progress your elbow needs to get "in line" as this alignment with the arrow allows your fingers to slip from the string in the most relaxed manner. (Tense draw fingers can cause arrows to fly sideways!) The sooner you can get into this position, the sooner everything else comes together to make great shots.

A key element in archery is achieving good form as quickly as possible because you do not want to practice doing it wrong! At some time or other in school one of your teachers had you rewrite all of your misspelled words on an assignment ten times. This is a fairly good rule of thumb: if you practice something incorrect, it will take ten times the work doing it correctly to fix the incorrect execution. So, if you shoot arrows 10 times incorrectly, it takes 100 correct shots to make doing it correctly somewhat of a habit (1000 incorrect shots requires 10,000 correct ones!).

This is the *Signpost* for achieving good alignment.

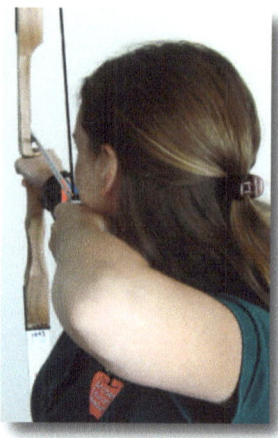

9. Exhibits good alignment .... ☐ Sometimes ☐ Often ☐ Always
At full draw, draw elbow lines up with the arrow line extended backward.

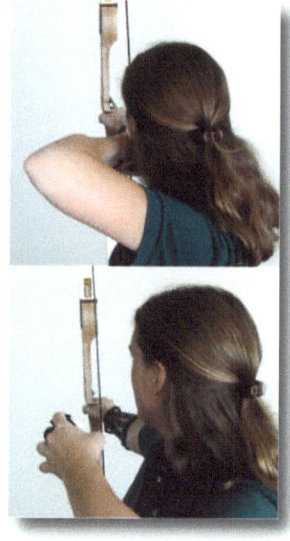

Good alignment (top) is essential for consistency; poor alignment (below) causes "plucked" releases (bottom) and poor consistency.

"Grouping" Your Shots When anyone first begins shooting arrows, we celebrate all "bull's eyes." But as time goes on, the goal is not just hitting the target's center, it is hitting it consistently, which is why the concept of "grouping" is introduced here. Shooting arrows that all land in (roughly) one place is even more important than hitting those bull's eyes, because if you can shoot arrows so they land all in the same place you can move those arrows to a new place using an aiming technique. (Most people prefer the center as a landing location.) But, if you can't "group" your arrows and you get a bull's eye, the next arrow will be somewhere else and each subsequent arrow in yet another location.

So, how do you get "good groups?" Grouping is an outcome of consistency; grouping is the outcome of doing the same thing, the same way, over and over. There is a very old saying: "Repetition is the Mother of Learning." This is true in archery, but repetition without good form and execution is worse than not practicing! You must strive to "do it right" over and over.

Be aware, though, that there is not a lot of "trying" involved. (Actually "trying

Line, line, line! Alignment ("Getting in Line") is the key to good form and accuracy. If the draw elbow is behind the arrow, the forces in the bow and archer's body are arrayed properly and the draw wrist and hand can be relaxed and the fingers can come off the string as a unit. If there is a "kink" in the alignment, there is no relaxation and no smooth release. A ragged release causes the string to swing wildly (you can see it in slow-motion video) and arrows to fly all over the place. The importance of line cannot be emphasized too much—to coaches. Athletes should not be thinking about "line" as it is too abstract; their thoughts are "reach to the target" (bow arm) and "swing elbow backward" (draw arm), both of which contribute to good "line."

Notes _____

_____

_____

too hard" blocks making progress in archery.) The target gives you feedback: either the arrows are in nice, tight groups, or they are not. If you are reasonably careful about how you shoot, even moderate amounts of practice will result in good groups in very little time.

Here is your first target-oriented *Signpost*:

10. Shoots good groups consistently .... ☐ Sometimes ☐ Often ☐ Always
    Three arrow groups fit into an eight inch circle two ends out of three at 10 yards. Must achieve "Often" to advance to the next Stage.

Aiming "Off the Point" Back when we addressed where an archer needs to put his head, the wrong idea of looking down the arrow shaft to aim was mentioned. The idea of using the arrow was good but the wrong part (the shaft) was being used. An accurate aiming system, that needs no additional equipment attached to the bow, is the technique of aiming off the point (the arrow point) which, by the way, was invented by a longbow archer.

Because we shoot arrows up into the air so they can arc down into the target (due to of the effect of gravity on relatively slow flying arrows), we hold the rear end of the arrow down under our eye so that the arrow shaft points upward. If we are executing shots with good alignment, a soft bow hand, and a decent followthrough your arrows will rarely miss left or right of a vertical centerline on the target. (We use a clock face orientation on circular targets. The very top is 12 o'clock, the bottom, 6 o'clock, the left edge 9 o'clock, and the right edge is 3 o'clock (see diagram). We can then specify any location on the target by naming the ring and the time, e.g. 6:30 in the red or 11 o'clock in the black. So, if you meet the requirements mentioned, your arrows will be in a narrow band from 12 o'clock to 6 o'clock and rarely left or right of that band. You will have solved the "windage problem" which is "How do I aim left and right?"

The other question: "How do I aim up and down?" is called the "elevation problem" and is more difficult to solve. You can do it by shooting many hundreds of arrows at each of a great many different dis-

You can encourage students to keep track of their groups by asking them "How big are your groups, normally?" They often will not include "flyers" (arrows that don't group) at the beginning, which is okay . . . in the beginning. Archers typically use phrases like "I am holding the red" (all arrows in the red and gold (7-10 rings) or "I usually hold the five ring" (all arrows in the blue, red, gold or 5-10 rings. Most people specify the yardage, too, but that comes later. As time goes on, more and more attention will be paid to the size of the groups. Right now attention is being paid to the act of grouping arrows and less so to their location. The key point is: if they can group their arrows they can move the group into the center with aiming techniques. If they can't group (a sign of inconsistent form), then aiming doesn't matter, so reasonable "grouping" must precede learning to aim.

Notes _____

_____

_____

_____

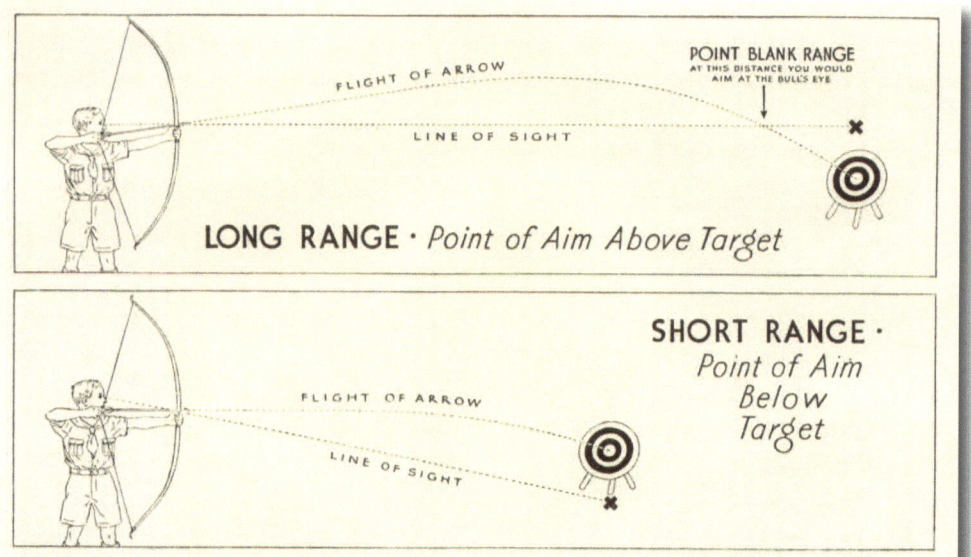

This point of aim diagram is from a pamphlet printed in 1932. The technique was invented in the mid-1800s.

tances, or you can use an aiming technique like *aiming off of the point*.

Here is how it works. Imagine that you are about to release the string on a perfect shot, one in which the arrow will strike the target dead center. Now imagine what you are seeing just before the arrow is shot. This is called your "sight picture." Because you are focused on the target, it is about the only thing you will notice, but in your field of view is part of the bow and also the arrow. The point of the arrow in your sight picture is in some position relative to the target, e.g. blue ring at 6 o'clock. (If you haven't mastered all of the previous steps or if your bow and arrows aren't perfectly matched (usually the case with class equipment) you may be to one side or the other of that 12 o'clock—6 o'clock line. In any case, it is somewhere on or near the target.) You release the arrow and it goes right into the center. Ah, but you want to do it again, don't you? Are their any clues as to how to get your body back into that perfect full draw position time after time? The answer is "the position of the arrow point in your sight picture." If your posture and shot execution are the same and the arrow point is at the same place in your sight picture, the arrow will land in the same location (roughly). This is aiming off of the point.

Traditional archers don't use bow sights, so they must use parts of their bows to aim with. Virtually every part of the bow visible to the archer's aiming eye while focused on the target has been used for this purpose. The arrow has benefits for us in that it looks a certain way when rested on top of our bow hand (or on the arrow shelf) that can help us gauge whether we are at full draw.

Notes _____

There is one distance at which if you put the point onto the center, the arrow goes into the center. This is called "point blank range." Archers usually refer to it as being at their "point on target" distance or their "point on" for short. At closer distances than this, the point of aim is lower than the center and at longer distances than the point on target distance, the point of aim is higher on the target. At very short distances, the POA (point of aim) may be on the ground or floor and for much longer distances it may be on the wall or the hill, or trees on top of the hill (*see the diagram*)!

This is the *Signpost* for aiming off of the point.

11. Uses arrow point to aim with .... ☐ Sometimes ☐ Often ☐ Always
    Must be able to find and use a point of aim for at least one distance (7-15 yards).

Notes _____

Signposts—Stage II Getting Better
Must have completed requirements of Stage I before beginning.

Congratulations! By making it out of *Stage I* you are now quite a good archer. You know how stand, fit an arrow to the string, raise up the bow, draw it smoothly, release the shot cleanly and followthrough . . . and your arrows go mostly into the center of the target at shorter distances. You can stop at this point and enjoy archery for the rest of your life this way. But, after you have acknowledged that you have come a long way, you might feel like there is more to learn . . . and there is. If you want to keep going then you are going to learn intermediate archery form and now it is time for you to acquire your own equipment.

The equipment you need is the same equipment you have been using: bow, arrows, armguard; but there is more you will have to get as you go. If you have been learning on a program recurve bow, it is time to get a longbow, traditional recurve, or modern recurve bow (for FITA Barebow). The reason you need your own equipment is the equipment now needs to be fitted to you. Now that your draw length has become regular, you don't need extra-long arrows (used by beginners for safety). You may need to adjust the bowstring's length or even change it for one made differently or from different materials. If you intend on buying your own gear, ask your AER Archery Coach if he does "Bow Fittings." This is a service in the form of a private lesson that measures you up for the equipment style you favor, so that you will know exactly what to buy as well as where you can shop and what you can reasonably expect to pay.

If you are borrowing equipment, the same criteria apply, so consult your coach as to what exactly you need to acquire.

When you have your own equipment, the first thing you are going to want to do is set it up correctly. The first step is to set the brace/string height (twisting the string makes it shorter which makes the brace/string height higher—check with your bow's manufacturer for the recommended brace/string height); note that new strings tend to stretch somewhat and have to be twisted from time to time to keep them the same length) and placing a nocking point locator (like on your class bow) on the string. If this has not been done when you acquired your equipment, your Coach will assist you. Then you can start shooting your way through the next *Stage*.

Now You Need Your Own ...

bow

arrows

armguard

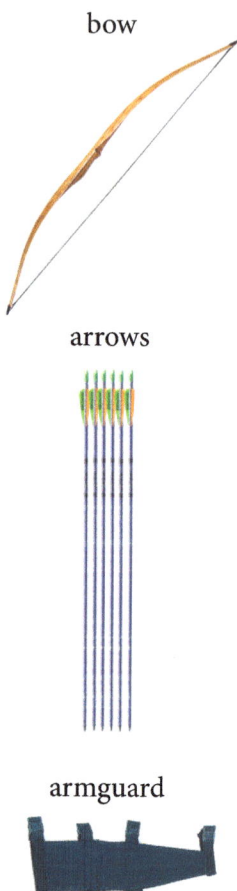

Notes _____

_____

_____

_____

_____

_____

_____

Intermediate Archery Form

Modifying Your Stance Everybody starts with a square stance but everybody is also different from everybody else. Sometimes a different stance can help you shoot better. Stances are classified as "even" or "square," which you have learned already or "open" or "closed." An open stance has the front foot swung around and or back from the square position. A closed stance has the rear foot swung around or back from the open stance. What we recommend is that you try these stances for a class or two to see if they make an improvement in your comfort or accuracy. It takes a class or two attempt because making any change is difficult.

A basic teaching principle of AER is that anytime you change something, your archery gets worse before it gets better. Because archery is a repetition sport, you have had many repetitions of your archery shot making it comfortable and "normal." Whenever you make a change, it feels uncomfortable and not "normal" which automatically makes you worse! It takes a fair number of repetitions to overcome this effect and make the new way seem at least reasonable. And you can't evaluate whether the change was good or bad until you have taken many shots. If the "result" of the change is your archery gets worse and then gets better than when you started, it is a good change. If it gets worse and never gets back to where you were before the change, it is a bad change. But without a fair chance, you will never make any changes. Don't be a archer who says, "I tried that for ten minutes and it wasn't as good!" Nothing in archery will be better after only ten minutes of trying. (Of course, if something creates pain, we recommend you stop doing it immediately!)

If you try, say, an open stance and it doesn't work for you, don't go straight to a closed stance and try that. Return to your "normal" stance for several lessons and get back to the feel of "normal" before you try the closed stance (or anything else).

Generally, an open stance is the most popular stance (although popularity is not a guarantee of anything as every individual is unique) and a closed stance makes it easier to get into line. So, if you are struggling with getting or keeping good alignment, try the closed stance. If you want to look like all of the other archers, try the open stance.

But realize, you do not have to change your stance! But if you don't try the other options you will never know if there is a better archery stance out there for you.

The prime criterion to evaluate form changes is can it be done the same way

> A basic AER learning principle is: *any-time you change something, your archery gets*

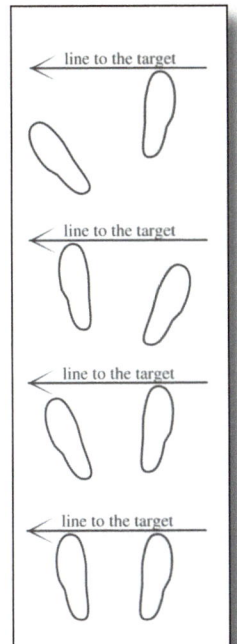

Stances (from bottom to top) can be "square," or "open," or "closed," or "wide open" or done other ways (not shown).

See the Appendix—*On Stances* for more detail. Many traditional archers are steeped in bowhunting technique which requires one to be able to shoot one's bow while standing awkwardly, or sitting, or even laying down. We are emphasizing target arch-ery where consistent foot placement is to our advantage. In competition, this was such an advantage that archers were allowed "foot pegs" to mark the positions of their feet on the shooting line. There were even commercial foot pegs, separated by a length of chain, to give consistent spacing from session to session, available. Today, some archers use golf tees for this purpose.

Notes _____

_____

_____

_____

each and every shot. This is the *Signpost* if you modify your stance.

1. Adopts a personal stance consistently .... ☐ Sometimes ☐ Often ☐ Always
   If open or closed stance is adopted, must adopt that stance consistently.

Modifying Your Posture Traditional archers can shoot arrows bending over, kneeling, even laying down! But these are postures used while bowhunting to avoid obstructions in the flight path of the arrow. In target archery, one always stands erect. A refinement of the form you have learned so far is the "hip tuck" or "hip tilt." If you rotate your hips slightly (bottom of your hips rotates forward, your back becomes flat (see photo) and you center of gravity drops slightly. The flat back allows your back muscles (instrumental in drawing the bowstring) freer reign and the lower center of gravity makes you more stable (less tendency to sway back and forth as you shoot). While this is a small change, so are all of the others as you build better form, but the sum of many small changes can be a big improvement in score! Here is the *Signpost* for your refined archery posture.<insert hip tuck photo>

2. Exhibits good archery posture .... ☐ Sometimes ☐ Often ☐ Always
   Stands relaxed and straight up and down, doesn't lean left or right, forward or backward. Knees straight but not locked. Shoulders down. Small of back flat.

Using a Finger Tab Bows used in beginner classes are very light drawing. As you gain experience the amount of draw weight you can handle goes up. But as the draw weight goes up, so does the tension on the bowstring along with the pressure it creates on your fingers during the draw. At very high draw weights, this pressure can damage the nerves in your fingers. Long before that would happen the discomfort of shooting leads on to some form of finger protection. The vast majority of target archers us a finger tab for this purpose. In addition to protecting your draw fingers, tabs also provide a slick surface for the string to slide from.

It makes no sense to stint when buying a tab because they do not cost much. The most expensive tabs cost almost $30, but a very good tab (the *Black Widow* tab made by the Wilson Brothers—*bottom photo at right*) typically can be had for around $10, if not under $10. If you are a very serious archer, you may want to buy two, not because they wear out fast but they are small enough to get lost and you want to have a backup tab. If you alternate days using them, the two tabs will be near identical in

Without the hip tuck, the archer's back is hollow; with it, it is flat.

If you are not familiar with the hip tuck, try this: stand straight up in front of a vertically hung mirror and then let your body flow "down." (We tend to hold ourselves "up" a little due to mom's or the military's posture exhortations. Then tilt your pelvis as described while looking straight forward in the mirror. You will see yourself drop a slight bit more. This is a lowering of your center of gravity which makes you slightly more stable and, more importantly, causes your lower back to line up with your upper back (with no "hollow" in your lower back—*see photos*). You can see this standing sideways to the mirror as you do the hip tuck. This "flat back" gives you a more rounded back which, in turn, gives your back muscles more range of motion to draw the bow. A stiff, military "chest out" posture uses much of the back muscles' range of motion to puff out the chest and does nothing to help an archer in his/her task, so it is to be avoided.

Some traditional archers scoff at such refinements as their equipment (self bows and wood arrows) is often not up to the precision standards of modern equipment. This attitude is not without basis . . . and we want to prepare our archers to choose between "old style" equipment and modern equipment, possibly on consecutive weekends if they want. And we want archery to be fun. If an archer wants to skip this *Signpost*, we wouldn't argue with him/her.

their performance (both will be "broken in" to the same extent). There are many styles of tabs, even from a single manufacturer, so consult with your coach or read the catalogs or online information carefully.

At the same time you break in a new tab, you will probably want to try a "split-finger" placement on the bowstring. This usually happens when you begin to shoot longer distances (outdoors). Placing one finger above the arrow (the other two below) instead of all three below the arrow and using the same anchor position, effectively lowers the back end of the arrow the width of your top finger. This is actually a great deal. The effect is to point the arrow upward more and thus greater "cast" or distance can be had. The *Black Widow* tab has leather flaps between the top two fingers that protect your fingers from developing calluses and reduce "finger pinch." The reason you were started "three fingers under" was that beginners tend to tense their hands when they draw, which if you use a "split-finger" position from the start a) causes the fingers to pinch the arrow and b) causes the string and the arrow to rotate away from (and fall off of!) the bow. This is very frustrating for beginning archers. The "three fingers under" approach eliminates this source of frustration and once beginning archers learn to relax their draw hands while drawing, a change to split finger is possible.

Having said this, if you intend to walk the string (*see Signpost #11 below*), there is no need to try a split-finger approach. But many people want to learn all they can and so try it anyway. It is your choice.

This is the *Signpost* for using a finger tab.

3. Uses an archery tab correctly .... ☐ Sometimes ☐ Often ☐ Always
   Can put on a fitted archery tab and use it properly as a guide to placing fingers on string.

Longbow Bowhand Technique Longbow grips come in a number of styles. In the old-fashion longbow, there was no arrow rest, the arrow was placed atop the top finger of the bow hand. More modern longbows provide an "arrow shelf" which is a ledge built into the bow. The arrow is then "shot off of the shelf." In FITA Barebow, which allows the use of an arrow rest, quite complicated arrow rests are employed. In FITA barebow, the grip is as you have learned. But, if you graduate to a true longbow, you may very well have to modify the way you "grip" the bow. Some

Finger tabs can be sources of problems but also sources of information. Tabs need to be fitted (the tab's material must wrap around the top and bottom fingers somewhat as the string wraps around them—only trim off unnecessary material) and worn snuggly. The draw fingers still need to be held in a fixed position (typically touching one another and the arrow), but without tension. As tabs wear, the indentations (from the pressure of the string) and wear patterns on the tab can tell you how that tab is being used. For example, if the indentation from the string is narrow, this indicates the tab being placed consistently on the string; if wide, maybe the archer is a little careless at this. The position of the indentation shows you where the string is regarding the fingers (you have to see where the archer wears his tab, of course) and the depth of the indentation shows you where the pressure is greatest and least.

See *The Magic Release* by Don Rabska in the Coach Resources section of the AER website (*www.archeryeducationresources.com*) for an excellent article about the finger release.

Again, this is for more modern equipment. Some "old style" folks think a piece of elk hide is the only tab they will ever need. We would not disagree with them.

wooden longbows have pistol grips and the can be shot using the grip you have already learned, but most longbows do not. Most longbows have either a cylindrical grip region or one that has a somewhat "molded" grip region. The larger ones were created originally by gluing a block of wood to the bow where it would be gripped. This block was called a "riser" block which has lead to us calling the middle sections of three piece longbows, recurve bows, and compound bows "risers" to this day.

Longbow advocates fall roughly into two groups when it comes to "gripping" the bow: those who advocate a "strong grip" and those who advocate a "weak grip" (who are in the majority). The strong grip folks recommend you grab the bow about as you would a hammer, fairly tightly. The weak grip people recommend you cradle the bow as if it were a baby bird. We recommend you try both approaches, as both can be done well, but be wary of too strong of a grip as it can cost you energy and the tension can spread up your arm.

And, if you are "shooting off of your hand" rather than off of an arrow shelf or an arrow rest, you must take care to have your hand in the same place on the bow for each shot, and that the top finger (your arrow rest!) is placed the same way every shot.

This is the *Signpost* for your new bow hand position.

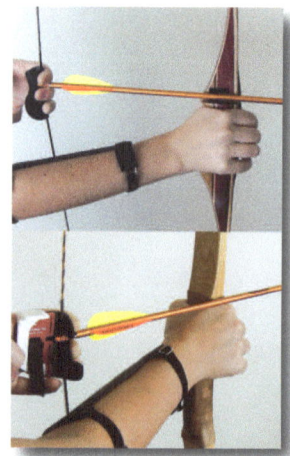

Some longbow have "shelves" that act as arrow rests, others require you to "shoot off of your knuckle."

1. Exhibits good bow hand .... ☐ Sometimes ☐ Often ☐ Always
   Bow hand is relaxed, in proper position with bow sitting on pad of thumb, fingers curled slightly and relaxed.

Drawing Smoothly There is little you have to change to bring your draw up to intermediate archer standards, if you have worked to get a quick smooth draw in the previous Stage. If you have changed your finger position to "split-finger" and changed your bowhand positioning and have more draw weight to handle, then it will take some time for all of those elements to become comfortable. Then with a little focus on your draw, you can get back to the smooth, controlled, but quick draw you had using a light-drawing program bow. This is *Signpost* makes sure you don't lose sight of the benefits of a smooth, strong drawing of the bowstring:

5. Draws the bow smoothly
   and in rhythm .... ☐ Sometimes ☐ Often ☐ Always
   Bow string is drawn smoothly and quickly without hurrying, draw elbow is high.

The draw is the major movement, with everything else being either smaller or involving less tension creation. In order for an archer to be relaxed (a requirement for performance) the draw must be smooth and strong, under control. Yanking on the string is a sign of fatigue (or cluelessness). Shaking while drawing or at full draw is a sign of being "overbowed" (too much draw weight) which pretty much kills any chance of achieving good form. Archers should be able to draw their bows smoothly and seemingly effortlessly with the bow held straight up and down (arrow level, pointed at target). Any other draw (higher, lower, draw elbow too low, etc.) is dangerous in the event of a premature loose of the string. If archers struggle to draw, they need less draw weight—this is an absolute.

Notes _____

_____

_____

_____

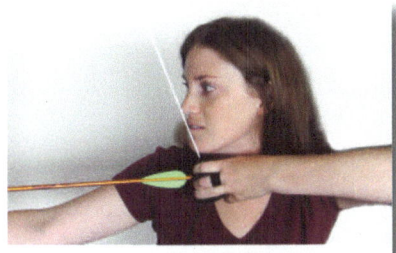

Anchors Away? It was mentioned in *Stage I* that there are other anchors and that we would be teaching you two. It is time to learn a low anchor. Actually this typically happens as you move to longer distances (as with the split-finger string grip). Moving your anchor position from alongside your face to under your jaw lowers the back end of the arrow far more than any other change you are making. It creates much greater "cast" (distance shot) because of this.

To execute the low or "Olympic-style" anchor we recommend you use a light-drawing practice bow at first (even without arrows; just draw, anchor, and then let down the bow—and repeat until comfortable). What you will find is that your head position has to be modified slightly. You must raise your chin a fraction of an inch. If you do not, your chin can block off your new hand position. The bow is drawn to slightly (1-2 inches) below the chin, then you "find your anchor" by raising your hand up until it presses against the bottom edge of your jaw (*see the photos left*).

Some people draw until the bowstring reaches the corner of their chin before they raise their draw hand and they say that in this manner they know whether they have drawn the string the correct amount. You do not want the bowstring any farther back along the edge of your jaw as the string will then drag on the skin of your face and worse, cause the arrow to fly offline!

Obviously, if this lower anchor gives you greater distance it is less useful at short distances. Adult Olympic-style archers do not shoot anything shorter than 30 meters (about 33 yards) but traditional and field archers shoot arrows as close as at ten yards or so, so traditional archers will often use the high anchor for short shots and the low anchor for the long ones. So, it is best to practice both.

This is the *Signpost* for evaluating your new low anchor.

6. Exhibits a tight anchor .... ☐ Sometimes ☐ Often ☐ Always
   Anchor position is consistent with draw hand pressed against face (high anchor) or jaw (low anchor) bringing the string in front of the aiming eye.

Still Following Through There is little you need to modify in your followthrough. We have included this signpost, though, because it is easy to let the followthrough work it's way back into the release. For example, one bad habit is called

What many beginners struggle with is that the anchor position requires the draw hand to be pressed firmly against the cheek (high anchor) or against the under jaw (low anchor). Hovering/floating the anchor hand is a major source of poor group sizes. The goal is to get the bowstring right in front of the aiming eye and "pressing the flesh" is a requirement for this and for the stability of the position. Head position cannot be affected by this. [Note that this does *not* apply to compound archers shooting mechanical release aids. The anchor position of a release aid is closer to a "touch point" than it is a firm anchor (due to the peep sight being the thing that keeps its position from shot it shot (as the bow goes up, the anchor point goes down (slightly), etc.). Be very leery of applying technique from one kind of bow to others that are significantly different (recurve bows and longbows are much alike, but compound bows (due to low string tension at full draw) can be quite different.]

Many traditional archers who pull substantial amounts of draw weight, use a "touch and go" anchor, which means they get their draw hand back to their anchor position and as soon as they touch down, the string is away. This requires a great deal of practice and is not recommended for long range shooting. If archers learn to pause at anchor, and make their anchor "tight," using a light drawing bow, they will have the option of this or a "touch and go" approach later. If they learn the "touch and go" approach first, it will be harder to learn this anchoring technique as they will have graduated to more draw weight by then. (It is typical that, when addressing form changes, one uses lighter drawing equipment to do so.)

"dropping your bow arm." This doesn't happen to longbow archers often because the bows are so light, but whether the cause is due to the weight of the bow or not, the flaw is to allow the bow to drop down immediately after the shot. The problem with this is: shoot drop, shoot drop, shoot drop can easily become: shoot, drop, shoot drop, drop shoot (ooops)! So, an archer does well at the time of releasing the string to be thinking about doing her followthrough correctly.

This is the *Signpost* for following through.

7. Exhibits good followthrough .... ☐ Sometimes ☐ Often ☐ Always
    After the string is released, bow arm stays up and draw hand moves backward along face.

Lining Up Alignment is, like the followthrough, something that you cannot just set and forget. Focus on it needs to be continual. You can check your own alignment with a mirror (an inexpensive closet door mirror propped against a wall will do) or you can ask your coach or even another knowledgeable archer to check it for you from time to time. The goal is to always have your elbow in or past line, so having your elbow on average slightly behind the arrow line is very desirable.

8. Exhibits good alignment .... ☐ Sometimes ☐ Often ☐ Always
    At full draw, draw elbow lines up with or is behind the arrow line extended backward.

Step-by-Step The key to consistent accuracy is to get accurate and then get consistent. Getting accurate with bow and arrow involves getting good form and good execution. Getting consistent is largely a mental task of being focused on doing things the same way each time. Being focused means not letting your mind drift. The question is: "How can I do this?" The answer is "With a strong mental game."

The start of the mental game in archery begins with what is called a "shot sequence" or a "shot routine." This is simply a list of the things you do to make a good archery shot. At first we will give you a set of steps to be learned, then as time goes on you will modify the sequence by changing steps or even adding or removing steps until it is your personal shot sequence.

Learning a basic shot sequence is the goal of this *Signpost*, but realize that a shot sequence is just a tool. The ultimate goal is to learn to use it to guarantee consistency. Here are what a shot sequence is to be used for:

• practice of the sequence ensures all of the steps are done (in the right order)

Because longbows and one-piece wood recurve bows are so light, it is rare for traditional archers to pick up the bad habit of "dropping their bow arms." Even so it does happen. You may hear the term "snap shooting" to describe the archer's technique. For target archery, we want to "hold form" for two seconds post shot (later it will be one sec–

The alignment goal for traditional archers is to get their draw elbow's behind arrow line. This is insurance for having the arrow ahead of line (the dreaded "flying elbow") which is a major cause of "plucking" the string. (See *Pluck, Pluck, Pluck* by Steve Ruis in the Coach Resources section of the AER website.) Archers are not robots, so if they are typically "in line" there are small percentages of the time when they will be behind and ahead of line—behind is okay, ahead is not. If the archer's elbow is typically behind arrow line, there are small percentages of the time when they will be even farther behind line or be "just in line"—both of which are okay.

Since traditional archers have the same shooting geometry considerations as Olympic-style archers, the same is true for them. You will hear advice that this is poppycock, but it will be coming from the "bow-hunting associated" traditional archers, not the target shooting traditional archers. bowhunt-ers rarely take shots over thirty yards. In the York round, a target round that has been shot for hundreds of years, two-thirds of the 12 dozen arrows are shot at a four-foot round target placed . . . *100 yards away*. Under these circumstances, good alignment is a must.

Notes _____

_____

_____

_____

_____

_____

_____

- the sequence provides a common set of terms for discussions with your coach
- each step of the sequence has physical and mental checks to occupy your mind
- the sequence can be used to diagnose problems in your shot
- The sequence is the foundation upon which your mental program will be built

> **The Rule of Discipline**
> *If anything, anything at all—mental or physical—intrudes from a prior step or from your environment, you must let down and start over.*

The last point is a little vague, but here is the rule that makes it work: *if anything, anything at all—mental or physical—intrudes from a prior step, you must let down and start over.* So, for example, if you are about to draw the bow but your feet/stance feels funny, you must let down. Without this discipline, it will be very hard to improve at all. Shooting a bad shot requires ten good shots to wash away it's influence. Not shooting a shot that feels wrong (somehow) actually will help you shoot good shots in the long run!

A Basic Shot Sequence On the next three pages a basic shot sequence is described for you to use shooting any kind of bow. You will personalize it later.

This is the *Signpost* for learning your shot sequence.

9. Knows and can demonstrate
   steps in shot sequence .... ☐ Sometimes ☐ Often ☐ Always
   Using a light-drawing bow or stretch band, can demonstrate steps in whatever shot sequence has been adopted.

Notes _____

Take Your Stance
Place your feet shoulder width apart, with your toes on line to target (a square stance), legs are straight (neither bent nor locked back at knees), shoulders are down, chest is down, head is balanced on top of spine and turned toward target; everything is relaxed.

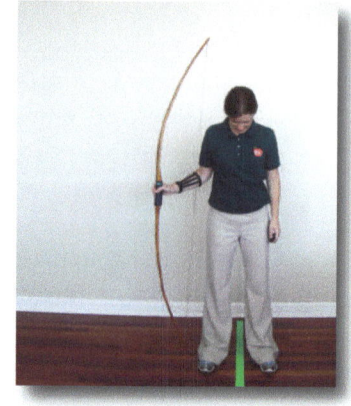

Nock an Arrow
Check to *hear* arrow snap onto string, *see* that arrow is on arrow rest, and *see* that index vane is pointing away from bow.

Set Your Hands
(*Draw Hand*) Fingers wrap around string in a "deep hook" (slightly behind first joint of fingers) and *not* on the fingertips; thumb reaches down to touch little finger tip. One yo two inches of draw keeps hands from moving to different positions. (*Bow Hand*) Palm flat to ground is slid into grip's throat, then wrist is bent until bow sits upon pad of the thumb. Other fingers are relaxed (curled); see that bowhand knuckles make 45° angle to ground.

Notes _____

_____

_____

_____

_____

_____

_____

Raise the Bow
Maintaining slight draw of string, bow is raised to a height at which draw hand is between chin and eye level, bow hand brings sight aperture to top of target or arrow point to top of target. Draw elbow must be as high or higher than draw hand.

Draw the String
Maintaining high draw elbow, the string is drawn to just under the chin. All muscles except shoulder and back muscles need to be as relaxed as possible with no extra tension. Both shoulders need to be kept in "down" position.

Find Your Anchor
Move your draw hand to its anchor position (here the high anchor is being used). Draw hand must be firmly pressed against bone. String must be visible in aiming eye. Increase tense feeling between shoulder blades by moving draw elbow around toward the back.

Notes _____
_____
_____
_____
_____
_____
_____

Aim

Move arrow point to where it is desired and increase tense feeling between shoulder blades by moving draw elbow around toward the back. Relax. Check to see arrow point is steady (not necessarily still). Once learned, aiming is natural and easy. (Later you will first check string alignment and adjust.)

Release the String

Continue to increase tense feeling between your shoulder blades by moving your draw elbow around toward the back as fingers of the draw hand are relaxed. Stop holding the string. This is not so much an activity as it is the stopping of the effort to keep the fingers curled.

Having your entire class doing the basic sequence either with mimetics (play acting) or with stretch bands while shouting out the names of the steps is not a bad idea at all. With younger students, be aware that they may want to snap other students when they loose they stretch bands. This is not to be tolerated—ever. Alternatively, you can walk around with a clipboard/binder and ask individual students to "stand and deliver" a shot sequence performance. There are AER Basic Shot Sequence handouts available for downloading in the Coach Resources section of the AER website (www.archeryeducationresources.com). Students with the Archer's Guide have these photos to learn from.

Follow Through

Allow bow to rock back while maintaining the position of the bow arm and both shoulders until the shot is completed. Due to the squeezing of the shoulder blades together, the draw hand's fingertips should finish moving when just below the ear.

Notes _____

Using the Point You have learned now to use the position of the arrow point in your sight picture to aim with. Now we want to expand your capabilities by using the technique to create all of the points of aim you need to shoot all of the distances you are currently shooting. It is not necessary to find POAs for every yard of those distances. Here is a suggested approach: find POAs for each ten yards of distance you are shooting. For example, if you are shooting at distances out to 40 yards, find a POA for 10, 20, 30, and 40 yards. Then try out intermediate yardages, like 25 yards. If you have a POA for 20 yards and one for 30 yards, try the point exactly half way in between. It should be perfect. Try 15 yards and 35 yards.

Getting at distances that are different requires a bit more imagination. For 26 yards, for example, the POA should be slightly higher than for 25 yards (specifically $6/10$ of the way up from your 20 yard POA to your 30 yard POA. For 27 yards it is slightly higher, for 28 yards higher still, and for 29 yards just below your 30 yard POA. This is called interpolation, and if you can do it (most people required just some practice, but for others it is hopelessly confusing) all you will ever need are your POAs for every 10 yards of distance you are shooting.

Another approach is to learn POAs for every five yards and then, for example, shoot 23, 24, 25, 26 and 27 yards as 25 yards. You can then make small adjustments (higher, lower) to your POA based on how the first arrow or arrows land.

Getting in Focus As you have been learning to shoot, you started by focusing on the target. When we introduced "aiming off of the point" you may have switched to focusing your eyes on the arrow point. Which is correct? There are arguments that can be made for focusing on the arrow point and arguments that can be made for focusing on the target. Rather than discuss the arguments, we recommend you try both. Take a very light drawing bow, stand in front of a target, draw the bow until you are in the point on target orientation, then shift your focus to the point and back to the target, then repeat. Try not to get too fatigued doing this. It is okay to let down, rest for 30 seconds, and then draw again. See if you have a preference for one of the two focal points. If you do, use that one consistently. If you do not, pick one and use that one consistently. After you have shot a while using this technique, check your preference again; it might have changed.

Meters or Yards? Should you "sight in" in meters or yards? The answer depends on the types of rounds you shoot. If the rounds specify distances in meters (typical

Notes

for international competition) then meters is more convenient. If the rounds specify distances in yards (typical for U.S. traditional archery competitions, for example) then yards is more convenient. If you want to shoot both, pick one or the other and then here's a simple conversion table (make all of the distance conversions before hand because doing math while shooting arrows is not a good idea):

Yards ▶	Meters	Meters ▶	Yards
10	9.14	10	10.94
20	18.29	20	21.87
30	27.43	30	32.95
40	36.58	40	43.75
50	45.72	50	54.92
60	54.86	60	65.90
70	64.01	70	76.88
80	73.15	80	87.49
90	82.30	90	98.85

If you want to do the calculations yourself:
1 yard = 0.9144 meters
1 meter = 1.0936 yards

This is the *Signpost* for "sighting in" off the point.

10. Uses arrow point to aim with .... ☐ Sometimes ☐ Often ☐ Always
   Must be able to find and use a point of aim at all reachable distances.

Walking the String An alternative to the method describe above is *string-walking*. In this aiming technique you still position the arrow point in your sight picture, but you place it in the same place every time (most people use the center of the target). This, of course, would work at your point blank range (point on target distance), but what about other distances? The others are dealt with by "walking" the string. Physically you move your tab and draw fingers down the string away from the arrow. You then draw to your normal anchor position and shoot. Every inch or fraction of an inch you move down the string moves the arrow nock higher by the

Most experts put the top of their shaft just touching the bottom of the central dot in their sight picture forming a "figure eight" that can be precisely repeated over and over.

Stringwalking is a very accurate technique which is used internationally by most barebow archers. If stringwalking is not allowed by shooting style rules, point of aim "gap shooting" is almost as accurate.

To make it even more accurate, experts use a very specific "sight picture." They make the arrow point and the aiming dot at the center of the target into a "figure 8" (*see diagram*). The arrow point is the bottom loop of the 8, and the central dot (gold or black or white aiming center) forms the top loop of the 8. There is one and only one position that forms this sight picture, the top of the arrow just touching (is tangent to) the bottom of the aiming circle. This attention to detail can only make an archer more accurate.

Notes _____

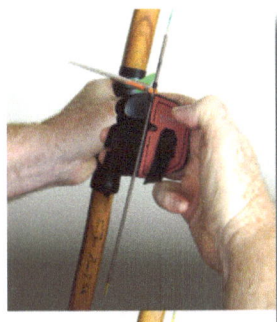

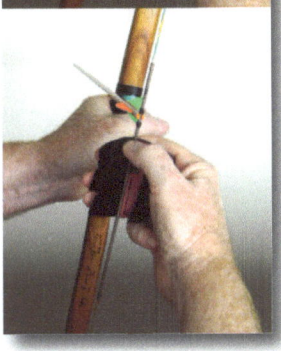

To "crawl" down the string, set the tab up against the arrow, count down how many stitches or serving wraps and insert thumbnail, then move tab to that position.

same amount. Raising the back end of the arrow point and keeping the point of the arrow at the same elevation (on your line of sight to the target) causes the arrow to strike the target lower. There is a correspondence between how much lower on the target and how far down the string and . . . there is a correspondence with lower on the target and bull's eyes at shorter distances. In other words, the distance you move down the string (called a "crawl" as in "you have to crawl before you can walk (or stringwalk)") correlates exactly to the shooting distance. From your "point on target" distance inward, there is a crawl that corresponds to each distance. And like the point of aim method, once you know the crawls for 20 and 30 yards, the crawl for 25 yards is half way in between.

Setting Your Crawls The accompanying photos show a crawl being set. To figure out how far down to go, people use two systems: tab stitches and serving wraps. Many finger tabs have a line of stitching that parallels the bowstring. By placing the tab up against the arrow, the stitches can be used to determine the crawls (a "point on" of forty yards is a zero crawl (by definition), 20 yards is eight stitches down, 30 yards is four stitches, etc. For those who like to count serving wraps instead, they serve the center of their bowstrings with "monofilament" serving material (essentially fishing line). This is harder than braided serving thread and you can run your thumbnail down such a serves bowstring and it will click, one click for each wrap of the string. Typically one wrap corresponds to a yard or a fraction of a yard.

Beyond Your Point On Crawls work for distances shorter than your point on distance. To reach distances beyond your point on, we will just change the point on distance . . . by changing anchors. You already have a point on target distance for your high anchor that will be used for shorter distances, and we will add a point on target distance for your low anchor that will be used for longer distances. The crawls for both distances will be similar in that a crawl that gives you a bull's eye for five yards closer than your high anchor "point on" distance will be very close to a bull's eye for a distance five yards closer than your low anchor "point on" distance. Hopefully, the two ranges of distances you can crawl do overlap. If not, there are additional techniques to employ but this is enough for now: two anchor positions (high and low) resulting in two point on target distances and two (very similar) sets of crawls for distances shorter than those.

Be sure to take notes on these things as they are easy to forget!

Notes _____

_____

_____

_____

_____

_____

_____

This is the *Signpost* for walking the string.

11. Can walk the string to aim .... ☐ Sometimes ☐ Often ☐ Always
    Able to identify moderate crawls and execute shots with them.

String Alignment There is another use for fixing the positions of things in your sight picture; it is called string alignment. This technique enables you to fine tune the windage (left-right) of a shot. In your sight picture all along there has been part of your bow, part of your arrow, and . . . part of the bowstring. Most people pay no attention to the bowstring because it is so close to your aiming eye that it is very fuzzy (out of focus). But if you do pay attention to it, it enables you to keep your head and your bow in the same relationship to one another. And if you are keeping your head straight up and down (no tilt!), you will be keeping your bow straight up and down, too.

You may have seen pictures of traditional hunters tilting their bows quite a bit. This is called *canting the bow*, and when you are aiming off of the point there is very little effect on your shot. (If you are using a bow sight on a bow there is a big effect!) The hunters tell us they do that to get a better look at the animal they are hunting (they don't have a target to shoot at, they have to imagine the spot they want the arrow to hit). In target archery, for the greatest accuracy we want the bow to be at the same angle each and every shot. Straight up and down is an angle we can find reliably (as gravity is our guide), which is something hard to say for other angles.

String alignment is simply lining up the fuzzy string image with something on the bow, such as the inside edge (or center or outside edge) of the bow or right over the arrow. Most people don't want to use the arrow because the string gets in the way of seeing the point, but you get the idea. If you practice lining up the string after you get to full draw each time you shoot, it will become a habit and less and less time needs to be devoted to it.

Start with a light drawing bow (10#), get to your full draw position, and look for the string in your sight picture. Play with it, see if you can get it to line up at various points on the bow or your bow hand. Don't stay at full draw so long you get fatigued. Let down, rest for 30 seconds and start over. After you get used to see the bowstring in your sight picture, try some shots at a close in target with your bow. Be consistent in your placement of the string in your sight picture.

With a 10# bow, you can draw and anchor facing a student to show them the position of the bowstring in front of your eye (from the target's point of view). Make sure you can see the string in your sight picture, that you are looking along the inside edge of the string, and that you are lined up over the arrow rest. Warn students before doing this as it can be disconcerting.

Notes _____

_____

_____

_____

_____

_____

_____

This is the *Signpost* for aligning the string.

12. Can identify string in sight picture
    and align with bow .... ☐ Sometimes ☐ Often ☐ Always
    Able to identify position of bowstring in sight picture at full draw and adjust accordingly.

Bracing Your Bow There are quite a few ways to brace a bow (set the string into position). We recommend only one way, the safest way, which is by using a *bow stringer*. Your coach will demonstrate how to do this safety and then ask you to do it a couple of times to be sure you are doing it correctly. From this point onward, you

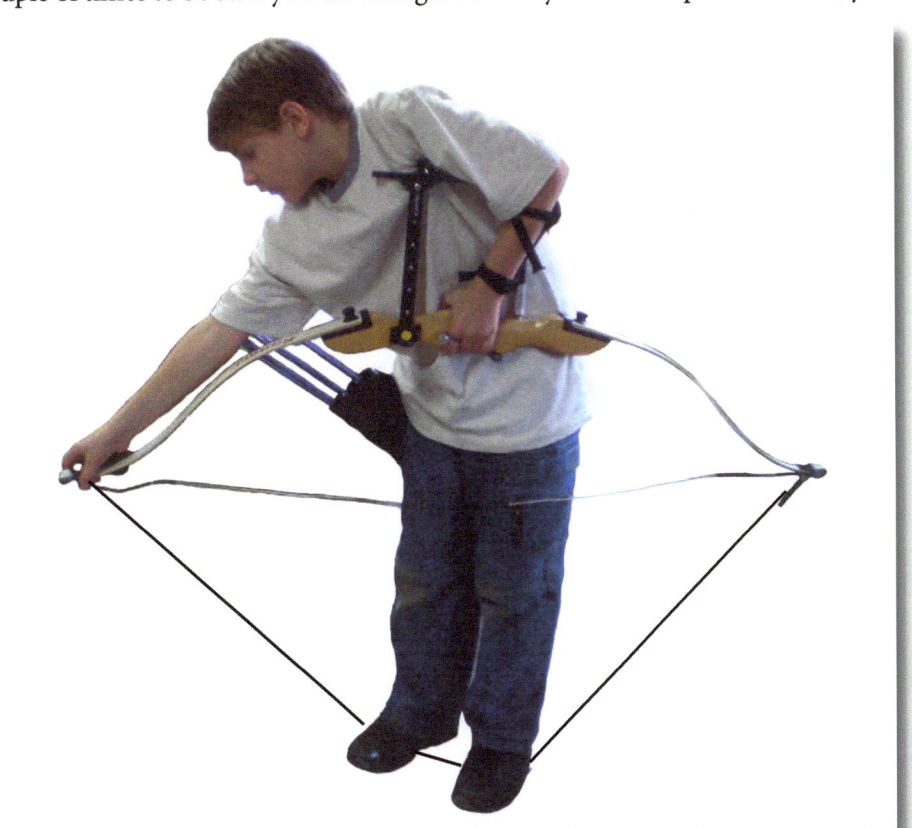

Here the boy is bracing a recurve bow, but the procedure is the same for a longbow. Your coach will demonstrate the use of a bowstringer and then ask you to try it.

Notes _____

_____

_____

_____

_____

_____

_____

can brace your own bow. You will want to acquire your own bowstringer for this purpose. This is the *Signpost* for being able to brace your longbow.

13. Able to brace the bow .... ☐ Sometimes ☐ Often ☐ Always
    Able to brace and unbrace bow safely using a bowstringer.

Equipment Inspection No matter how good the equipment you have it does suffer wear and tear. It is necessary for you to inspect your equipment often, even while shooting! When you brace your bow, pull back the string a couple of inches and let go; it should twang nicely and your ear is capable of detecting changes in that "twang." If your bow sounds different, it may indicate a stretched or defective bowstring or that your bow has changed. If your longbow is a "self bow" that is made out of a single piece of wood (not laminations), the limbs might be changing or even near failure. If you detect a significant difference in the "twang" of your bow upon bracing, here is how to test it. On a folded towel or soft carpet, lay the bow down so you can pull the string while holding the bow down with your foot (see photo). This way, if the bow breaks (self bows can break!), the pieces will fly into the floor instead of into you! Draw the bow smoothly and listen for any sounds the bow makes. If you hear any kind of cracking sound, let down and take you bow to a good bowyer to see if it can be repaired. If you hear no sound, draw the bow 1-2 inches past your normal draw length. If still no sounds, then the bow is probably sound and the problem is more than likely with the string. Try replacing the string to see if it restores things to the prior condition.

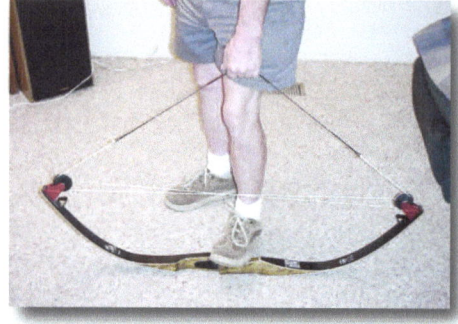

Don't just pull a suspicious bow using normal form—do a safety pull test instead as is being shown with this old compound bow.

Inspecting Strings Strings that have broken stands sticking out obviously need to be replaced. When archers buy bowstrings they often buy two to make sure they have a "backup" in case the primary string fails. They set each string up with nock locators in the same places with enough twists to make the two strings the same length. Both are "shot in" that is quite a number of shots are taken with each (to do this just change strings each day you shoot), the "spare" is stored in a plastic bag in a safe place with a safety pin holding the two loops together (so the twists won't come out).

See the Appendix— Equipment Maintenance and Repair.

Checking Brace Height A check on whether the string is stretched or damaged

Notes _____

_____

_____

_____

_____

_____

_____

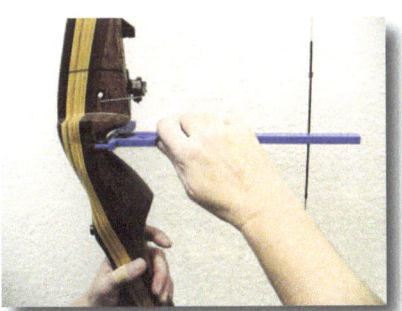

Check your brace height every time you brace your bow. A bow square works great but you can also use a ruler.

is measuring the brace height of the bow. This should be done each time the bow is strung. You might want to acquire a bow square for this purpose but you can also do it with a simple ruler (*see photo*). Bow squares can also help you set your nocking point locator and check its location, too. This is another check on whether your bowstring has changed.

Checking Wood Arrows If you have chosen to shoot wood arrows, you are accepting the fact that wood arrows are less durable than arrows made out of modern materials (carbon fiber, aluminum, etc.). If one of your arrows hits anything other than the target, it should be inspected. Look it over for cracks or dents. Gently flex it and listen for cracking sounds. If you see or hear a crack, do not shoot that arrow again! Shooting flawed arrows can cause them to shatter upon release! Traditionally people have accepted these facts by simply breaking in half cracked or even suspect arrows so they cannot even accidentally be shot again. Be careful about throwing away the pieces as curious children are attracted to arrows. Many people take the pieces home and dispose of them there.

Checking Aluminum Arrows If an aluminum arrow gets damaged, it is usually easy to spot (broken nocks, lost arrow points, ripped fletches, etc.). What aren't easy to spot are slight bends, which can be a source of danger as bent arrows may fly very erratically. There are any number of ways to check an arrow to see if it is bent. If you lay the shaft on a flat table (fletches hanging over the edge) a straight arrow should roll fairly easily. Alternatively you can balance an arrow on your palm you can spin it with your fingers (*see photo*) and the arrow shouldn't wobble. Or you can make a "V" out of the fingernails on your off thumb and index finger then spin the shaft and push it so it rides up the groove (*see photo*) and it shouldn't wobble . . . or you can use the same "V" and rest the point in your palm and blow on the fletches to spin the arrow and it shouldn't wobble. (All of these tests take practice. Use a perfectly straight arrow and a slightly bent one for practice.)

Checking Carbon Arrows If you have chosen to acquire carbon arrows, you are accepting the fact that carbon arrows, while being durable and are almost impossible to bend, may crack. If one of your arrows hits anything other than the target, it should be inspected. Look it over for cracks. Gently flex it, while rolling it between your fingers, and listen for cracking sounds. If you see or hear a crack, do not shoot

Notes

that arrow again! Shooting flawed arrows can cause them to shatter upon release! If you break an arrow, be careful about throwing away the pieces as curious children are attracted to arrows and the carbon fibers making up the shaft can be razor sharp!. Many people take the pieces home and dispose of them there.

This is the *Signpost* for inspecting your own equipment.

14. Can identify flawed arrows, bow parts ...... ☐ Sometimes ☐ Often ☐ Always
    Able to identify arrows with damaged points, nocks or which are bent, also damaged or worn bowstrings, nock locators, etc.

Grouping Better The ultimate sign of consistency is shooting small groups. If the groups aren't in the center, you can move them there. But if your groups are not small, all of the arrows won't be in the highest scoring zone of the target. Group size is the universal gauge of consistency in archery. With all of the refinements to your form, execution, and aiming systems you should be able to meet this new criterion. Good shooting! This is the *Signpost* for grouping at the intermediate level.

13. Shoots good groups consistently .... ☐ Sometimes ☐ Often ☐ Always
    Three arrow groups fit into an eight inch circle two ends out of three at 20 yards. Must achieve "Often" to advance to the next Stage.

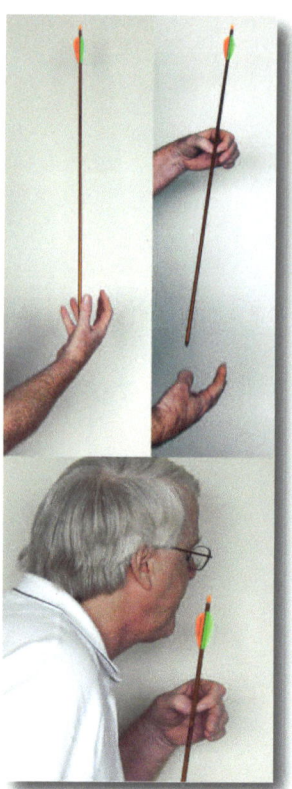

Stage II Mental Aspects

In the next *Stage* we will spend a great deal of time on how your mind controls your ability to shoot (whether you acknowledge it or not). We have introduced the shot sequence and the rule of discipline into your shot. For now there are a couple of more tools of the mind you can use to good effect.

Talking to Yourself People who talk to themselves out loud are consider a bit odd. Mostly we keep our comments to ourselves by not saying things out loud or muttering to ourselves, especially if the comments are uncomplimentary. Here we are limiting the discuss to what you to yourself about yourself. This is called *self talk*. Self talk, either out loud or in the privacy of your own mind, has an effect and that effect can be good or bad depending on whether the self talk is positive or negative.

If you have ever muttered to your self "I am such an idiot!" or "Here I go again!" You are experiencing *negative self talk*. This can be motivating in a kind of "pick

A fun way to evaluate the "Grouping Better" *Signpost* is to buy some inexpensive 8" paper plates. place a small aiming dot (2-3" press on sticker dots work well) in the center of the plate. Pin these to a target butt and have your archers verify each end that results in all three arrows hitting the plate. Doing this two out of three ends or four or more times out of six ends, etc. meets the *Signpost* criterion. (Alternatively, you could have them shoot three ends of three arrows and show you at least six arrow holes in the plate at the end.) Doing this at least three times in three different sessions (with no lapses) and you get an "Always." Obviously records must be kept. And, younger students may want to decorate/ personalize their plates with their names or drawings, but no human likenesses are allowed on a target.

If you find this is too much of a challenge for your group, change the distance to 15 yards.

Notes _____

_____

_____

yourself up by your own bootstraps" kind of way but it is more likely to hurt your performance in archery. It does nothing to change the situation, certainly nothing to make it better. *Positive self talk*, on the other hand, can actually help you perform. Here is an example:

Consider that you are having a good time and competing well at an event you typically enjoy. And then the skies darken and it begins to rain. Here are two possible responses to the change in the weather:

Self Talk Example 1 Oh, no! I hate shooting in the rain! It always lowers my score. There goes my personal best score and I probably won't win, either!

Self Talk Example 2 Oh, I had better get my rain gear out; I'm glad I came prepared. I probably won't shoot a personal best, but I could still win this thing, especially if the two people ahead of me get bent out of shape because of the rain. Woo hoo!

> Once you introduce "self talk" and "being positive" you really, really have to be careful how you address your students and yourself because they will call you on your lapses, which is good for you, like eating your vegetables.

We are all capable of the disappointment, disgust, and fear associated with Self Talk Example 1. We are all also capable of learning how to achieve Self Talk Example 2 with its apparent happiness (came prepared, might win) and reasonable logic (might win if the two people ahead of me get bent out of shape because of the rain).

The point is that *you can choose how you talk to yourself*. But it is necessary, like all aspects of archery, to practice this. Whenever you think or say something negative about yourself, try rephrasing it as a positive statement. Look for the opportunity to do something better. Here's the self talk *Signpost*.

1. Exhibits positive self talk .... ☐ Sometimes ☐ Often ☐ Always
   Exhibits positive self talk and can take negative references and make them positive. Must achieve "Often" to advance to the next Stage.

Goals This sounds like a boring topic. True, it can be, but we are only talking about a specific kind of goal here, a kind of goal that can actually help you become a better archer. The goals we address here are called *process goals*. Process goals are about how things happen, not what actually happens. If you have a goal of shoot-

Notes

ing a particular score or making a team, those are what are called outcome goals. Either you get the score or you don't; either you make the team or you don't. There is a role for outcome goals . . . but not for now. We are focusing on goals that can actually result in you doing better in some way.

Here is an example of a process goal: "In practice today I will have a strong bow arm for 90% of all shots." A goal like this focuses your attention on making your bow arm stronger. Keeping track of whether you did or didn't have a strong bow arm on each of your shots focuses more of your attention and the results are not necessarily cut and dried. What if it comes out to 89% of your shots you had a strong bow arm. Good enough? (Yes) What about 92%? What about 13%? There is food for thought here.

Process goals focus on what you are doing, not on the results of you doing it. If you want to compete on an AER Archery Team, you will have to have at least one process goal based on your shooting and one deportment goal, too, for each competition. For your first deportment goal at your first archery competition, we recommend "Have fun!" But if you get distracted talking trash to another competitor at this competition, don't be surprised if your coach tells you that you will have the deportment goal of "I will not talk trash at the tournament" at your next tournament.

Because your form is becoming more and more refined, your process goals can also become more and more refined. Ask your coach for help drafting some for you to use.

A Word of Caution: Having more than 1-2 process goals for any practice session or tournament is a recipe for disaster. You just can't focus on that many things at one time. Work on something. Switch to something else. Come back to the first topic at a later time. Make progress slowly and steadily and you will end up at the top.

This is the *Signpost* regarding process goals for the intermediate level.

> As students get more and more serious, it becomes more and more important that there be process goals for each practice session and each competition. This is true for recreational archers striving to get better and mandatory for competitive archers learning how to win.

2. Helps draft and uses process goals .... ☐ Sometimes ☐ Often ☐ Always
   Can help create process goals and then exhibits using them through self evaluation.

Notes _____
_____
_____
_____
_____
_____
_____

Signposts—Stage III Achieving Mastery
Must have completed requirements of Stage II before beginning.

Congratulations are again in order. You have come a long way and now are ready to pursue the goal of becoming an expert archer. Do you think you are ready? (Even if you don't think you are, if you have followed the plan to this point, you are ready!)

There are always new things to learn about the physical elements of shooting arrows. We are convinced that you can never know it all, but at this point you know a great deal about yourself and how you shoot arrows. Now we have to turn to things that will improve your performance which are more about the equipment and the role your mind plays.

Advanced Archery Skills

Tuning You probably know what it means to give a car a tune-up but tuning your archery equipment is probably a mystery. Tuning the bow-arrow-archer system involves a couple of stages. For simplicity we will call them basic tuning, fine tuning, and microtuning. Here we address ourselves to basic tuning.

So what is tuning? Tuning is making adjustments in the bow-arrow system to fit them to the archer better. No archer is perfect; each makes mistakes (of aiming, of releasing, of . . .). The goal of tuning is to create a bow-arrow setup that minimizes the impact of those mistakes. Consequently the exact same bow-arrow combination will shoot differently in the hands of different archers. Otherwise all archers need only shoot what this year's traditional champions shoot or the champion archer who is closest to them in size and equipment shoots.

The goal of tuning therefore is a "forgiving" bow-arrow system in the sense that it forgives the archer's mistakes. In "basic" tuning for longbow archers, we tune three things: nocking point height, brace height, and arrow spine. Arrow spine is a measure of how resilient (or stiff) your arrows are.

Blank Bale Testing In this form of "tune testing" you stand about 3-5 yards in front of a blank target butt. It is preferred that the target have no "grain," that is the arrow penetrates according to its direction of flight and not because of the target material's grain. Examples of grainy target butts are compressed straw target

Notes

butts and wound or stacked foam (*e.g.* American Whitetail target butts). Examples of target butts with no grain are piles of sand and solid foam (Ethafoam™) targets.

You then shoot several arrows and depending on the angle the arrows enter the butt, you can draw certain conclusions. In essence the target butt interrupts the flight of the arrows as they are leaving the bow. Here is what you can learn:

- If the nock end of the arrow sticks *up* above the impact point, your nocking point is too high.
- If the nock end of the arrow sticks *down* below the impact point, your nocking point is too low.
- If the nock end of the arrow sticks out *left* of the impact point, your arrow's spine is too weak.
- If the nock end of the arrow sticks out *right* of the impact point, your arrow's spine is too strong (stiff).
- If the nock end of the arrow sticks out in any other way rather then being directly in line with the arrow point, you have a combination of adjustments to make.

Bare Shaft Tuning Here is a somewhat better tuning test (also called the bare shaft planing test). In bare shaft tuning, you need to have two arrows with no fletches. If you've already fletched them all, you'll need to strip two of them. From about 15 yards shoot arrows until you are warmed up and so you can get a good group of three arrows in the center of a target. Then shoot the two bare shafts. (You shoot two to tell if you shot good shots with the bare shafts; they should each group! If not, it is a "do over.")

- If the bare shafts strike the target *above* the fletched group, your nocking point is too low.
- If the bare shafts strike the target *below* the fletched group, your nocking point is too high.
- If the bare shafts strike the target to the *left* of the fletched group, your arrows are too strong (stiff).

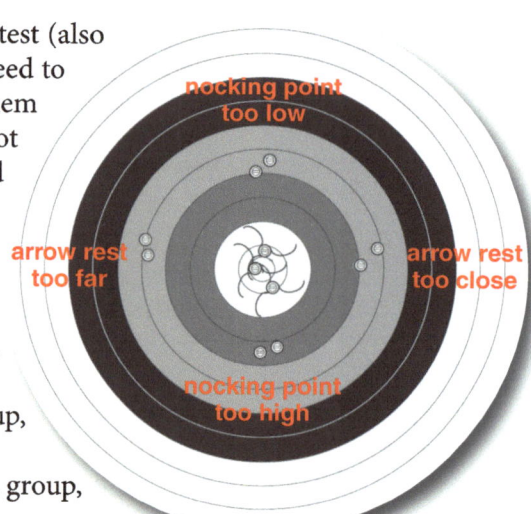

Notes _____
_____
_____
_____
_____
_____
_____
_____

- If the bare shafts strike the target to the *right* of the fletched group, your arrows are too weak.
- If the bare shafts strike the target anywhere else except as part of the fletched group, you have a combination of adjustments to make.

The farther out the arrows are, the bigger the problem. Just a couple of inches of separation between the group of bare shafts and the fletched shafts indicates a pretty good tune.

Making Corrections—Nocking Point Location If your nocking point needs adjusting, you need to consider your bow carefully. If you shoot off of an arrow shelf from a solid nocking point location, simply move the nocking point locator(s) a little bit in the corrective direction and retest. (Always start by adjusting the nocking point.)

If you shoot off of your knuckle, you might be able to make the adjustment by moving your hand ever so slightly up or down (if your nocking point is too low, lower your hand a fraction of an inch and retest). This is a little tricky as your hand position affects other things as well. If you don't want to change your hand position, move your nocking point locator(s) and test again.

Making Corrections—Brace Height Sometimes it is possible to tune in your arrows by changing your brace height. These changes are made like this:
- To make the brace height *higher* add twists to the string to make it shorter (twist in the same direction as the twists already there).
- To make the brace height *lower* remove twists from the string to make it longer (twist in the opposite direction from the twists already there).

This can be a little tricky as which of these you do depends on where your brace height is to start with. If it is too high already, making it higher rarely fixes anything. Similarly, if it is too low already, making it lower doesn't help. So, here is the strategy: try the basic fix . . . and if it does work, try making a change the other way. Here are the basic brace height fixes:
- If you arrows test too weak try making the brace height higher (add twists to the string to make it shorter)
- If you arrows test too strong/stiff try making the brace height lower (remove twists to the string to make it longer)

The basic rule when making changes, make them large (at first). If you are

Notes

sneaking up an a big problem with itty bitty changes, you are going to be at it a long time. If you are too low, make a big change and now you are too high. Good! You now have an lower and an upper limit to your adjustments. Split the difference between those two settings until you get what you want.

When adding or removing twists start with eight twists at a time, later you can try four, two, or even one twist at a time. But, start with a big change and retest, if there is no effect from the change, maybe that's the wrong "fix."

Also, be very careful not to exceed the manufacturer's brace height (and draw length) range. This could result in your bow breaking.

Making Corrections—Bowstrings You can affect the characteristics of your bow by changing bowstrings. The physical principles are: a lighter bowstring will provide more energy to the arrow, and a more resilient bowstring will provide more energy.

So, if your arrows test too strong/stiff:
- switch from a Flemish twist string to a continuous loop string (recurve style)—be sure to check with the bow's documentation to see if this is allowed. Some bows cannot use modern bowstrings or bowstrings made from modern materials.
- switch from a continuous loop string made of Dacron to one made of a more modern string material—be sure to check with the bow's documentation to see if this is allowed. Some bows cannot use modern bowstrings or bowstrings made from modern materials.
- switch from a continuous loop string of more stands (16-18) to fewer strands (10-12-14).

If your arrows test too weak:
- switch from a continuous loop string (recurve style) to a Flemish twist string.
- switch from a continuous loop string made of a more modern string material to one made of Dacron.
- switch from a continuous loop string of fewer stands (10-12-14) to more strands (16-18).

A Flemish twist bowstring

Making Corrections—Arrow Spine In making changes in arrow spine, you again need to consider your equipment carefully, but this time it is the arrows.

Stiffening Arrows—If you need a stiffer arrow, you are in luck: arrows are easier to stiffen than to weaken. The simple things you can do to stiffen arrows (in order

Tuning is quite a complex subject, so the more you can learn about it the better. It is especially important that you, yourself, have done these procedures with your own equipment. We simply are going to refer you to the traditional archery literature as a starting point (try either *Beginner's Guide to Traditional Archery* by Brian J. Sorrells or *Traditional Archery* by Sam Fadala) and strongly encourage you to read up on this topic. Realize that a well set up bow (see the appropriate Appendix) is all that is needed to shoot very good scores.

We also refer you to the very fine (and free!) *Reference Guide for Recurve Archers*, by Murray Elliot, available on the AER website and elsewhere on the internet. *The Reference Guide* includes tuning information and a little bit of everything else about Olympic-style archery, but don't hold that against it. Much of it applies to traditional recurve bows, FITA barebow style (for sure), and even longbows.

Notes _____

_____

_____

of the effect) are:
1. Cut them shorter.
2. Use lighter arrow points.
3. Switch from feathers to plastic vanes.

If these don't work, you may have to buy new arrows. Buying new arrows isn't uncommon for beginners, because as you change draw weight, you need stiffer arrows to handle the forces. The rule on cutting arrows is a little at a time, cut a half an inch off of a small number of arrows and retest. If you cut them too short, they can only be given away as they will be of no further use to you. (Also, too short arrows can be a safety hazard!)

Weakening Arrows—Weakening arrows is harder because there is no opposite to "cut them shorter." Making them longer will certainly weaken them but you would have to be a magician to do it! Here are basic some things you can do to weaken your arrows:
1. Use heavier arrow points.
2. If you have wood arrows you can sand them to make them thinner (smaller in diameter). If you want to try this, consult with your coach as it is a little tricky.
3. Switch from plastic vanes to feathers.

This is the *Signpost* for tuning at the intermediate level.

1. Able to tune bow/arrow system (basic) ..... ☐ Sometimes ☐ Often ☐ Always
   Basic tuning involves shooting shafts into a "neutral" butt and deciphering the angles of impacting arrows and is followed by bare shaft tuning. Longbows are tuned by making brace height adjustments and occasionally by switching string types (Flemish twist vs. continuous loop) or string materials (Dacron vs. Fastflight). Arrows are tuned by adjusting their lengths and point weights.

Shooting Cool This *Signpost* you have seen before, but as you have made progress you have been shooting longer and longer distances, at least if it is "outdoor" season. (Your coach is taught to encourage this.) This is the *Signpost* for "making distance" at the intermediate level. The goal is to shoot comfortably and well at all competitive distances that you would shoot in competition. Bear in mind that if you do not want to shoot longer distances, you can work with your coach to adjust this *Signpost* (you can't eliminate this one as it is required to reach the next *Stage*).

Here's your *Signpost*:

This *Signpost* (Shooting Cool) can be a real struggle for youths at a particular level of development (especially when they have changed competitive categories (to greater distances) before they were physically ready) and more mature archers with short draw lengths (short draw length means low power). A techno-fix is to buy/acquire barreled wood arrows or light weight carbon arrows (if allowed) but sometimes even that doesn't work. Often more draw weight is needed.

Notes

2. Can shoot comfortably at
   all appropriate distances .... ☐ Sometimes ☐ Often ☐ Always
   This includes the longest distances required by competitive category (even if not competing). Must achieve "Often" to advance to the next Stage.

Shooting Rhythmically This is a fairly advanced skill and takes quite a bit of time to do, but you may want to attempt this anyway. Most people shoot in a particular rhythm which can be refined by identifying it and using your shot sequence to make it regular.

It is okay for archers to skip this Signpost. An archer can come back to it at a later time.

Finding Your Rhythm This is the hard part. You either need to have someone with a stopwatch help you or you can use a metronome to figure it out. In the stopwatch approach, you have somebody time how many seconds (without you noticing them doing it) it takes from raising your bow to releasing the string. After each shot, you say "yes" if the shot felt good and was in rhythm or "no" if it didn't feel good or was out of rhythm.

After recording the times of many dozens of shots from more than one session, you try to correlate the number of seconds to the quality of the shot. (One way to do this is to enter the number of seconds and the yes's and no's into a two-column spread sheet, sort the rows for time shot and see if the yes's cluster around any particular shot time. For the sake of this discussion. Let's say that most of the yes's were from 4-6 seconds. Then there are a number of ways to lock in that rhythm (see below).

The metronome approach is to play a metronome and count off your shot, so many "clicks" for each step of the shot sequence. If the metronome is set too fast, you will feel rushed or unable to count fast enough. If it is set too slow, you will feel sluggish and impatient. Eventually you get it set right and then you want to lock in that rhythm.

Locking in Your Rhythm There are a couple of ways to lock in your personal shot rhythm. One way is through feedback. Again, you need somebody with a stop watch. If your slice of time is 4-6 seconds from raising to bow to loose, your helper practices with you and times each shot. If you shoot quicker than the four seconds, she tells you. If you reach 6 seconds before shooting, she announces "let down" and you must let down the string. The feedback eventually gets you to shoot in your best

Notes _____
_____
_____
_____
_____
_____
_____

rhythm. You may need several sessions to do this and you may need to test yourself at intervals to check on your status.

Another method is you may have a snippet of music in your head that is in the same tempo as your shot rhythm (or you may hear it an recognize it then). A great many archers use a sample of a song as part of their shot sequence. It helps them to stay in rhythm.

This is the *Signpost* for shooting rhythmically at the intermediate level.

3. Uses shot sequence to create
   regular shooting rhythm .... ☐ Sometimes ☐ Often ☐ Always
   Shooting rhythm can be made regular by use of creative shot sequence elements which can only be found by trial and test.

Scoring Now that you have refined form and much practice shooting arrows under your belt, it is time for your first scoring Signpost. There are any number of scoring rounds available. You may want to choose on of the classic traditional archery rounds—the York Round, the Hereford Round, the Columbia Round or you might prefer something more modern (the FITA 30m Round or even an NFAA field archery round).

Your goal is to score at least as much as 75% of the age group record for that round. Most age group records can be found on the internet and your coach can help you find yours. Good luck and good shooting! (And, yes, this is an "outcome" goal.)

This is the *Signpost* for scoring at the intermediate level.

4. Can shoot scores of 75% of record level ... ☐ Sometimes ☐ Often ☐ Always
   These can be competition or practice scores shot under competition conditions. Any rounds may be used but must include outdoor rounds. Must achieve "Often" to advance to the next Stage.

Stage III Mental Aspects

You will have to work closely with your coach to see which of these you are willing to attempt. Some will work better than others and some won't work at all . . . for you. You may have to try each of them to see, but start with a discussion with your coach.

You may want to set students loose on the Internet looking for the U.S. age level records of USA Archery (*www.usarchery. org*) on the common international rounds. There are buttons leading to their records but they can be reached directly at *www. usarcheryrecords.org*. For explanations of their age classifications, there is no better source than a table available at *www.texasarchery.org/Documents/Distances/DistanceSummary.htm*.

FITA, the International Archery Federation, also has a record search engine at their website www.archery.org under Results and Records/Best Scores.

Many traditional rounds are either not shot very often or are not shot at all. What might be fun is to use historical scores (often found in the backs of old archery books) to make comparisons.

Notes _____

_____

_____

Journaling Have you ever had anyone ask "How's archery going?" and you answered "Okay, I guess." This is certainly not a good answer if it is your coach asking the question or, worse, a prominent guest coach who might be able to help you a lot! One of the ways to be aware of what you are doing is to keep a journal. No, not a diary! This is a journal in which you write all of the import stuff you are doing. Here are some recommendations:

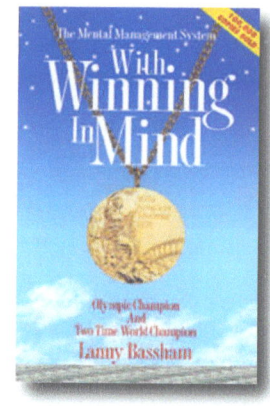

1. Set aside the back of your journal (any small notebook will do) to write down all of the critical numbers about your equipment (your brace height, how many strands (of what material) in your string, arrow length, etc.
2. Have a separate place for your practice and competition goals. Always write them down and write an evaluation of how well you met each goal.
3. Have a place to write down the particulars of your "testing" sessions. If you are tuning or testing some new arrows, write down the results. Before you make a change, in brace height, whatever, write down the old value. Write down the numbers of twists put in or taken out of your string. It may seem silly but if you mess things up, such notes may make it possible for you to make your bow "right" again.
4. Never, ever write anything negative in your journal. (Yes, we know this is a negative statement. It is for emphasis.) Writing things down gives them power, so writing about how you want to do things better and doing them better is good because it makes progress easier. If you complain in your journal (It was raining . . . I was so miserable . . .) it doesn't help you, it simply focuses your attention on what you were doing wrong. Try to make positive comments like, "The next time it rains, I am going to practice and see if I can figure out what went wrong . . . I found out that my windbreaker was catching the bowstring causing my arrows to go low-left. I snugged up the sleeve with some rubber bands and shot really good!" These observations can really help and reviewing them later on can show you how you solved problems and made progress.

Here is the *Signpost* for journaling at the intermediate level.

1. Keeps a journal for practice/competition ..... ☐ Sometimes ☐ Often ☐ Always
Journal entries focus on record keeping and finding solutions (not problems) and are positive in nature.

Of all the things that could be said to underscore the importance of the mental landscape to archers, we simply encourage you to read *With Winning in Mind* by Lanny Bassham. If you think "winning" is too crass of a goal, please open up your thinking. Your student's goals are your focus as a coach and the only person who has the power to defeat your archer . . . is himself or herself. Archers compete without any defense from the other archers, the only opposition they have is within themselves. To excel, they must come to know and accept themselves as never before. This is a journey that has more to do with their lives than with archery; archery is just the vehicle.

Notes _____

_____

_____

_____

Getting Help from Others As you interact with other archers, you will have the opportunity to learn from others. You are encouraged to engage other archers and talk about archery. If you get a good idea, you might find it helpful o your improvement. And, as with all other topics you can also find a lot of misinformation floating around. You can even find good information on the internet, but the warning about misinformation goes double for the internet. Any fool can post anything, apparently.

If you are not sure about something you have read or heard from another archer, discuss it with your coach. If he or she can't help, they likely can point you to someone who can.

A Warning About Advice Many adults like to see kids starting up in their favorite sport, so if you are young, you will attract all kinds of advice from older archers. When an adult gives advice to a youth and the youth does not immediately accept or test out the advice, they can be perceived as being "standoffish," or "aloof," or "stuck up." (The old expect the young to take their advice.) Here is how you can diffuse any potential criticism. If you are given advice from an older archer ("You know what you ought to do . . .") say to him or her, "Thanks for the advice, I will tell my coach when I see him next week." This mollifies older advice givers apparently because they think you have your own personal older, wiser person to guide you? We don't know, but the phrase does work . . . like magic! So, if you are young, you might want to have that phrase in your back pocket when nosey older folks get in your face. (The same is true for female beginners who tend to attract advice from older males.)

This is the *Signpost* for learning from others at the intermediate level.

> Don't forget that many of your students won't acquire the *Archer's Guide* so teaching them the "Thanks for the advice, I will tell my coach when I see him/her next week" trick is worth doing face to face. Of course this recommendation applies to everything else in this guide also.

2. Interacts with other archers
   in style to learn .... ☐ Sometimes ☐ Often ☐ Always

   Much can be learned from other archers of the same style. Archers wanting to improve need to seek out useful information and try to apply it to their own game. Must achieve "Often" to advance to the next Stage.

Imagine This It seems like a shooting sport like archery would have no room for imagination. Archers are solidly embedded in reality! Well, not exactly. You may already know some uses of imagination in sports and archery is no exception. Most successful archers start out each and every shot by imagining the look, feel, smell,

Notes _____

_____

_____

_____

_____

_____

_____

sound, etc. of a perfect shot. This imagery works. It works because you operate mostly subconsciously and a basic aspect of your subconscious mind is it can't tell the difference between reality and something vividly imagined.

The advantage here is that each shot you take is preceded by a perfect shot and followed by a perfect shot. It is much easier to do something just after you have done it well. And it is very hard to do something right just after you have done it wrong. *Imagery in the form of imagining perfect shots before shooting them, enables archers to shoot significantly more consistently.*

You will see the same behavior from football kickers as they take practice swings of the legs before the kick field goals (they imaging the impact of the ball and seeing it tumble through the goalposts). Golfers taking practice swings (the imagine the ball sailing through the air and landing just where they want), and basketballers hooting free throws (they imagine the feel of the ball, the ball's flight, and it settling gently into the net).

This takes practice a) to do it well and b) to make it a habit.

This is the *Signpost* for imagery at the intermediate level.

3. Uses imagery as part of shot sequence ...... ☐ Sometimes ☐ Often ☐ Always
   Good shots are imaged/imagined as an early stage in shot sequence (practice and competition). Must achieve "Often" to advance to the next Stage.

Affirmations Affirmations are short statements of personal beliefs that are designed to help you feel better about yourself and your abilities, thus reinforcing those abilities. They may take many forms, but they must always be drafted in:
- first person (I . . .)
- be positive, and
- are written in the present tense.

They state exactly what you will do in a positive manner. Do not use the words no, never, not or don't. For example, an affirmation for baseball "I never strike out" is poor as it focuses energy and attention on striking out. It is far better to affirm what you want to happen (focus on the solution, not the problem) like this: "I hit the ball with a high batting average pretty much where I want it to go."

The classic method involves writing your affirmations on 3x5 cards, but you might want to write them daily in a journal or read them to yourself or aloud, or

Notes _____

record affirmations so you can listen to them, or do all of these. Some people post copies of their affirmations where they will see them throughout the day and stop what they are doing to read them each and every time they encounter one. Use your imagery skills as you read or listen; the more senses (sight, smell, touch, etc.) you invoke in the imagery, the more effective it is.

Here are some examples. An archer-athlete who gets overly upset when he makes mistakes (which imprints the mistakes causing them to be repeated), might make an affirmation "It's normal to make mistakes from time to time, as I am improving." If you are affected greatly by the pressure you feel during competitions, you might say, "I appreciate pressure-packed situations because the pressure tells me I am close to winning."

Typically these are archery-related things, but if you have personal issues to deal with, this works on them, too. If you are using 3x5 cards, read each card first thing each morning, and last thing each day. Read them just before each practice and competition, and again immediately afterward. Of course, you may also read them any other time you like (waiting for a bus, just before a doctor appointment, but not while you are driving your car!).

This is the *Signpost* for using affirmations at the intermediate level.

4. Uses affirmations to achieve goals .... ☐ Sometimes ☐ Often ☐ Always
   Affirmations are used in a prescribed process to achieve goals.

Shot Thoughts We have borrowed this idea from golfers (along with the names for "open" and "closed" stances). Golfers have what are called "swing thoughts." Since a golf swing happens too fast to be thought about consciously, they happen subconsciously. But thoughts in the conscious mind can guide the subconscious. They have to be short thoughts because things are happening fast. So, a golfer might think "relaxed hands" or "balanced followthrough" as they swing. They have similar "thoughts" for their putting routines. If you get a chance to watch golf on TV, watch any golfer. He/she will have a pre-shot and pre-putt routine on display. Golfers, like archers, use shot sequences.

So, you too, may use "shot thoughts" to help your form. This is usually in the context of dealing with a problem. Foe example, if your bowhand was getting tense as you drew the string, you might think "soft bow hand" to yourself as you draw. Or,

Notes

if your bow shoulder has begun to creep into the "up" position, you might think "shoulders down" as you raise your bow.

This is the *Signpost* for shot thoughts at the intermediate level.

5. Uses shot thoughts as part
   of shot sequence .... ☐ Sometimes ☐ Often ☐ Always
   Shot thoughts are used in any stage in shot sequence (practice and competition) to address weaknesses or lack of focus.

More on Goals If you feel that goals really work for you, learn more about the goal setting and goal getting process. Here are some important points to consider.

- Let's say you want to win a national championship (an outcome goal). This is too far removed from where you are now to make in a single leap. So, break it down. What kinds of scores do you have to shoot (on what rounds) to win? What was last year's winning score? What is your score on that round now? Create a series of goals for scores on the round, which will tell you about the progress you are making. This is a framework for a plan to achieve your ultimate goal.
- A handy way to describe the desirable characteristics of your goals is the word SMART. *SMART goals* are:
  - Specific
  - Measureable
  - Attainable/Adjustable/Action-based
  - Realistic
  - Time-based

If your goals aren't specific, how can you know whether you have met them? If they aren't measurable, what will you use as an indicator of success? If they aren't attainable (I want to jump to the Moon!), what good are they? If you can't adjust them, you can feel trapped and out of control. If they aren't action-based, they won't encourage the actions you need to take to get where you want to go. If they aren't realistic, they will only frustrate you. If they don't have a timeline associated with them (By June, I will . . .), there is no sense of urgency.

There has been much written about goal setting and goal getting and much of it is available on the Internet. Try to learn what you can to help you with this.

Notes _____
_____
_____
_____
_____
_____
_____
_____

This is the *Signpost* for goal setting and getting at the intermediate level.

6. Helps draft and uses process goals .... ☐ Sometimes ☐ Often ☐ Always
   Can help create process goals and then exhibits using them through self evaluation. Must achieve "Often" to advance to the next Stage.

Notes

Signposts—Stage IV Owning the Sport
Must have completed requirements of Stage III before beginning.

Wow! You have come a long way. You are now a really accomplished archer. You can shoot high scores and you are in command of your shot. This doesn't mean there isn't more to learn, just that you have come more than 80% of the way. At this point it gets harder to make improvements. This is not a problem, in fact it is normal. When you have done 50% of a task, you have doubled your progress since when you had done 25% of that task. But when you are at the 80% mark, only a 25% improvement is now possible. Hence the farther along you get, the less far there is to go, but often the harder it is to do, because we have already done the easier tasks. It would be stupid to not do the easiest tasks that give the greatest progress first, no?

In this *Stage* you take over total control of your sport. Coaches are now your partners who work with you on what you want to work on. At this stage you become independent of systems and teachers. You know enough to learn on your own and to seek out new knowledge, test it, and incorporate into your archery. All of these Stages can be done in just a few years or it can take longer. How long you have taken to get to this point is not a sign of anything; it just is.

In this *Stage*, there are just a few physical skills, and the same list of mental skills as in *Stage III*, but instead of us teaching you, we are going to refer you to really good references for you to explore based on what you think works best for you. You can still consult your AER Coach and other coaches as well. Welcome to the wide world of archery!

Oh, now, the *Signposts* are for *you* to evaluate and sign off on. As before, your coach is there to help, if you need.

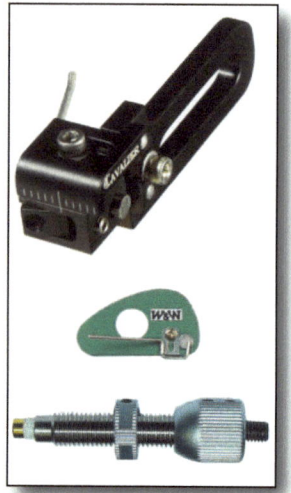

If you are going to shoot "modern traditional" you may want to add to your bow a wrap around arrow rest (*top*) or stick on metal rest (*middle*) with a pressure button (*bottom*). If you are more "traditional" you are probably all set, except it is now time to try out wood arrows.

Finishing Your Kit
If you are a traditional longbow or recurve archer, you may have everything you need at this point. If you choose FITA Barebow, you may want to invest in a better arrow rest at this point. Most FITA Barebow archers use a more involved arrow rest including a "cushion plunger" and these can cost anywhere from $30-175. Whatever you decide on, set it up according to the manufacturer's instructions.

Students always need help with acquiring new gear. If you are so lucky as to have a quality archery shop in your vicinity, one that has a target archery specialist, you can send your students there. The odds against this being the case are so large, though, that we urge you to get as familiar as you can with target archery gear so you can make informed recommendations. Check out the AER website (*www.archeryeducationresources.com*). We are trying to have all of the beginner-level stuff there, but for more advanced equipment, ask the kind folks at 3Rivers Archery Supply (*www.3riversarchery.com*, 866.732. 8783) to send you a catalog. If you don't have a traditional target archery-minded shop in your locale, you will find 3RiversArchery Supply to be a virtual "one stop shop" for all things traditional and target. If you do have a target archery-minded shop in your locale, pay them a visit, strike up a relationship. Shop owners often see the wisdom of encouraging new archers (your students!) with discounts and services. If you are this lucky, don't pass on this opportunity! Also, if they don't get your business, they may not be there the next time you need them.

Notes _____

_____

_____

You may also want to purchase a custom bow grip or modify the one you have so it fits your hand better. Expert archers are known to modify their bow's grip using auto body dent filler, tennis racquet wraps, tape, and other substances it make it exactly as they want.

Whatever you might want to do to finish out your setup, maybe you wantto try wood arrows, whatever, now is a good time to do it.

Changing Gear Be aware that many target archers tend to change accessories on their bows often, or even change bows/arrows often, looking for better performance. If you are one of these people, do yourself a favor and devise standards to compare the "befores" and "afters" of any such changes. For example, you can use the score on your favorite competitive round. Look up the last three scores for that round in your journal (if you don't have three, shoot them) and take an average. Make the change (new rest, new sight, whatever . . . but only one thing at a time!). Then, after some practice time to get acquainted to your new gewgaw, shoot three more rounds (on different days, not back to back) and average the scores. Any improvement? If not, then maybe spending that money was not a good idea. If yes, then maybe that change was good. We say maybe, because of what is called the *Hawthorne Effect*: which is any time a change is made that is supposed to make things better, things do get better . . . for a while. This effect is just the "new toy" factor. Any time you have a new something or other, it fascinates you and raises your interest level, until you get used to it. The short term gain in interest and focus can be a source of improvement which disappears later when the change becomes the norm.

> Beware the *Hawthorne Effect*! Any time a change is made that is supposed to make things better, things do get better . . . for a while.

This is about the only way you can tell you are wisely investing your time and money in new equipment, so devise a test before each equipment change (group size, standard round scores, something) and check to see if things really got better or whether you just thought they did.

Refining Your Archery Skills

Advanced Tuning Tuning recurve bows takes considerably more time than tuning longbows, and probably a little less than compound bows, but at this point, most of the tuning will be done on the arrows. There is a free arrow tuning resource from the Easton Archery company which is available at the AER web site. This guide is

Notes _____

for modern arrows (shafts of aluminum, carbon, and carbon-aluminum). For wood arrows the information is spread out more and you will have to look for what is available to you. A good place to start is *www.rosecityarchery.com/bowhunting_with_wood.htm* which is directed at bowhunters but the concepts are the same for target archers. Rose City Archery is a major distributor of wood arrows. You may also want to look in *Beginner's Guide to Traditional Archery* by Brian J. Sorrells which has a nice tuning section in it or *Traditional Archery* by Sam Fadala.

Group Tuning Any advanced tuning procedure must include group tuning. Basically, you examine your groups at all distances you shoot. The groups should be round and proportional. Being round means the arrows making the group would fit in a circle and would be distributed as much left as right, as much up as down, and be more concentrated toward the center of the group. By proportional, it means the diameters (widths or heights) of the circles should correspond to the distances. If you shoot six arrows in a 10 inch group at 20 yards they should be in a 20 inch circle at 40 yards and a 30 inch circle at 60 yards (*see diagram*). If the groups are smaller or larger than they should be at either end of the distance range, there is something wrong with your tune. You can tune for better performance at longer distances but with a sacrifice in performance at shorter, and vice-versa, but generally we would like our equipment to perform equally well over all of the distances we shoot.

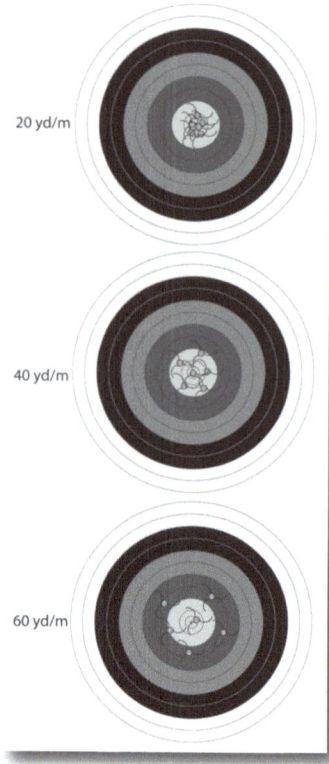

Group tuning can be exhausting as you have to shoot many groups (dozens) to establish a normal group size and you have to do this at a number of distances. Then if you make a tuning change (for example, moving the nocking point locator down just a tiny bit), you have to do it over again. Each change requires a test and the basic rule of tuning is: never make more than one change at a time! If you make two or more changes at one time and there is an improvement, you won't be able to tell which change caused the improvement; maybe Change A caused a big improvement and Change B made it less! There is no way to tell, so one change at a time, then test.

Here is the tuning *Signpost*:

> The basic rule of tuning is: *never make more than one change at a time*! If you make two or more changes at one time and there is an improvement, you won't be able to tell which change caused the improvement.

Notes _____

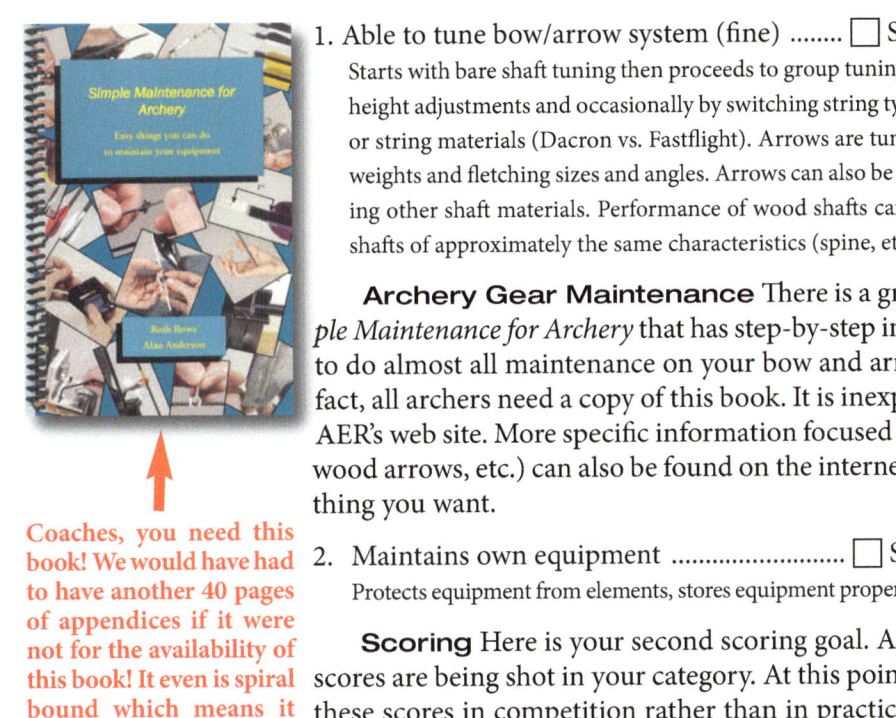

1. Able to tune bow/arrow system (fine) .... ☐ Sometimes ☐ Often ☐ Always
   Starts with bare shaft tuning then proceeds to group tuning. Longbows are tuned by making brace height adjustments and occasionally by switching string types (Flemish twist vs. continuous loop) or string materials (Dacron vs. Fastflight). Arrows are tuned by adjusting their lengths and point weights and fletching sizes and angles. Arrows can also be tuned by sanding, barreling, and choosing other shaft materials. Performance of wood shafts can be compared to aluminum or carbon shafts of approximately the same characteristics (spine, etc.).

Archery Gear Maintenance There is a great little book with the title *Simple Maintenance for Archery* that has step-by-step instructions (with photos) on how to do almost all maintenance on your bow and arrows. It is highly recommend, in fact, all archers need a copy of this book. It is inexpensive and can be purchased on AER's web site. More specific information focused on traditional archery (barreling wood arrows, etc.) can also be found on the internet. Try key word searches for anything you want.

Coaches, you need this book! We would have had to have another 40 pages of appendices if it were not for the availability of this book! It even is spiral bound which means it lays flat while you are using it to walk through a procedure. This is a must have "Coach's Friend" even though their focus is on modern equipment. You can find directions for making your own traditional bows, arrows, and bowstrings at numerous places on the internet and in your local library. Also check the Coach Resources section of the AER website.

2. Maintains own equipment .... ☐ Sometimes ☐ Often ☐ Always
   Protects equipment from elements, stores equipment properly, and repairs/maintains all archery gear.

Scoring Here is your second scoring goal. Again, it is set relative to what top scores are being shot in your category. At this point you should be looking to shoot these scores in competition rather than in practice. Keeping track of your process goals while you are shooting will probably give you information about what you need to improve you scores. Don't expect huge improvements in short time spans, the higher you go, the slower the progress seems! Also realize that any journey, such as your archery, has ups and downs (and plateaus as well). Sometimes we get stuck and can go up without going down first! (This is usually a sign of trying too hard.)

Here is your *Signpost*:

3. Can shoot scores of 90% of record level .... ☐ Sometimes ☐ Often ☐ Always
   These can be competition or practice scores shot under competition conditions. Any rounds may be used but must include both indoor and outdoor rounds.

This scoring goal is a high but not drastically high goal. Don't be surprised if your better archers sail right on by this *Signpost*.

Notes _____

_____

_____

_____

_____

_____

Stage IV Mental Aspects

If you are going to explore the mental side of archery further the one book you need to read (and read again) is Lanny Bassham's, *With Winning In Mind* (available on the AER website (*www.archeryeducationresources.com*) and at most online booksellers or ask your local book shop to order it for you). His story borders on the fantastic and his methods are proven. It will open up a great many new concepts and practices.

Here are the *Signposts* for you to sign off on:

1. Keeps a journal for practice/competition ...... ☐ Sometimes ☐ Often ☐ Always
   Journal entries focus on record keeping and finding solutions (not problems) and are positive in nature.

2. Interacts with other archers in style to learn .. ☐ Sometimes ☐ Often ☐ Always
   Much can be learned from other archers of the same style. Archers wanting to improve need to seek out useful information and try to apply it to their own game.

3. Uses imagery as part of shot sequence ...... ☐ Sometimes ☐ Often ☐ Always
   Good shots are imaged/imagined as an early stage in shot sequence (practice and competition).

4. Uses affirmations to achieve goals .... ☐ Sometimes ☐ Often ☐ Always
   Affirmations are used in a prescribed process to achieve goals.

5. Uses shot thoughts as part of shot sequence ... ☐ Sometimes ☐ Often ☐ Always
   Shot thoughts are used in any stage in shot sequence (practice and competition) to address weaknesses or lack of focus.

6. Uses shot sequence to create regular shooting rhythm .... ☐ Sometimes ☐ Often ☐ Always
   Shooting rhythm can be made regular by use of creative shot sequence elements which can only be found by trial and test.

7. Helps draft and uses process and outcome goals .... ☐ Sometimes ☐ Often ☐ Always
   Can help create process and outcome goals and then exhibits using them through self evaluation

Notes _____

Archery Education Resources
Recreational Archery Curriculum
Appendices

168

Archery Education Resources
Recreational Archery Curriculum
Appendices

Types of Styles/Targets/Scoring

These Appendices are also in the Archer's Guide; following these are additional Appendices for Coaches Only.

There are a great many different ways to shoot arrows from a bow. First, there are different kinds of bows, then there are quite a different number of techniques to be used in shooting any one of the kinds. For example, for just compound bow archers, the National Field Archery Association recognizes six shooting styles (*see graphic on the next page for details*):

Freestyle
Freestyle Limited
Bowhunter
Bowhunter Freestyle
Bowhunter Freestyle Limited, and
Barebow

and this is just one association (and there are others for recurve and longbow archers)! Then there are the **Divisions**—Youth (three-four age groups), Adult, Seniors (two age groups), and **Gender** (male-female). Each of these shooting styles has its own set of rules in addition to the common rules all archers must follow in competition.

Then there are differences in targets shot at. Most associations have created their own targets. In most cases, the distinction is not where to shoot (if the target is paper, try the middle) but in how to score it. USA Archery has targets with 10 scoring rings (worth 1-10 points, sensibly) while the NFAA has targets with five scoring rings (worth 1-5 points) but somehow left off the rings worth one and two points on many of their targets making them 5-4-3-0 targets (*see the diagrams on p. 72*).

Many archers shoot simulated hunting scenarios with three dimensional (3-D) targets (life-like turkeys and deer, etc.). There are several different scoring schemes associated with these animal targets.

As a general rule, if an arrow touches a higher scoring ring on a target, it gets the higher score. For more details on scoring consult the organizations themselves.

Notes _____

_____

_____

_____

_____

_____

NFAA Shooting Styles

If You Shoot ... and you are an ...	Adult	Young Adult/Youth/Cub/PeeWee
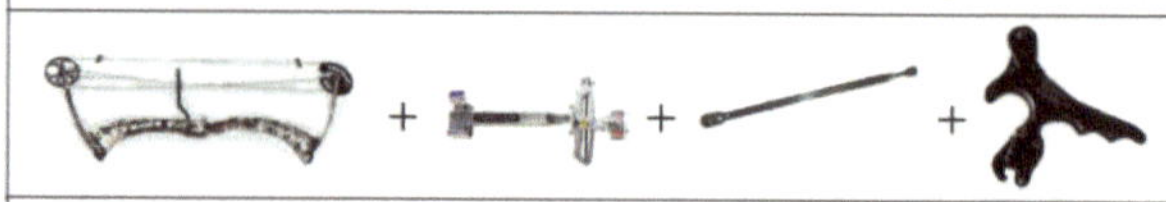 compound bow + sight + stabilizer + release	FS	FS
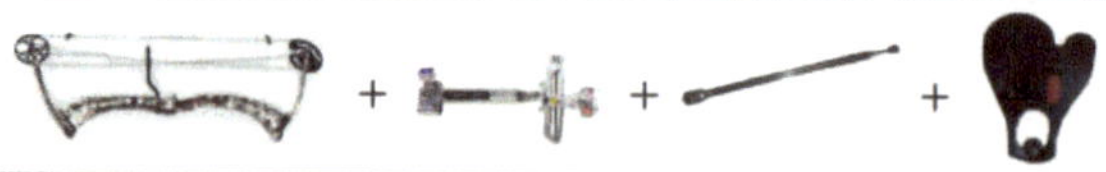 compound bow + sight + stabilizer + tab	FSL	FSL
 compound bow + sight + release	BHFS	FS
 compound bow + sight + tab	BHFSL	FSL
 compound bow + sight + tab	BH	BB
 compound bow + stabilizer + tab	BB	BB
 recurve + tab	Trad-RC	BB
 longbow + tab	Trad-LB	BB
 recurve + sight + stabilizer + tab	FSL-R/LB	FSL-R/LB

Key
FS = freestyle
BH = bowhunter
BHFS = bowhunter freestyle
Trad-RC = traditional recurve
FSL-R/L = freestyle limited–recurve longbow (basically FITA Freestyle)
FSL = freestyle limited
BHFSL = bowhunter freestyle limited
BB = barebow
Trad-LB = traditional longbow

Notes _____

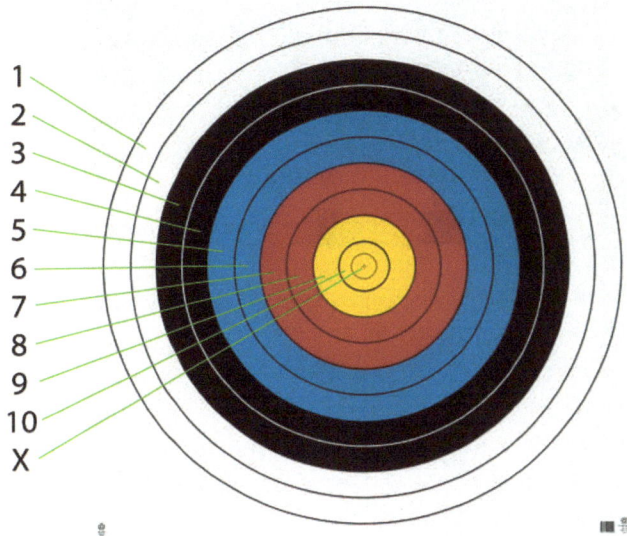

USA Archery scoring (above) as in NFAA target scoring (below) allows that as long as the arrow touches a higher scoring ring, even if it just touches the line separating rings, the arrow receives the higher score.

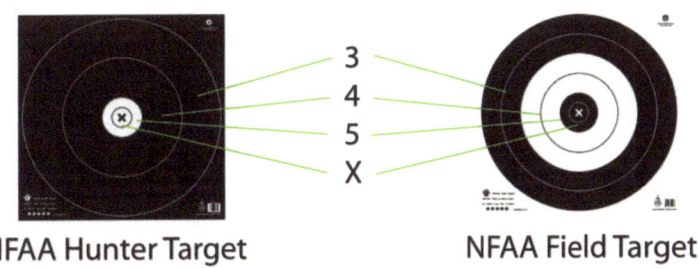

NFAA Hunter Target   NFAA Field Target

Notes

It is important to note that human or humanoid targets are never used in archery. Young students have a great deal of fun making up their own targets to shoot at, but they may not represent human beings.

3-D targets come in many shapes and sizes (some quite fictional, such as "Bigfoot"). The scoring systems vary from organization to organization.

Notes

Glossary

Adapter	An arrow part that allows screw in points on wooden shafts or glue on points for aluminum shafts.
Anchor point	The reference point that a person pulls the bow string to before releasing. This point should be the same for each shot and may be the side of the mouth, corner of the chin, or other reference point.
Armguard	Device attached to the forearm of the bow arm to protect it from a string burn or keeps the sleeve from catching on the string.
Arrow shaft	The main body of the arrow before the nock, fletching, or point is installed. It can be made from several materials including wood, aluminum, carbon, and composites.
Arrow shelf	The area of the bow above the handle or grip where the arrow sits.
Arrow straighter	A tool used to straighten arrow shafts which are only slightly bent.
Back of the bow	The side farthest away from you when you hold bow in shooting position.
Bare shaft	An arrow shaft without fletching, nocks, inserts, points, paint, or cresting.
Belly of the bow	The side closest to you when you hold the bow in shooting position.
Bow square	Tool that is T-shaped and used to determine where to place nocking point locators, measure brace height, and tiller.
Bow string	Several strands of material twisted together to form a strong string used to launch an arrow.
Bow stringer	An aid that helps to prevent limb twist and tip damage while installing the bow string.
Boyer	A person who makes bows.
Brace height	The distance from the string to the deepest part of the handle or grip. This distance can be changed by twisting the

Notes _____

_____

_____

_____

_____

_____

_____

_____

	string tighter to increase the height and untwisting it to decrease the height. Also called "string height."
Cable guard	The rod on compound bows which keeps the cables away from the center of the bow so the arrow can pass by without hitting the cables.
Cam	The wheel or pulley on the end of compound bow's limb used to provide let-off and power. They may be round, elliptical, or very complex in shape.
Center shot	A feature of a bow with a sight window that is inset past the centerline that allows the arrow to be placed in the exact center of the the bow's axis.
Clicker	A device attached to the bow which clicks when you are at your desired draw length.
Cock feather/vane	The odd colored or marked feather/vane which faces away from the bow when the arrow is on the string. Also called the "index feather/vane." Compound bow arrow rests may require a different orientation.
Compound bow	A bow with one or two cams which provide let-off and power.
Crossbow bolt	The shaft or arrow fired from a crossbow.
Crossbow	A small, strong bow, held and shot like a rifle. The stronger ones have a device to help cock it.
Dacron	A type of material used to make bowstrings.
D-Loop	A string in a U shape tied on the bow string around the nock point that a release aid is attached to when shooting.
Draw length	The distance a person draws a bow, measured from the bottom of the arrow nock to 1¾" past the arrow rest (approximately the back of a bow) when in shooting position.
Draw weight	Amount of pull force, measured in pounds, that it takes to pull a bow string a certain distance.
Fast Flight	A lightweight bowstring material that has little stretch and is used to make bowstrings and cables for newer bows.
Field points	Points that are round with a sharp point, usually used for

Notes _____

_____

_____

_____

_____

_____

_____

_____

	field archery and hunting practice.
Finger pinch	Having your fingers pinched against one another and the arrow's nock by the bow string when pulling the string back (typically due to a bow which is too short).
Fistmele	An older term for the brace/string height.
Fletching clamp	The clamp that the fletching is placed into before being attached to a fletching jig.
Fletching jig	A tool used to hold the fletching clamp(s) which hold fletching to an arrow shaft until the fletching cement dries.
Fletching	The feathers or vanes used to stabilize an arrow in flight.
Ground quiver	A piece of archery equipment that holds arrows. It may be stuck into the ground or merely rest upon it.
Index feather/vane	See Cock feather/vane.
Insert	An arrow part that accepts a screw-in point or a nock.
Kisser button	A button placed on a bow string to hold your anchor point consistently in the same position.
Let-off	The percent that a bow's holding weight is reduced from its peak pulling weight when a compound bow is properly drawn fully.
Limb tip notch	The notches at the end of the bow limbs where the bow string is placed. Also called a "string groove."
Limb	The parts of the bow that bend when the string is pulled back.
Longbow	An archery bow with no cams and when strung, the string only touches the limb tip notches.
Nock	Arrow part glued onto or pressed into the back of an arrow shaft that the bow string fits into. On early or very traditional arrows, the nock is cut into the shaft itself.
Nocking pliers	Special pliers used to install or remove brass string nocks.
Nocking point locator	A mark put on bow string to mark the nocking point of the arrow. Sometimes a simple knot in a string is used, sometimes the point is marked with a brass clip with a plastic insert.

Notes

Nocking point	The spot on bow string where the arrow nock is placed to be shot.
Peep sight	The rear sight of a compound bow. A piece of metal, plastic, or rubber with a hole in it placed into the string, which then allows the archer to look through the string.
Quiver	A piece of archery equipment that holds arrows. It may be attached to the bow, placed on a belt, or carried on your shoulder or back.
Recurve bow	A bow that has no cams which when strung is such that the string contacts the bow limbs a short distance from the limb tips.
Release aid	A tool that is used to pull the bow string and provide a better release by a trigger of some type.
Release	The act of letting go of the string to shoot an arrow.
Riser	The middle part of a bow that has the grip, shelf, sight window and other parts. Also called the "handle."
Serving jig	A tool used to apply serving string to bowstrings and cables.
Serving	String material applied to the bow string to make the string last longer in the nock area (center serving) and used also to make loops in the string/cable ends (end serving).
Shooting glove	A three- fingered leather glove used to protect the fingers while shooting bows. Not recommended for target archers.
Sight window	The area of the bow above the grip and arrow shelf where you would mount a bow sight.
Spin tester	A tool that checks the straightness of an arrow.
Spine	A term that describes the stiffness of an arrow shaft and tells if the shaft is strong enough to be shot in a bow of known poundage. Too weak or too stiff arrows can cause erratic arrow flight.
Stabilizer	A rod of various lengths and weights that is attached to a bow to make for a more stable bow and, secondarily, to reduce vibrations from shot arrows.

Notes _____

_____

_____

_____

_____

_____

_____

Tab	A small piece of material placed between fingers and bow string to protect the fingers while shooting a bow and to provide a slick surface for the string to slide from.
Take down bow	A long bow or recurve bow which can be taken apart for transportation, usually into two or three pieces.
Tiller	The distance from the string perpendicular to each limb at the ends of the riser/handle. These measursents can be adjusted on modern recurve and compound bows.
Tuning	Making small adjustments to bow and/or arrows to make a bow perform at its optimal level.

Scores, Scoring, and Competition

AER programs are directed at recreational archers as being different from competitive archers, the difference between the two is the competitive archer is training with the goal of winning competitions while the recreation archer's goals are different: often it is simply to participate, to enjoy the shooting, to test him- or herself, and almost always to "have fun," etc.

Competitive archers undergo rigorous physical training, equipment testing, and high arrow count shooting sessions, etc. as regular aspects of their practice. Recreational archers are unlikely to do such things.

We encourage recreational archers to attend competitions. Why? Because competitions are fun and instructive. For example, they are instructive in that the pressure one puts on oneself can illuminate flaws in one's technique. And there are many ways to compete, that don't involve a goal of "winning." Here are a few examples.

Competing Against Oneself Archery is a sport in which there is no defense. In this it is like golf and trapshooting. Consequently, one can't stop someone else from beating them; the only person you can triumph over is . . . yourself. This is done by keeping track of one's personal best score, often called a "personal best" or PB for short. If your PB goes up on a particular round on a consistent basis, you are making considerable improvement in your archery, whether that score is close to a winning score or not.

Competing Against Record Scores You will notice that the scoring goals in this curriculum are given as a percent of a record score, e.g. 75% or 90% of a particular

Notes

round's local, state, or national record. (Students get to choose which based on how ambitious they are.) Knowing that you can shoot a high percentage of a record score is a solid indicator of achievement. The record scores themselves include handicapping for the ages, types of equipment, and genders of the archers involved, which makes these comparisons valid. Traditional archers can even compete against famous archers of the past as records have been kept for hundreds of years.

Competing Against Fellow Competitors Archery is a social sport and part of that is "friendly competitions." One picks someone about equal in ability (or not!) and offers a competition. This can be during practice or at a formal competitive event. If the two archers are of different skill levels, a "handicap" (typically as a number of points) is negotiated. And a prize for winning the contest is also typically negotiated, the most common prize decided on is the loser buys the winner a soda. (Competing for things worth more than this is discouraged.)

Competing Against the Field Attending a competition sponsored by an archery organization to test oneself against the field can result in a recreational archer becoming a competitive archer. This has happened time and time again. An archer shows up and competes and shocks him- or herself by placing very high in the field. The idea that enhanced training might put the archer on top of the field can lead to higher level competitions, more intense practices, specialized coaching, physical and mental training, etc. and the transformation to a competitive archer is made.

Notes

Some Individual Competition Rounds

Current Rounds

Outdoor Rounds

	Men	Women	Youths
NFAA Hunter Round	14 targets, four arrows per target, scored 5-4-3 on NFAA Hunter targets in 1 yd increments	same	Shot from shorter distances based on age
NFAA Field Round	14 targets, four arrows per target, scored 5-4-3 on NFAA Field targets in 5 yd increments	same	Shot from shorter distances based on age
NFAA Animal Round	14 targets, 1-3 arrows per target, scored based on first scoring arrow on NFAA Animal (paper) targets in 1 yd increments	same	Shot from shorter distances based on age
FITA International Round	6x6 arrows at 90 and 70 meters at 122 cm target, then 12x3 arrows at 50 and 30 meters at 80 cm target, scored 10-0	6x6 arrows at 70 and 60 meters at 122 cm target, then 12x3 arrows at 50 and 30 meters at 80 cm target	Shot from shorter distances based on age
American Round (900 Round)	5x6 arrows at 60, 50, and 40 yards, scored 10-0 on 122 cm FITA target	same	Shot from shorter distances based on age
Metric 900 Round (FITA 900)	5x6 arrows at 60, 50, and 40 meters, scored 10-0 on 122 cm FITA target	same	Shot from shorter distances based on age

Notes

Indoor Rounds

	Men	Women	Youths
NFAA 300 Round	12x5 arrows at 20 yards, at the 40 cm target scored 5,4,3 (or NFAA five spot)	same	same
Vegas 300 Round	10x3 arrows at 18 meters, scored 10-0 on 40 cm FITA target (or triangular three spot)	same	same
FITA 18 m	10x3 arrows scored 10-0 on 40 cm FITA target	same	same
FITA 25 m	10x3 arrows scored 10-0 on 60 cm FITA target	same	same

Notes

Historic Rounds

Outdoor Rounds

	Men	Women	Youths
York Round	12x6 arrows at 100 yards, 8x6 arrows at 80 yards, 4x6 arrows at 60 yards, at the 122 cm target scored 9,7,5,3,1,0	N/A	N/A
Hereford Round	N/A	12x6 arrows at 80 yards, 8x6 arrows at 60 yards, 4x6 arrows at 50 yards, at the 122 cm target scored 9,7,5,3,1,0	N/A
American Round	5x6 arrows at 60, 50, and 40 yards, scored 9,7,5,3,1,0 on 122 cm FITA target	same	N/A
Columbia Round	N/A	4x6 arrows at 50, 40, 30 yards, scored 9,7,5,3,1,0 on 122 cm FITA target	N/A
Metropolitan Round	5x6 arrows at 100, 80, 60, 50, 40 yards, scored 9,7,5,3,1,0 on 122 cm FITA target	5x6 arrows at 60, 50, 40, 30 yards, scored 9,7,5,3,1,0 on 122 cm FITA target	5x6 arrows at 40, 30, 20 yards, scored 9,7,5,3,1,0 on 122 cm FITA target
National Round	N/A	8x6 arrows at 60 yards, 4x6 arrows at 50 yards, scored 9,7,5,3,1,0 on 122 cm FITA target	N/A
St. George's Round	6x6 arrows at 100, 80, 60 yards, scored 9,7,5,3,1,0 on 122 cm FITA target	N/A	N/A

Notes

Indoor Rounds

	Men	Women	Youths
Chicago Round	16x6 arrows, scored 9,7,5,3,1,0 on 40 cm/16 inch FITA target	same	N/A

Notes _____

_____

_____

_____

_____

_____

_____

_____

Archery Education Resources
Recreational Archery Curriculum
Coaches Appendices

184

Archery Education Resources
Comprehensive Archery Curriculum
Coaches Appendices

These Appendices do not appear in the Archer's Guide!

This section of the *Coach's Guide* has major treatments of many of the things coaches will need to know to deliver the AER Archery Curriculum well. Even so, there is much that is not included here and which can enhance your coaching journey, so you are encouraged to explore the books recommended in the Introduction and any other resources you find helpful.

The First Three Arrows
All AER archery students begin with *The First Three Arrows* as described in your *AER Basic Course Training Manual*. There are no exceptions. Because you have those instructions already, they are not repeated here.

Setting Up Bow Accessories
Bow Sights Sighting in a target sight has been covered elsewhere in this guide. The initial installation and setup are covered by the manufacturer's literature and in *Simple Maintenance for Archery* by Ruth Rowe Alan and Henderson beginning on page 71. Pin sights are not addressed in *Simple Maintenance for Archery* so pay close attention to the manufacturer's instructions for their setup and adjustment. *Note: There is more on bow sights below.*

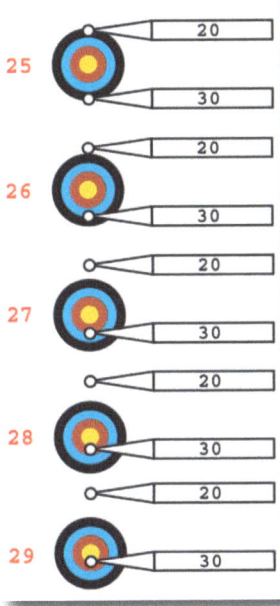

Pins can be positioned so the imagined distance lines up between two pins. Here are the pin positions for 25 through 29 yards.

Kinds of Bow Sights There are very many kinds of bow sights that have been developed and hundreds of different sights available for purchase today. The first sights appeared in the early 1900's and were relatively crude. Most often they consisted of a piece of thick tape stuck just above the handle of the archer's longbow (modern recurve and compound bows had not been invented yet). A hat pin was slid through the tape (sideways) so the ball of the pin stuck out to the left of the bow (for a right-handed archer). To make a windage (left-right) change the pin was slid left or right in its position as inserted. To make elevation (up-down) changes, the pin was pulled out and reinserted in a different position. The approximate distances associated with each pin position were written on the tape. As with any other inno-

Notes _____

_____

_____

_____

_____

_____

_____

vation, people who used such devices were initially accused of cheating, but after some rather spectacular competition scores were shot, general acceptance followed. Today the vast majority of archers shoot with sights.

The two most common sights are *pin sights* and *target sights*. Pin sights are often used by bowhunters but are used in target competitions, too. Target sights are almost never used by bowhunters, so the only place you will see them is on a competition field.

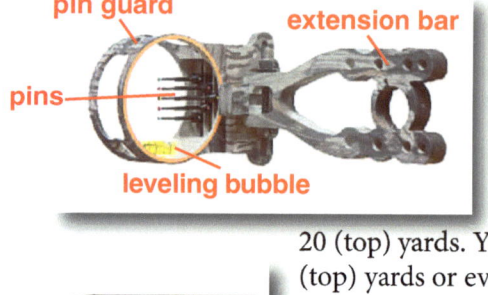

Pin Sights Pin or "fixed" sights involve a rack of pins whose heads are in a vertical line but the pins themselves are spread out top and bottom (*see photo*). A typical pin sight might have five pins. These pins can be assigned to any distances you want. A typical set of target distances to assign the pins is (bottom) 60, 50, 40, 30, and 20 (top) yards. Young archers might have pins set at (bottom) 50, 40, 30, 20, and 10 (top) yards or even (bottom) 30, 25, 20, 15, and 10 (top) yards. Bowhunters usually use fewer pins (some as few as one) set for yardages much closer in. The pins can be made of metal or, more common now, fiber optic strands. The fiber optic "pins" channel so much light to the ends that the pin "heads" seem to be glowing.

Sighting In a Pin Sight The procedure for setting the pins to correspond to distances is exactly the same as for the target sight except that with the target sight the aperture pin is moved to new positions for each distance, where with a pin sight you move each pin to its own location.

Using a Pin Sight Shooting with a pin sight can be confusing. Many archers make the mistake of "using the wrong pin" to aim with, so some practice is required to use them well. If the distance being shot corresponds to one of the distances of your pins, you just line up the head of the corresponding pin to the center of the target (using the correct pin, of course). If the distance is between pins, you have to "interpolate." If the target is at 25 yards and you have your pins set for 10, 20, 30, 40, and 50 yards for example, you need to line the center of the target with "half way" between the 20 and 30 yard pins. If it is 24 yards, then sight a tiny bit closer to the 20 yard pin from half way. Imagination is required!

If you are over the distance of your highest pin, you may have to "stack your pins." For example, if shooting 60 yards with a 50 yard (maximum distance) pin, you set your "stack" of pins so that the 50 yard pin is on the center of the target.

Pins can be "Stacked." here the forty yard pin, with the 50 yard pin positioned on center, suggests a POA for a 60 yard shot.

Notes

Then you look to see where the 40 yard pin is on the target, that provides an aiming spot (a point of aim!) to place the 50 yard pin when shooting the 60 yard target (the 50 yard pin is about 10 yards higher than the 60 yard pin when used this way). Again, imagination . . . and practice are required.

Target Sights Target, or moveable, sights generally have an "extension bar" which extends the sight itself out in front of the bow. At right angles to the end of the extension bar is the "sight bar." The sighting aperture moves up and down on a moveable "block" attached to the sight bar. The aperture is usually on a threaded rod so that windage (left-right) changes can be made using the screw threads. Elevation changes are made by moving the sight block up and down on the sight bar. Sometimes the block is merely slid up and down on the sight bar (typically on less expensive sights) and sometimes it "rides up and down upon a threaded shaft." The knobs to turn the shaft (and thus move the aperture up and down) typically have click stops in them that enable each turn to be divided into a number of clicks (typically 10 or 20). On a "10 click" sight, 1 click is 1/10 of a turn on the knob (and a corresponding movement of the sight aperture up or down), 2 clicks is 2/10 of a turn, 10 clicks is a whole turn, etc. In this manner, very fine adjustments in elevation of the sight's aperture can be made.

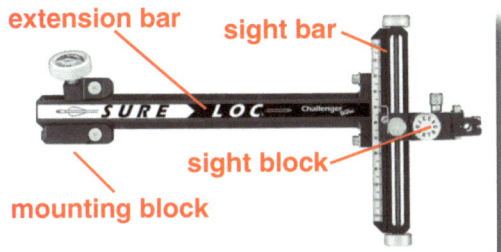

Target Sight Apertures What is used to line up the sight with the target is called the aperture (corresponding to the ball on the end of the hat pin). The style of competition determines what apertures are allowed. Olympic competition allows only pins or small loops at the end of a straight pin. Compound archery allows the use of telescopic sight apertures in some of its styles. Telescopic apertures include lenses that magnify the target. Typical magnifications are roughly 2X, 4X, and 6X ("roughly" because the actual magnification depends on the draw length of the archer). Higher magnification apertures magnify not only the target but the normal movements of the archer! It is very disconcerting to see the target jumping around through such a high magnification aperture. Only the steadiest of archers can use the higher power "scopes." A typical starting magnification is 2X-4X.

Some compound shooting styles allow telescopic apertures (like these two) which magnify the target.

Notes

A bubble level helps you keep a bow vertical at all times.

Some compound shooting styles allow peep sights which allow archers to look right through the string!

Some styles are allowed to use leveling bubbles (*see photo*) which, if set up properly, tell the archer when the sight is level and the bow is held straight up and down, since the bubble level is at right angles to the bow. Leveling bubbles are not allowed in many styles, for example Olympic-style archery.

Using Bow Sights No matter what kind of sight is used, their use follows some basic guidelines. Here are some of the more important ones:

- *No Sight Can Correct for Inconsistent Form* The bow sight generally sticks outward from the front of the bow, providing a consistent front sighting reference. But, if the archer's anchor position is inconsistent, inaccuracy is the result. The anchor position serves as the equivalent of the rear sight of a rifle. Having a consistent anchor point is therefore crucial. Compound bow shooters, in many of the classes allowing sights, are allowed to use what is called a "peep sight." This is typically a plastic or metal lozenge embedded into the string with a hole in it (the exact equivalent of a rear "peep" sight on a rifle). A properly positioned peep site can significantly increase accuracy—but if the archer's anchor position is inconsistent, inaccuracy is the result, even with a peep sight.

- *Sighting In is a Simple Procedure . . . But* Sighting in *is* simple, but there is a great deal of tinkering involved. The procedure for "sighting in" (assigning sight aperture positions to all (or most) distances to be shot) is:

1. Start up close to the target (10 yards) so you won't miss. The aperture being set will be high on the sight bar (or the top pin in the stack set near the top of its enclosure). Using best shooting form, three or more arrows are shot aiming dead center at the target. (Obviously, if the first shot misses the target altogether an adjustment is in order!)

2. Make adjustments according to the following scheme:
   (all orientations are from the viewpoint of the archer behind the bow)
   a. If the arrow hits high, move the aperture higher.
   b. If the arrow hits low, move the aperture lower.
   c. If the arrow hits left, move the aperture to the left.
   d. If the arrow hits right, move the aperture to the right.

   The rule of thumb is: *the aperture followschases the arrow.*

3. Repeat for the other distances.

   Be aware it is not necessary to sight in every distance. If you find a sight mark

Notes _____

for 30 yards and then one for 20 yards, the sight mark for 25 yards will be very close to (but not exactly) halfway in between. Most people get 4-5 sight marks and then interpolate the rest. There are even computer programs to do the work for you! Google "Archer's Advantage" if you are curious.

- *Peep Sights Increase Accuracy* Peep sights increase accuracy, not simply because they allow archers to look right through the string! When at full draw, the circular hole in the peep sight is visually aligned with the circular housing of the telescopic aperture (or circular pin guard on a pin sight) resulting in consistent alignment of the sight (and hence bow) with the archer's line of sight. Peep sights are not allowed in all styles, *e.g.* Olympic-style archery does not allow peep sights.
- Commercial jigs are available that guarantee that the extension bar is at right angles to the sight bar and the aperture block and shaft are at right angles to the sight bar. Also see *Simple Maintenance for Archery* by Ruth Rowe and Alan Anderson.

When used with a pin sight, the peep's hole has to line up with the sight's housing or the pin being used has to be centered in the peep's hole

Quivers Typically when archers first acquire their own equipment, they also invest in a quiver. Target archers typically choose to use a "target quiver" (hip quiver). There are two general styles, both worn on the hip oppositet he bow: pocket quivers, in which the arrows stick up and backward to be out of the way, and tube quivers, in which the arrows stick out to the front to be out of the way. Traditional archers also have back quivers available. Quivers that attach to the bow are typically only used for hunting and not for target archery (arrows attached to the bow change the weight of the bow from shot to shot (as they are removed and shot) which is not good for consistency). Arrows are kept in the quiver when not being shot. When arrows are bring pulled, the rule is "pull one, quiver one," that is pull one arrow at a time and place it into your quiver before you pull another. This is the safest procedure to follow.

Release Aids There are so many release aids available on the market, it would be extremely difficult to say anything specific about many of them. Instead here are some general aspects of using release aids:

1. *Your Release Must Fit Your Hand* This may be obvious but a great many people shoot with releases that are too big or too small and pay a score price thereby.
2. *All Releases Can Be Shot With (or Without) Back Tension* Some releases are sold as "back tension releases," which is incorrect because "back tension" is something the archer does, not the release. Typically they are referring to what are called

Notes _____

_____

_____

_____

_____

_____

_____

"triggerless" releases.

3. *Trigger Releases: The draw is executed with finger/thumb* off *of the trigger*; this is a must. Accidents happen to those who do not do this!
4. *Trigger Releases: The release must be set up "slow."* This means having a high trigger pressure with a very low "throw" (the distance the trigger travels). Fast or "hair" triggers create mental problems that prove difficult to solve. In other words, the trigger should be hard to "pull" with little movement between being "on" and "off" of the bow string.
5. *Always Test a New Release Aid with a Rope Loop* Take your rope loop with you any time you want check out a new release aid. If you try one with your bow and the release goes off too soon, the surprise can result in physical damage to your face! See the Appendix on *Training with Release Aids* below.

Finger Tabs Finger tabs must be fit to the archer's hand. Most tabs come with some capability to help the archer hold his/her fingers in the same place each shot. This may be a spacer meant to keep the top and middle fingers from "pinching" the arrow or some other device. Tabs come in various sizes: XS, S, M, L, XL, etc. A tab must be big enough so that the material laps over the top and bottom fingers, otherwise calluses will develop where the string presses against skin (*see photo*). Many people buy the next larger size and then trim away any unwanted material.

The tab must be thin enough to give the archer some feel of the string, yet thick enough to provide protect from the string's pressure. It must wear well, as few people enjoy breaking in new tabs. It should perform about as well in wet weather as it does in dry.

Once you have settled on a choice of tab, buy at least two. Shoot them on alternating days so they are all in about the same stage of wear. In this manner, if a tab is broken, or more likely lost, you will have a "backup tab" ready to use. Recommend the same to your serious students.

Kisser Buttons A "button" attached to your bow string that touches your lips (hence "kisser") to help you find your anchor position. Installation is covered in *Simple Maintenance for Archery* by Ruth Rowe and Alan Anderson (page 63). Probably more trouble than they are worth as anchor position based on feel of the hand on the jaw or face is more reliable. Definitely not for use with a peep sight as they will conflict with each other.

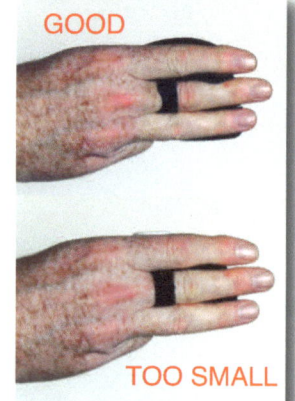

The tab material must be able to protect the tops of your fingers as well—see text.

Notes _____

_____

_____

_____

_____

_____

_____

Equipment Maintenance and Repair

Rather than make this appendix book-sized, we are relying on a very valuable resource that we want you to acquire, namely a copy of *Simple Maintenance for Archery* by Ruth Rowe and Alan Anderson. We will merely establish the value and importance of various techniques and procedures and refer you to the appropriate pages in that book. We end with a recommendation as to which coaches/instructors may want to do that particular procedure.

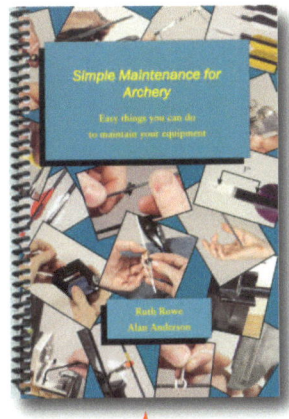

Checking Arrows (page 32) here is a nice summary of techniques that can be used to check arrows as to their being safe to shoot. All Coaches need to be able to do this.

Installing and Replacing Nocks (page 2) There are various kinds of nocks and they all can be replaced quite easily. Being able to do this means you do not have to take such simple repairs to a shop or another person and then pick them up when done and pay for the repairs, etc. The supplies (nocks, glue, etc.) for ordinary program equipment should be available from the AER website (*www.archeryeducationresources.com*) as well as the usual sources. All Coaches should be able to do this.

You need this book! We would have had to have another 40 pages of appendices if it were not for the availability of this book!

Fletching Arrows (page 8) Fletches, being made of feathers or soft plastic, often get damaged. On an aluminum arrow, all that is needed to repair the fletches is to replace them: they are cut off with a sharp knife, the residual glue removed by scraping and solvent, and a jig (<$25) and glue (<$5) are used to glue on new fletches. This can be done while watching TV or doing other tasks. The tools and supplies aren't expensive but this is time consuming. Recommended to coaches needing to make occasional repairs or to coaches without an archery shop nearby.

Installing and Replacing Points (page 29) Arrow points are easily lost and easily replaced. If you consider yourself to be "handy," you can do this.

Replacing a Center Serving (page 43 and page 36) The center serving on bowstrings wears out more often than any other part. It is the part the fingers, arrow, and armguard interact with. It can be replaced several times before the string itself wears out. The tools and materials needed are relatively inexpensive (<$25) and are paid back when you have "saved" three bowstrings (~$10-12) from the trash can. If you consider yourself to be "handy," you can do this.

Serving on a Nocking Point (page 52) With just a little serving thread,

Notes

you can "tie on" a nocking point locator that serves as well as the brass clamp-on variety (or better). This can be done very inexpensively, on the field, and quickly. This may not be worth the trouble, but if you consider yourself to be "handy," you can do this.

Making the Nocking Point Fit the Nock (page 56) As center servings wear, the nocks of the arrows fit more and more loosely, to the point they cause the arrows to fall from the bow. Old timers used to just bite on the "ears" of the nock making the groove in the nock a tad bit smaller and they were good to go. This is not recommended, though, because then those nocks are too tight for bows without worn center servings. This is a little procedure to fix this problem that all can do. All Coaches should be able to do this.

Installing a Peep Sight (page 58) All Compound Coaches should be able to do this.

Adding a D-Loop to a Compound Serving (page 58) All coaches who want to coach archers who shoot release aids need to be able to install a "D Loop." If you are a traditional or recurve specialist and are trying to help a compound archer with this, bring the book (and some release rope—available on the AER website—and a butane lighter and a pair of needle nose pliers) to a class and learn with your student as partner as you install one of these on his bow. This is a great "teaching moment" showing your student that we all have things to learn. (The needle nose pliers are used to "test" the loop. Insert the "noses" between loop and nocking point and spread them apart as strongly as you can. If the loop holds, you are good to use it while shooting. Don't forget to align the loop with the hole in the peep sight to aid in peep rotation.) All Compound Coaches should be able to do this.

The Rest of the Book It is all good stuff. There is a nice section starting on page 71 on setting up bow sights, for example.

Training with Release Aids (Compound Only)

The Preliminaries A release aid must fit the archer's hand. If it is too big, or too small, or too thick, or fits the wrist (wrist strap variety) too loosely or can't be adjusted to fit his hand, etc. he will struggle using it. Release aids are not inexpensive pieces of archery equipment and you will do well to send archers to get professional help at a quality archery shop when considering which to purchase. If they sell your

Notes

archer a release aid that does not fit, they can exchange it for one that does. If you buy one off of the internet and it doesn't fit, well, we hope they can sell it to someone it does fit as we will not waste your time or their time trying to train them to use a release aid that will not work well.

Release Aid Training We start all release shooters on a "rope bow" which is a loop of nylon clothesline such that the archer can loop it over his hand and get to a full draw position with the release attached. This takes the target and the expectation of the arrows landing somewhere out of the training. We then move to the bow but with a blank bale to shoot arrows, again we take the target and the expectation of the arrows "landing somewhere" out of the training. See Larry Wise's wonderful articles about training (and retraining) release aid archers on the AER website (*www.archeryeducationresources.com*).

Eye Dominance

Just as you are right- or left-handed, you are right- or left-eyed, that is your brain favors one of your two eyes for visual information. The eye your brain favors is called your *dominant eye*. The preferred situation for archers is to have the dominant hand and eye match ("right-right" who will shoot right-handed or "left-left" who will shoot left-handed). If an archer is *cross-dominant* ("right-left" or "left-right"), they must choose whether to favor their eye or hand. Some argue that being cross dominant is an advantage (especially for compound archers) as you get to aim with your dominant eye and hold the bow with dominant arm, a steady bow arm being very important for accuracy.

For beginner classes, some instructors like to check for eye dominance and some do not. Either way is acceptable but you should know the signs of somebody fighting a cross dominant situation (drawing string to wrong side of face, shooting arrows three feet to the left (RH archer), or closing the "normal" aiming eye while aiming).

For intermediate archers, eye dominance testing at least supplies information that may be used for equipment acquisition. Archers getting a right-handed kit might be more than a little upset if they find out they can shoot more comfortably left-handed, etc.

Notes _____
_____
_____
_____
_____
_____
_____

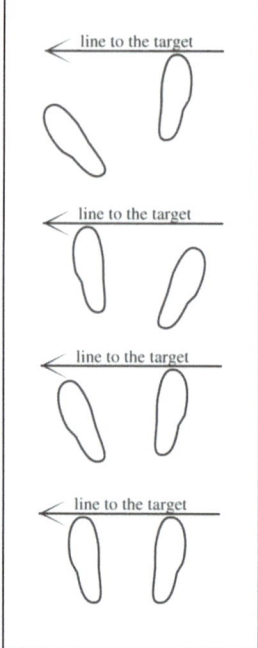

Can you put names to these stances?

On Stances

The Arabs were writing about the pros and cons of various stances 500 years ago. Not much has been settled since then. Whatever you read about stances, including this, is highly opinion-based, so be warned.

There Is Nothing Wrong With the Square Stance The greatest handicap the square stance has is it is considered a stance for beginners. After all, who wants to be taunted for using a "baby stance?" Contrarily, in 2008, the Korean Olympic coaches indicated that they were going to recommend the square stance more to their elite archers. And the Koreans are the most decorated Olympic archers on the planet (at least the women are).

The Other Stances Argh, there are dozens! The main categories are:
- a *square stance* is one in which a line extended across the tips of the archer's shoes points directly to the centerline of the target (*see figure*)
- an *open stance* is one in which a line extended across the tips of the archer's shoes points to the left of the centerline of the target (for right-handed archers, again *see figure*)
- a *closed stance* is one in which a line extended across the tips of the archer's shoes points to the right of the centerline of the target (for right-handed archers, again *see figure*)

The Natural Stance The point here is that your body has a natural tendency built in regarding where to point the bow. If you position your body other than in your natural stance, you will have to tense muscles to swing the bow onto the target. The procedure goes like this: take your stance in front of a far off target and close your eyes; bring your bow up, draw and anchor and "settle in" using your best form, then open your eyes. If your arrow/sight isn't pointed exactly at the centerline of the target (in the left-right sense, not up-down) move your feet until it is. You then repeat this process until you can draw on the target with your eyes closed and then when you opened them, you are pointed in the right direction. This stance is your natural stance. Take out your cell phone and take a picture of it or stand on a piece of cardboard while you do the exercise and then have someone outline your shoes onto the cardboard (shooting and target lines already being drawn on and oriented properly).

This procedure has to be repeated from time to time as the stance could change

Notes

due to injuries or weight gains or other effects.

The Open Stance for Compound Archers Compound archers have preferred an open stance because the power of a compound bow is determined by leverage built into the design and is not at all like how the power of a recurve bow is generated. In a recurve bow, the power of the bow is determined by two large factors: draw weight/force and draw length. Since the archer is bending the limbs directly, a premium is put upon draw length, more is better (more draw length increases the power stroke (the distance the arrow moves while on the string), which creates more stored energy, which increases arrow speed). Therefore recurve archers must get as close to their bows as is possible to maximize their draw lengths. This creates a flat "force triangle" at full draw (*see figure left*) with one side of the triangle consisting of the bow hand, bow arm, and the bones across the shoulders, the second side consists of the upper draw arm, and the third is the draw hand and forearm to the elbow. This brings the bowstring very close to the chest (which is why recurve archers wear chest protectors) and very close to the bow forearm (which is why recurve archers wear armguards).

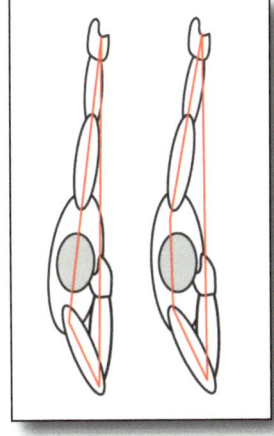

The full draw positions are different for recurve (left) and compound (right) archers. Compound archers have their shoulders roughly parallel to their arrows whereas recurve archers have to strain a bit more to line up their shoulders with their bow arms.

Compound archers, on the other hand, have more of a "force trapezoid" at full draw. By not standing so close to the bow, the bow arm and the shoulders make an angle adding another side to the force pathways (*see figure again*). Side one of the trapezoid consists of the bow hand and the bow arm, side two being the bones across the shoulders, the third side consists of the upper draw arm, and the fourth is the draw hand and forearm to the elbow.

Compound archers' body positions are different from recurve archers simply because this posture is more comfortable. The open stance and the slightly open bow shoulder means compound archers do not have to turn their heads so far over their shoulders, eliminating strain on the neck. This comes about because the power of a compound bow is determined largely by the design of the eccentrics and limbs used and not so much on draw length. The eccentric design provides "letoff," the lessening of the draw force to 20-35% of peak weight, which provides more time to aim, which requires more relaxation at full draw to do effectively.

The things to watch out for if you coach compound archers, is that an open stance can lead to a torso that is too open (a shoulder angle too small) which can lead to bow shoulder injuries and poor groups. Make sure your student's torso faces down the

Notes _____
_____
_____
_____
_____
_____

shooting line to prevent this (a good cue is "point your belly button down the line").

The Open Stance for Recurve Archers Olympic-style archers with good line have their draw elbows past (toward the back) the point where a line through the arrow (the "arrow line") extends rearward, or at the very least their elbows are on that line. Archers with poor line (their elbows are outside of arrow line) are almost required to "pluck" the string by opening their fingers when releasing. The best release of the string comes when the fingers are simply relaxed and the string leaves of its own accord. This is extremely difficult to do if the archer is not "in line." Getting "past line" is insurance for being "short of line." If one's elbow is behind the arrow line, the normal variation from shot to shot will not be great enough to get you out of line. Normal variation when the archer is merely "in line" means that a sizable percentage of the shots will be made with the elbow slightly outside of line (bad).

So, what does line have to do with stance? Consider the following two points (all for a right-handed archers, reverse everything for left-handers): 1) In order for the draw forearm and elbow to be in line, the side of the force triangle containing the shoulders must point to the right of the target (assuming the arrow is pointing at the target, of course—if you don't understand this, study the figure). 2) Archers failing to get their shoulders into that alignment will have their draw elbows outside of the arrow line.

Now rotating your stance to the left of the target (creating an open stance) can't help you get your shoulders onto a line to the right of the target. In fact, it makes it more difficult. Some claim that all of the twisting (between stance and shoulders) is supposed to be from the waist up and the purpose of the twisting is to provide stability (especially from wind forces), but if an archer isn't in line (or better, beyond it), what good is stability? Also, since youngsters are particularly flexible, their torso twisting doesn't even provide help with the wind, so recommending an open stance for this purpose to youngsters is dubious at best. There is more to unfold here.

The Closed Stance for Recurve Archers Now consider the closed stance. Does rotating your stance to the right of the target help you get your shoulders aligned to the right of the target? The answer is "yes." Your shoulders naturally align with your hips. So, the closed stance helps you get in line, so if getting "in line" is a problem, a stance more closed may help.

Certainly getting in line is far more important that any advantage in wind shoot-

Notes

ing early on in an archer's career, so starting with a more closed stance could be followed by a more open stance later after the correct upper body position has been instilled.

Stance Rules The rules regarding stances vary from organization to organization. You have been given the most all-encompassing definition that will keep you out of trouble. And, for example, in the NFAA, if any part of either foot is on the shooting line (or you straddle the line), you are okay. In some field archery competitions, you may stand anywhere behind the shooting line. Since there are so many rules, ask lots of questions and get copies of the rules from the sponsoring organization before attending a competition or counseling an attending student.

Fine Tuning a Stance The procedure above under the description of the "natural stance" is more than a little imprecise. There are at least two more precise procedures by which the best stance for a specific archer can be determined. One has a compound archer shooting when closing his eyes after acquiring the target in the bow sight, then adjusted his stance until he could shoot good groups in the center of the target that way. This is way too advanced for any but the most expert archers. The other technique is provided by Larry Wise, one of the finest compound coaches in the world. In Larry's technique you take two three dot (40 cm) target strips and mount them sideways and end-to-end (*see diagram*). You then take a square stance

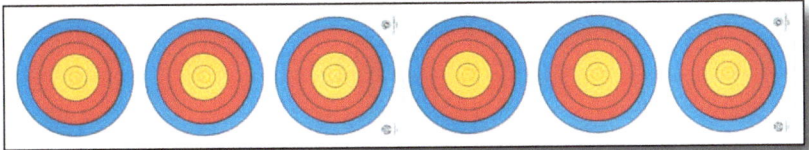

aligned to the middle of that strip and shoot arrows at whatever distance you can perform well at. The shots must be in a nonsequential order—all of the targets can be shot from left to right one time then from right to left, then in random sequences, etc. but you can't keep shooting in the same sequence. (If you shoot them always from left to right, for example, and your fourth shot is technically weak (due to shot timing, breathing, fatigue, etc.), you will get poor performance on the fourth target every time for reasons that are unrelated to stance.)

The archer shoots these same targets for a number of days or weeks and then looks at the patterns made. The three targets to the left represent three degrees of

Notes

closed stance; the three targets on the right represent three degrees of open stance. If one of the targets shows clearly superior grouping, the stance associated with that target is your best stance. If the leftmost or rightmost target shows best grouping you will want to repeat the experiment aligning your square stance with the left edge (if the rightmost target proved superior) or right edge (if the leftmost target proved superior). This will give you six degrees of open stances or closed stances, respectively, to compare.

This also is an advanced (and time consuming) technique, but some will be interested anyway.

More on Bow Sights

Rather than make these appendices book-sized, we are relying on a very valuable resource that we want you to acquire, namely a copy of *Simple Maintenance for Archery* by Ruth Rowe and Alan Anderson. There is a nice section starting on page 71 of that book on setting up bow sights, for example, which means we do not have to duplicate that information here. And, since there is so much more valuable information in that book, we simply encourage you to get a copy. We will, however, comment on a number of general aspects of using sights.

Extending Sights The first bow sights were attached directly to the belly of the bow. Later, the sight was extended out in front of the bow. To see what advantage or disadvantage there is in making that extension, consider a little experiment. While looking at a large FITA target that is quite far off, hold up thumb and forefinger aligned with the top and bottom edges of that circle while at arm's length. Your thumb and finger tips will only be about an inch part. If you bring your hand closer to your aiming eye while keeping visual contact with the top and bottom of the target round, the gap between thumb and finger tips gets smaller. So, the image of an object that is three or four feet high at a distance appears to only an inch or so high at arm's length. This is not exactly shocking, but it does explain what extension does for a bow sight. The farther apart the bow and sight are, the more spread out the image and, consequently, so are the aperture/pin positions. The more distance between, say the 40 and 50 yard/meter marks, the more room for intermediate marks and the more room to set the sight accurately. If the 40 and 50 yard/meter marks are right next to one another, where is 43 yards or 48 yards?

Notes

But this is a disadvantage for young archers trying to "make distance." To reach a particularly far target the bow has to be held high, which means the aperture must be slid down low on the sight and it can go so low that it is in the path of the arrow! (The initial left-right position of the aperture being directly above the arrow shaft.) One source of solutions to this problem is to move the sight closer to the bow or even to the back of the bow (if the attachment block allows this configuration). This can be done just for the "too long" distance or for all.

There are even finer points here. If your archer is inserting torque (twisting force) on the bow through a poor bow hand (called "bow hand torque"), this can cause left-right misses. When using a sight, if the bow is twisted to the left (counterclockwise from above), it will cause the arrow to go to the left when shot. But, with a bow sight, twisting the bow to the left, causes the aperture to move to the left, which causes the archer to move the bow to the right, canceling out some of the effect of the bow torque. There are some who believe that there is an optimal extension distance in which the two effects cancel out exactly creating the ultimate forgiving set up. (This is an advanced topic.)

More on Pin Sights The positions of the pins in a pin sight can tell you a great deal about how the bow is set up. Ideally the tips of the pins should lie on a straight line and that line should be parallel to the bow's bowstring. If they are not, something is wrong. For example, if the line slants (off of plumb) it may be an indication that the archer "cants" or tilts his bow while shooting. Some archers actually prefer this situation, but beginning or new archers should avoid this complication.

The spacing between the pins follows a mathematical scheme. The gap between the top two pins is slightly smaller than the gap between the next two, which is slight smaller than the gap between the next two, etc. We are assuming that the pin distances are set up in a regular increment here, *e.g.* (top) 5, 10, 15, 20, 25 (bottom) yards or (top) 20, 30, 40, 50, 60 (bottom) yards. The mathematics is irrelevant to our purpose, but there is a little graph (*see graph on next page*) that can be used to check the gaps. The pin stack is held against the lines in the graph with the highest and lowest pins on their respective lines, then the other pins should also line up. If any of the pins do not line up, that pin's setting is questionable. Some folks photocopy the graph onto plastic transparency sheeting so they can look *through* the graph

Notes

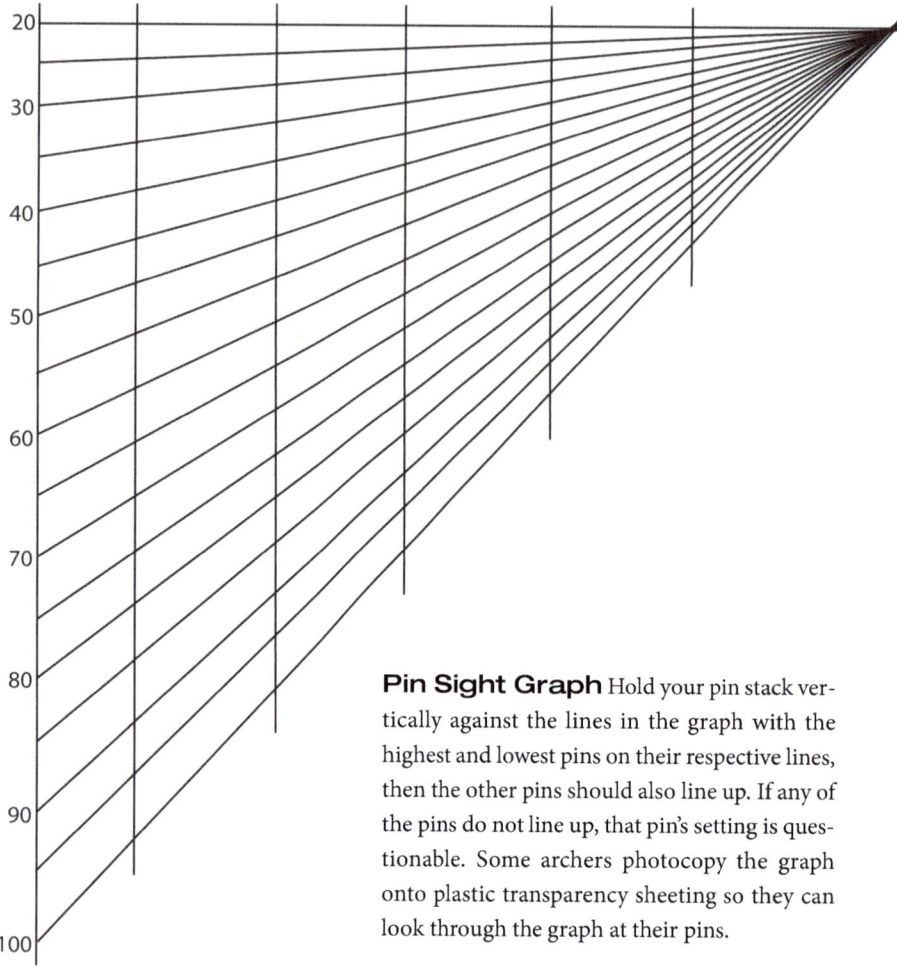

Pin Sight Graph Hold your pin stack vertically against the lines in the graph with the highest and lowest pins on their respective lines, then the other pins should also line up. If any of the pins do not line up, that pin's setting is questionable. Some archers photocopy the graph onto plastic transparency sheeting so they can look through the graph at their pins.

at their pins. This is a great little checking tool.

Notes _____

_____

_____

_____

_____

_____

_____

Bow Fitting
Preparing a bow to perform can be separated into three steps:
- bow/arrow fitting
- bow/arrow setup, and
- bow/arrow tuning.

The first stage "bow/arrow fitting" involves making sure that the equipment acquired for an archer is suitable is size (length, mass) and draw force (draw weight), especially as it regards selecting arrows to match the bow and archer.

For a complete description of how to do this, see *Bow Fitting* by Steve Ruis, available in Coach Resources on the AER website (*www.archeryeducationresources.com*).

Bow Setup
We separate bow preparation into three steps:
- bow/arrow fitting
- bow/arrow setup, and
- bow/arrow tuning.

The second stage "bow/arrow setup" is best taught when an archer gets a new bow, which typically occurs at the beginning of *Stage II*. The archer may be being lent a bow, rather than buying one, but it must be with the understanding that the bow will be adjusted to fit the archer.

There are a number of things needing to be set in reasonable places on any new bow.

Setting Up a New Recurve Bow
Getting a new recurve bow is great fun. Here is how to set up a new recurve bow. We will be adjusting brace height, centershot (arrow rest position), and nocking point.

Assembling the Bow If your bow is a one piece bow, there is just a little to do. If the bow is a traditional bow designed to be "shot off of the shelf," there should be some soft material (felt or leather) on the arrow shelf itself and up against the bow at the arrow shelf. This serves two purposes: protecting the bow and correcting for slips while shooting (the arrows rebound softly when banging into these materials). The arrow shelf materials may already be installed or they may be provided for you

Notes

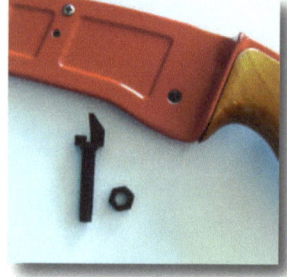

to install; check the manufacturer's instructions for installing these materials.

If your bow is designed to be shot off of an arrow rest, it may need to be installed. If a screw hole is provided to install the arrow rest, we recommend an inexpensive plastic screw-in arrow rest for the time being (*see photo*). Later you may want to install a more elaborate rest, but the plastic ones work surprisingly well.

If your bow is a three piece bow, the limbs need to be attached to the bow. On some bows there is a bolt that goes through a hole in the limb and then it is made finger tight. Other bows have limbs that slide or click into place. If the bow has "adjustable limb pockets" read the manufacturer's instructions carefully to make sure the limbs are inserted into their proper positions and are aligned correctly (this can be quite complicated). The goal is to have the bowstring visually bisect both the riser/handle and the limbs of the strung bow when viewed from behind.

Next up is stringing the bow and checking the brace height. If a string didn't come with the bow, one must be purchased. This can actually be an advantage as strings that come with bows are typically of low quality and wear out quickly; even so, if one came with the bow, there is no reason not to use it. In any case, archers often order a second bowstring for a bow so as to have a backup. If this was done, the factory supplied string can be used as a backup (or not used at all). To begin, slip the larger loop of the string over the top limb tip and then put 8-10 twists in the string before putting on the bottom loop. (Some argue that the twists should be in the same direction that your fingers curl around the bowstring so that you are "tightening" the twists when your fingers are on the string.) Now, using a bow stringer, brace the bow. Some stretching of the bowstring through use is expected (especially if the bowstring is made from Dacron) so it may be a little shorter than it will be after you have taken 20-30 shots, but the brace height of the bow should be within the manufacturer's specification. If the brace height is nowhere near the range specified, you may want to use another string. If it is close to being "in spec," shooting the bow in, also called "shooting in the bow," will result in the string stretching and the brace height dropping some.

Setting the Nocking Point Location A good starting point for a recurve bow nock locator is ½" above square for your nocking point locator. If you don't have a bow square yet, you can use a piece of stiff paper. Mark a spot ½" in from the corner of a piece of paper and line the edge of the paper with the mark with the

Notes _____

_____

_____

_____

_____

_____

_____

bowstring and the adjacent edge lined up with where the arrow will sit on the arrow rest. The mark on the paper shows you where the bottom of the nocking point locator should be. Clamp on a brass nock locator or tie on a thread locator (instructions are available in *Simple Maintenance for Archery*). Many people add a second nock locator slightly below the nock when one is snugged up against the primary nock locator. If you choose to do this, you may want to wait to do it until you have checked the position of nocking point with a bare shaft test.

Setting the Centershot The only thing left to do is to set the position of the arrow rest. A screw hole is provided to install the arrow rest; we recommend an inexpensive plastic screw-in arrow rest for the time being (*see photo previous page*). Later you may want to install a more elaborate rest, but the plastic ones work surprisingly well. Here we just loosen the lock nut on the screw-in arrow rest and screw the rest in or out to make the setting. The position we are looking for is one in which the right side of the arrow point is just visible to the left side of the bowstring when the string visually bisects both the riser/handle and the limbs when viewed from behind (switch left and right if you are left-handed). The easiest way to do this is to put an arrow on the string at the nocking point and arrow rest and then prop the top bow tip on the back of a chair or against a tree so that you can sight down the string onto the bow until the string exactly splits the bow. The arrow point should be just peeking out from behind the string on the outboard side (*see photo*). (The reason for this setting is the string is sliding slightly sideways when it leaves the fingers and we want the rear end of the arrow to be behind the front end. So if the rear is slightly to the left when it leaves the fingers, we want the point to also be slightly to the left (reverse for left-hand archers).)

The First Shots The bow now needs to be "shot in" by taking several dozen shots. This can be done blank bale at close range. This should "set" the bowstring and get you ready for a bare shaft test, which will give you feedback on whether the starting positions of the limbs, arrow rest, and nocking point locator are good or need to be "tweaked" for better performance.

When you have set the initial centershot of a recurve bow you should just see the right edge of the arrow's point lining up with the left edge of the string when the string visually bisects the limbs from behind the bow (reverse for left-handed archers).

Notes

Setting Up a New Longbow

Getting a new longbow is great fun. Here is how to set up a new longbow. The beauty of the longbow is its simplicity; the only things to consider are setting the proper brace height, setting the initial nocking point location, and the type of rest you intend to use.

Setting the Brace Height Most new bows will come with an owner's manual with brace height recommendations. If you bought the bow used, try looking for a copy of the manufacturer's owner's manual on the Internet. Typically, a modern fiberglass laminated longbow having a length of 66 inches will have a brace height recommended from 7 to 7¾ inches. Shorter bows will have somewhat smaller recommended brace heights; but most are above 6½ inches. These are just suggested brace heights. Understand that a lower brace height will increase the power stroke of the bow and, usually, the speed of the arrow.

A recurve archer knows they have gone too low on the brace height if the sound of the recoil of the limbs after the shot gets noticeably noisier than it was with a larger brace height. This noise comes from the excessive slapping of the string on the recurve part of the limbs. A longbow string, however, only makes contact with the limb at the string notches. You may not notice much difference in the sound of the shot from one height to the other. It becomes evident if you went too low if you start noticing the string slapping near your bow arm wrist after the shot.

Brace heights are adjusted by either twisting or untwisting the bow string to make it shorter or longer. Be careful not to untwist a Flemish bow string too much or you will unwind the end loops. This is not a danger with a continuous double loop bow string. If you need to twist the string 40 to 50 twists or more to get a desirable brace height that is both quiet and does not slap the wrist, you probably need a shorter string.

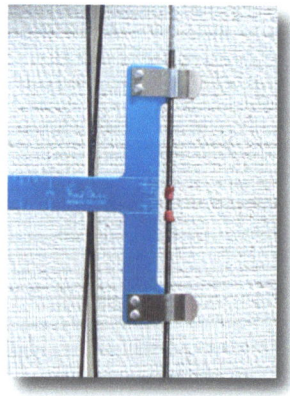

Having and using a bow square makes setting nocking point heights very easy.

Setting the Nocking Point Location A good starting point for a recurve bow nock locator is ½" above square for your nocking point locator. If you don't have a bow square yet, you can use a piece of stiff paper. Mark a spot ½" in from the corner of a piece of paper and line the edge of the paper with the mark with the bowstring and the adjacent edge lined up with where the arrow will sit on the arrow rest. The mark on the paper shows you where the bottom of the nocking point locator should be. Clamp on a brass nock locator or tie on a thread locator (instructions are available in *Simple Maintenance for Archery*). Many people add a second

Notes _____

_____

_____

_____

_____

_____

_____

nock locator slightly below the nock when one is snugged up against the primary nock locator. If you choose to do this, you may want to wait to do it until you have checked the position of nocking point with a bare shaft test.

If you are shooting off of your knuckle, you may want a little extra height in your nocking point location because a "too low" nocking point will cause the feathers/fletches to slide across your hand (painfully!). Use part of the handle wrap or a piece of tape to fix the location of the arrow when you set the nocking point locator.

The Arrow Rest Most longbow archers choose to shoot "off the shelf" rather than sticking on an elevated arrow rest. A "rug" rest with a leather "strike plate," placed just above the rug rest, will quiet the arrow and protect the finish of the bow (*see photo*). If the rug rest is made of horse hair, make sure the hair points in the direction the arrow is leaving the rest. Shooting "off the shelf" is best suited to the use of feather fletching. To get better arrow flight using plastic vanes, an elevated rest is recommended.

Bows which are designed to be shot off of the shelf have a crowned shelf, that is, the shelf bows upward in the middle. If your arrow shelf is flat it was not designed to be shot off of the shelf (but you can build a little crown for the shelf out of felt or leather and do it anyway).

If you are shooting off of your hand or knuckle, your arrow rest is already installed!

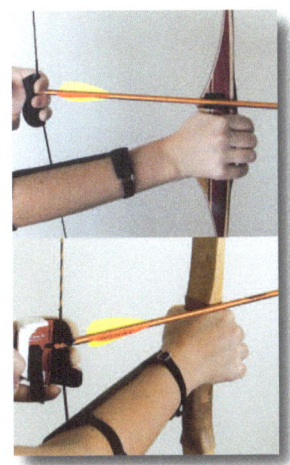

Some longbow have "shelves" that act as arrow rests, others require you to "shoot off of your knuckle."

The First Shots The bow now needs to be "shot in" by taken several dozen shots. This can be done blank bale at close range. This should "set" the bowstring and get you ready for a neutral bale or bare shaft testing, which will give you feedback on whether the starting positions of the arrow rest and nocking point locator are good or need to be "tweaked" for better performance.

Setting Up a New Compound Bow

Getting a new compound bow is great fun. Here is how to set up a new compound bow. We will be adjusting draw weight, nocking point height, and centershot (arrow rest position).

Assembling the Bow One of the things nice about compound bows is that there is very little assembly required. About the only thing required is to set the

Notes _____

_____

_____

_____

_____

_____

_____

draw weight. We hope you bought your bow so that it's lowest draw weight setting is where you will start shooting. If so, take an Allen wrench and screw the limb bolts all of the way in (the typical shipping position) and then back them out the maximum number of turns that the manufacturer allows. (If they didn't send you this information, check their website or call them. Backing out the limb bolts too far is dangerous.)

If there is a specific draw weight you need, you will need to use a bow scale. If you do not have one or the one you have is unreliable (a common problem), you can use a bathroom scale. All you need is a small board about three feet long of which you can put a small notch in the end. The board is stood on scale, notch end up, and the bow hangs from its bowstring placed in the notch where the arrow would go. With two hands on the riser, push down slowly. You will see the scale reading go up and then come down (let off!). Start from the top, slowly pushing down, look for the peak (highest) weight reading. Repeat this several times to get a consistent reading. This is your "peak draw weight" and it is as good as your bathroom scale is capable of measuring. If the value is too high for you, back the limb bolts out. If it is too small, screw them down/in and retest. Do not exceed the number of turns backed out specified by the manufacturer.

Setting the Nocking Point Location A good starting point for a compound bow is $3/16"$ to $1/4"$ above square for your nocking point locator ($1/2"$ above square for "fingers" archers). If you don't have a bow square yet, you can use a piece of stiff paper. Mark a spot $3/16"$ to $1/4"$ (or $1/2"$) in from the corner of a piece of paper and line edge of the paper with the mark with the bowstring and the adjacent edge lined up with where the arrow will sit on the arrow rest. The mark on the paper shows you where the bottom of the nocking point locator should be. Clamp on a brass nock locator or tie on a thread locator (instructions are available in *Simple Maintenance for Archery*). Many people add a second nock locator slightly below the nock when one is snugged up against the primary nock locator. You may want to wait to do this until you have checked the position of nocking point with a bare shaft test.

Setting the Centershot The only thing left to do is to set the position of the arrow rest. Here we just loosen the lock nut on the screw-in arrow rest and screw the rest in or out to make the setting. The position we are looking for depends on whether you are shooting with your fingers on the string ("fingers") or with a me-

Notes _____
_____
_____
_____
_____
_____
_____

chanical release aid ("release").

For "Fingers" Archers—The position we are looking for is the one in which the right side of the arrow point is just visible to the left side of the bowstring when the string visually bisects both the riser/handle and the limbs when viewed from behind (switch left and right if you are left-handed). The easiest way to do this is to put an arrow on the string at the nocking point and arrow rest and then prop the top bow tip on the back of a chair or against a tree so that you can sight down the string onto the bow until the string exactly splits the bow. The arrow point should be just peeking out from behind the string on the outboard side. (The reason for this setting is the string is sliding slightly sideways when it leaves the fingers and we want the rear end of the arrow to be behind the front end. So if the rear is slightly to the left when it leaves the fingers, we want the point to also be slightly to the left (reverse for left-hand archers).)

For "Release" Archers—The position we are looking for is the one in which the arrow shaft is directly behind the bowstring when the string visually bisects both the riser/handle and the limbs when viewed from behind (*see photo*).

The First Shots The bow now needs to be "shot in" by taken several dozen shots. This can be done blank bale at close range. This should "set" the bowstring and cables and get you ready for a bare shaft test, which will give you feedback on whether the starting positions of the arrow rest and nocking point locator are good or need to be "tweaked" for better performance.

Mechanical Complications Because compound bows have so many more parts than recurve bows or longbows, and because there are so many different designs, have the shop you acquired the bow from check it out to make sure all settings are appropriate. If you acquired the bow second hand, take it to a good bow technician at an archery shop for a similar check-up. Expect to pay for this service and for any parts (strings, cables, etc.) that need replacing.

Bow/Arrow Tuning
We separate bow preparation into three steps:
- bow/arrow fitting
- bow/arrow setup, and
- bow/arrow tuning.

To set the centershot for a release aid, the rest must be moved in a bit more so the arrow is right behind the string.

Notes _____

The third stage "bow/arrow tuning" is best done in stages also, starting (typically) with bare shaft tuning techniques. This is definitely not done until your archer's equipment setup is complete and his form is solid. The recommended tuning procedures are described in the *Archer's Guide*, so they won't be repeated here. But there are some general concepts that may help you understand what is going on during tuning; we address those here.

What is Tuning? Tuning is making adjustments in the bow-arrow system to fit them to the archer better. No archer is perfect; each makes mistakes (of aiming, of releasing, of . . .). The goal of tuning is to create a bow-arrow setup that minimizes the impact of those mistakes. Consequently the exact same bow-arrow combination will shoot differently in the hands of different archers. Otherwise all archers need only shoot what the world champion, or the archer who is closest to them in size and style of equipment, shoots. The goal of tuning therefore is a "forgiving" bow-arrow system in the sense that it forgives the archer's mistakes.

Tuning Concepts

Bow/Arrow Fitting This step is making sure that the bow and arrows are fit to the archer. The critical factors for the bow are draw weight and draw length. If we are talking about a compound bow, add physical mass to the list. If the bow has too much or too little draw weight, there is little to no chance you can teach the shooter of that bow good form. Too much draw weight and all the wrong muscles will be engaged in shooting the bow. If too little, they will have trouble getting off of the string. If the draw length is too long or too short, good form is impossible. With recurve bows, this manifests itself (usually) in bow length. Someone under five feet tall trying to shoot a 70 inch recurve bow will find they can't work the limbs sufficiently to get performance out of it. With compound bows this involves cams, cam modules, and string and cable lengths.

If you are working with a child or an adult with little upper body strength, the mass of a compound bow is also a factor. Holding a 4-6 pound weight at arm's length is an impediment to finding any kind of successful archery form.

With regard to arrows, having arrows suitably spined and long enough is critical to having a forgiving setup. Many students are working with hand-me-down equipment and the arrows are typically overspined. You also need to be sure nock

Notes

fit (nock on string) is good. (Dad's or Mom's bowstring is typically much thicker than junior's.) There is no way you can "tune in" poorly spined arrows or arrows that are too tight or too loose on the string. All you will get is erratic arrow flight.

Tuning Concept: *If the bow and arrows are not suitable to the archer, attempts to tune will be futile.*

Bow/Arrow Setup The initial setup of the bow involves setting a starting nocking point position and the centershot of the bow. If you are working with a recurve bow, add brace height to the list. And, if there are accessories: bow sight, stabilizers, clickers, etc., they need to be fitted, too. Since there is such a wide variety of such accessories, we will focus on the adjustments mad to the bows and arrows themselves.

You may not know that there are two or three points around which a recurve bow can be tuned. These are typically different brace height settings because if you change anything else, you are either creating a new bow (new limbs, different string, etc.) or you are tuning. A basic principle of tuning is if you change something and it gets worse, change it back. This is how we find the optimal bow setup and tune—

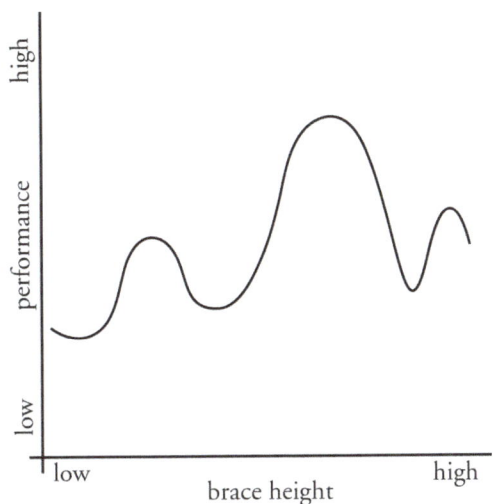

Notes _____

_____

_____

_____

_____

_____

_____

a little more, a little more, oops, too much! But because there are a number of different points to tune a bow, you want to be sure your basic setup has you near that optimal point you want to find. Consider the following graph.

The graph represents the performance of a hypothetical recurve bow (measured by cast or chronograph) as a function of brace height. This bow has three desirable points of tune. The highest peak is the optimal tuning point with the very best performance you can get out of this bow. You want to be sure you are close to the mountain and not just one of hills before you begin any tuning process. Mind you there are very good reasons why you might want to tune on one of the hills, for example, shooting short distances indoors, where arrow speed is not so important and a higher brace height may make for a more forgiving setup. But for most, either use the bow manufacturer's string and brace height settings or do some brace height tuning before you begin.

Compound bows also can be adjusted for brace height, but that topic is too advanced for this guide.

> Tuning Concept: *If the bow is not set up well initially, your chances of tuning the bow well are limited.*

Unfortunately you can tune a bow, well-fitted but slightly poorly set up. You typically end up with a "bad tune" which means your or your student's equipment is not as forgiving as it could be.

Bow/Arrow Tuning Here is where minor adjustments in the bow-arrow system are made to optimize the setup. These adjustments are in nocking point height and centershot typically and, if a recurve bow, some minor adjustments in brace height). If you are having to adjust draw weight, arrow spine (by cutting arrows shorter or adjusting point weight or vane size). You are really doing bow setup.

> Tuning Concept: *You Can't Tune Better Than You Shoot.*

This is probably the source of many misspent hours tuning. Archers with poor form aren't going to acquire it by going through tuning procedures. If you can't shoot a decent group, tuning the bow probably won't help. In fact, consistently shooting decent groups of arrows is a prerequisite for tuning. (Which is why beginners don't tune.)

Notes _____

_____

_____

_____

_____

_____

_____

Tuning Concept: *If You Change Something and It Gets Worse, Change It Back.*

This may seem obvious. It is the basis of all tuning procedures. It is simply the trial and error (trial and test) procedure.

Tuning Concept: *When You Make Adjustments, Make Them Large (At First).*

Another basic tuning principle is when you make adjustments, make them large (at first). If you are sneaking up on a big problem with itty bitty changes, you are going to be at it a long time. If you are too low, make a big change and now you are too high. Good! You now have an lower and an upper limit to your adjustments. Split the difference between those two settings until you get what you want.

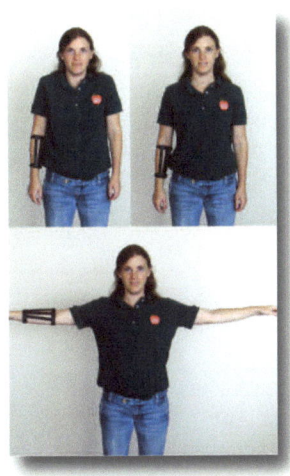

AER Archery Drills

Shoulders Up, Shoulders Down Drill
Purpose To teach basic shoulder position to beginners
Signs It Is Needed Beginners often hunch their bow shoulders to help hold the bow up. If they are really struggling with the mass of the bow, spread their stance out 1-3" and use the least heavy bow available (*e.g.* recurve rather than *Genesis* bow).
How to Do It Start by standing (no bow) and raising both shoulders while saying "Shoulders Up" then lowering the shoulders and saying 'Shoulders Down." Ask the student to follow for 1-2 repetitions. Then show how the arms are raised from the shoulders down position. Ask the student to do this also.
What It Does Students often have very little body awareness. More than a few drills are just to switch back and forth between extreme body positions so students can feel the difference. (Sometimes one of the extremes is the goal (as here), other times you are looking for a "happy medium" position between the two extremes.

Rotate That Elbow Drill
Purpose Protecting bow arms and elbows from bowstrings.
Signs It Is Needed If student has a bow elbow crease pointed upward or any part of bow arm that is too close to the path of the bowstring. If you pick up from *The First*

Notes _____

_____

_____

_____

_____

_____

_____

BAD

GOOD

Three Arrows that a number of students need this drill, do it for the whole class.
How to Do It You need an outward pointing wall corner or a small diameter post or door frame to lean against (which simulates the bow and some small draw force on the bow arm). Place the bow hand on the corner/post/door frame as you would on a bow (in good T Form), lean slightly against the edge and then rotate the bow elbow back and forth (to establish the range of motion) and then into a safe position (elbow crease is near vertical).
What It Does The elbow is wider when it is sideways and this puts the unprotected elbow close (too close) to the path of the bowstring. Rotating the elbow moves the vulnerable region out of the way. Note: There are some whose arm geometry is such that the elbow crease faces upward and this cannot be corrected. Some kind of neoprene sleeve can be used to protect the vulnerable elbow until they have enough experience that the string can be avoided (as they gain experience, the path the bowstring takes becomes more narrow and more regular).

Elbow Rotation Test
Purpose To test whether an "elbow rotation" step needs to be inserted into an archer's shot sequence (typically after the "set hands stage" whether the sequence has been taught yet or not).
Signs It Is Needed If student has an elbow crease pointed upward or any part of bow arm too close to the path of the bowstring.
How to Do It Hold the bow at arm's length as if shooting. Bend the bow elbow, bringing the bow toward the archer's body. If the bow swings in toward the chest (good); if the bow swings up toward the head (bad).
What It Does Gives the archer the ability to test whether their own bow arm elbow is in the correct orientation.

Arm Relaxation Drill
Purpose Student has unnecessary tension in draw hand and draw arm.
Signs It Is Needed Tension in back of draw hand indicated by arching of hand or wrist.
How to Do It Have student make "deep hook" and merge

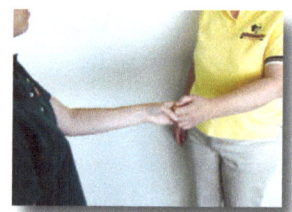

Notes

your deep hook with his. Wiggle his arm with your arm relaxed until his arm relaxes. Then say "this is the feeling you want to have in your forearm, wrist, and hand."
What It Does Provides feedback necessarily to feeling what a relaxed bow arm feels like.

Finger Release Drill
Purpose Practice relaxing the draw fingers for the release of the string.
Signs It Is Needed Plucking (hand flying away from face) while shooting.
How to Do It Stand recurve bow/longbow on shoot top. Set draw fingers into hook, hook onto end serving/string near top limb tip, pull slightly, the relax hook.
What It Does Provides the sensation of relaxing the fingers while under tension. Good practice.

Back Tension Drill #1
Purpose Student needs better idea of what is involved in using back muscles to draw bow.
Signs It Is Needed No or little movement of scapulae/shoulder blades during draw.
How to Do It Lay down on carpet or floor facing up. Using mimetics (play acting), stretch band, or very light drawing bow, go through the motions of drawing the bow. Students should feel considerable movement of their shoulder blades. Note: if you do this on grass, expect major grass stains!
What It Does The floor supplies tactile feedback as to what is happening in the student's back.

Back Tension Drill #2
Purpose Student needs better idea of what is involved in using back muscles to draw bow.
Signs It Is Needed No or little movement of scapulae/shoulder blades during draw.
How to Do It While student draws a light drawing bow, place your finger tips on their scapulae/shoulder blades. Instruct them to bring your fingers together as they draw the bow. Alternatively, you can put thumb or finger between the scapulae and instruct the student to "pinch my thumb/finger."
What It Does The touches supply tactile feedback as to what is happening in the student's back.

Notes _____

Back Tension Drill #3

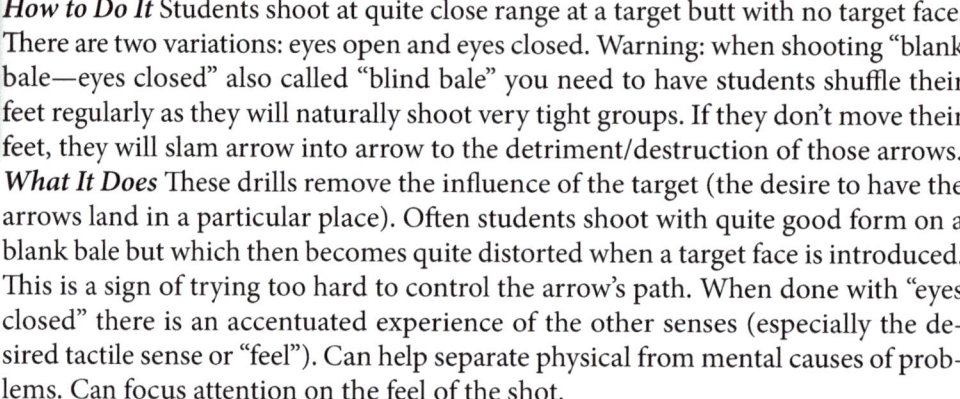

Purpose Student needs better idea of what is involved in using back muscles to draw bow.

Signs It Is Needed No or little movement of scapulae/shoulder blades during draw.

How to Do It Instruct the student to stand in the letter T. Have them bend both arms at the elbow. Instruct them to try to touch their elbows together behind their back.

What It Does The drill creates a very tight feeling between the shoulder blades, the feeling of which can then be incorporated into the student's shooting.

Blank Bale Routines

Purpose Various

Signs It Is Needed various

How to Do It Students shoot at quite close range at a target butt with no target face. There are two variations: eyes open and eyes closed. Warning: when shooting "blank bale—eyes closed" also called "blind bale" you need to have students shuffle their feet regularly as they will naturally shoot very tight groups. If they don't move their feet, they will slam arrow into arrow to the detriment/destruction of those arrows.

What It Does These drills remove the influence of the target (the desire to have the arrows land in a particular place). Often students shoot with quite good form on a blank bale but which then becomes quite distorted when a target face is introduced. This is a sign of trying too hard to control the arrow's path. When done with "eyes closed" there is an accentuated experience of the other senses (especially the desired tactile sense or "feel"). Can help separate physical from mental causes of problems. Can focus attention on the feel of the shot.

Used, for example, when student first gets to use a release aid with his compound bow, to allow the focus to be on the use of the release (for a while). Later the focus shifts to the target, but only after the release aid's use is comfortable.

Notes _____

_____

_____

_____

_____

_____

_____

Mirror Drill

Purpose Connects the feel of an archer's posture to correct posture.
Signs It Is Needed Student wants to make more progress than they are making or seems disconnected from his/her shot.
How to Do It A large mirror is mounted vertically (as a closet mirror is) and with a stretch band or light drawing bow, the archer "shoots" at the mirror. Archers can check their stance, hip position, shoulder position, head position and alignment.
What It Does Archery is a "feel" sport. When shooting the only check on an archer's form is how it feels to them. This drill provides great feedback visually that archers can then associate with the feel of their shot. This is a good drill to do daily during practice in that it "reminds" the subconscious mind of what it is trying to achieve.

Photo Courtesy of Andy Macdonald

AER Basic Coaching Approaches

This is an incomplete list of AER Basic Coaching Approaches. It is incomplete as we are always looking for ways to improve what we do.

1. Safe archery practices must be taught, reinforced, and enforced in all *Stages* of archery instruction. There are no exceptions.
2. All archers, no matter their age, need to be begin archery with a very low draw weight bow (10# draw for recurve, 15# draw for compound). Much of archery is learning how to achieve certain body positions, *e.g.* T Form at full draw, while relaxing yet being under the tension of the draw. To encourage rapid progress, draw weight must be kept to a minimum at the beginning. If the students allow, instruction may begin with stretch bands or form straps.
3. Shooting begins, almost always, up close at a fairly large target. The purpose is for archers of all levels to experience success, here in the form of the arrows hitting the target. This is not a "lowering of the bar" but, at least in part, training of the archers' self image to expect that their arrows will hit the target, at or near the center. As an archer, young or old, progresses in developing consistent form, targets are moved farther away or switched out for smaller target faces at the same distance until the archer is shooting at standard-sized targets, at standard shooting distances.
4. Changes in significant parameters (draw weight, draw length, bow mass in the form of back weights, etc.) must occur in small increments, *e.g.* 2# of draw weight

Notes

at a time, spread out over several shooting sessions. Large changes in such parameters distort good form, reversing progress made prior to the change.

5. When making adjustments in body positions, or accessory settings (these are less significant parameters as compared with those in #4 above), make changes in large increments at first, then smaller ones. This is the *Goldilocks' Principle* (This porridge is too hot! This porridge is too cold! This one is just right!). For example, if you are making a sight setting change because the arrows are hitting the target too high, you need to raise the aperture. Move it a half an inch or so. If that doesn't get you to center, move it another half of an inch. Often that first half an inch makes you low where you were high before—perfect! You now know the sight setting you are looking for is below the second one and above the first. Split that gap in half and test. If you are still "too high" spilt the difference between the new mark and the "too low mark." And you will be closer. In this manner, you will make smaller and smaller changes until the setting is correct.

On the other hand, if you need to move the aperture up one whole inch and you push it up $1/16$ of an inch, it will take you 16 tries to get it right.

The hard part for beginning coaches is to figure out what "a little" and "a lot" are—only experience will teach you that.

6. In all matters, it is recommended that coach and archer view each other as partners in achieving "better archery" for the archer. "Better archery" may mean the archer has more fun, or the archer gets better scores, or the archer simply feels better about participating. The archer sets the goal and the team works toward it in good communication. Coaches do not have to approve of the goal, but if you actually disapprove, you probably should not work with that archer.

Archery is an individual sport and the goal is for the archer to become independent. Independence does not mean "to be free from the need for coaching" but to be free to choose coaching or any other service the archer may feel is beneficial.

AER Coaching Principles

This is an incomplete list of AER Coaching Principles. It is incomplete as we are always looking for ways to improve what we do.

1. *Teach safety by building safe archery habits*, because you don't have to think about

Notes

a habit, it is just something you do.
2. *If something creates pain, stop doing it!* This is only common sense . . . good common sense.
3. *If you practice something incorrect, it will take ten times the work doing it correctly to fix the incorrect execution.* This is not a scientific principle, just a fairly good rule of thumb. The point is we want to be able to trust our training and in times of stress, it is easy to revert to other "options," therefore those other options need to poorly practiced (no repetitions lately).
4. *A key element in archery is achieving good form as quickly as possible because you do not want to practice doing it wrong!* Archers who receive solid coaching make very rapid progress due to this simple principle. If one doesn't pick up bad habits, one doesn't have to work to overcome them. Having stated that, it is unwise to try to correct everything a beginning archer is not doing well. The objective is to get them started well, and then make corrections in their order of importance (and generally in the order of the shot sequence) to get them into some semblance of good form rapidly.
5. *A basic rule of archery is: never make more than one change at a time!* This is also the rule for adding new or different accessories to your bow or kit. Its basis is you won't be able to tell which change had which effect if you do more than one at a time.
6. *Your subconscious mind (responsible for the consistency of your shot execution) cannot tell the difference between reality and something vividly imagined.* This is the foundation for imagery and many other mental training techniques.
7. *While an archer is shooting, if anything, anything at all—mental or physical—intrudes from a prior step, they must let down and start over.* This is "the rule of discipline" which is the foundation of a strong mental program. Archers willing to shoot shots they know aren't correct will not achieve any sort of consistent performance.
8. A basic teaching principle of AER is that *anytime you change something, your archery gets worse before it gets better.* Because archery is a repetition sport, archers have many repetitions of their archery shot making it comfortable and "normal." Whenever they make a change, it feels uncomfortable and not "normal" which automatically makes them worse. It takes a fair number of repetitions to overcome

Notes

this effect and make the new way seem at least reasonable. If the "result" of the change is your archery gets worse and then gets better than when you started, it is a good change. If it gets worse and never gets back to where you were before the change, it is a bad change. But without giving a change a fair chance, no one will ever make any changes.

9. A key point is: *if archers can group their arrows we can move that group into the center with aiming techniques.* If an archer can't group (a sign of inconsistent form), then aiming doesn't matter, so reasonable "grouping" must precede learning to aim.

10. *If archers struggle to draw, they need less draw weight.* Too much draw weight can prevent good form from being created and can destroy good form already created. Watch out for boys wanting to prove their manhood! Draw weight increases need to be gradual.

11. *Stepwise procedures, such as shooting arrows, need to be done by emphasizing the separate steps in the beginning.* This is fundamental. There are physical and mental activities that accompany each step. If the steps are blended or slurred one into the next, the attachment of the physical and mental activities may be incorrect. Later, if troubles occur in an archer's shot, reverting to "the fundamentals" is a diagnostic tool archers use to fix problems.

Field Archery

An introduction to field archery should occur as soon as is possible/desired. Of course, this is dependent on there being a field archery range available nearby. On the NFAA website (*www.fieldarchery.org*) you can find under "Archery Links" links

to all of the state organizations. Contact your state organization to find out if there is a field range near you (their websites often have a list). Contact the club which owns the range to see if someone will host a visit. It doesn't hurt to go out and pay a courtesy visit before you take students.

A primary consideration for student-archers being introduced to field archery is that they should not not necessarily shoot at predetermined shooting stakes but at distances where they are very likely to hit the target. (The alternative is to spend a lot of time looking for arrows in the woods and repairing those which hit something hard.)

Notes

Field archery is a great source of fun for archers of all ages; if there is a field range near you, it is worth the trip. Archers cannot choose what style or form of archery they prefer until they are aware of what those styles and forms are.

Anatomy of an Archery Session

This is a modular approach to designing archery class sessions. Various activities are combined in various ways to make for interesting and diverse practice formats. Coaches will probably need to adjust combinations of modules by how much time they take with his/her own students. Coaches are encouraged to design new modules and share them (see the Coaches Resources section of the AER website: *www.archeryeducationresources.com*). The basic design is:
- Session Time: 1-1.5 hrs (adjust as necessary)
- Setup-takedown time 10-15 min before and after session
- *Session Time is Broken Down into Thirds* (30 minutes for 1.5 hr session, 20 minutes for 1 hr session, etc.) which are filled by modular activities. Any module can be used during any third, but we recommend some general approaches:

First Third Modules

We do not recommend any session be started with paperwork or teaching. The start of session will necessarily include warm-up and stretching activities, and shooting some arrows to make sure student's subconscious and conscious minds are notified as to the task at hand. Typical first third modules are:
- Warm-up and Stretching Activities
- Fitness Routines
- Warm-up Shooting
- Specialized Routines (Self Image Drills, Target Panic drills, etc.)
- Blank Bale Work
- …

Second Third Modules

The second third segment of any lesson is the meat of your class session. Teaching modules need to be sandwiched between initial physical activity (acclimating and focusing students on task) and a final physical activity in which students attempt to

Notes _____

_____

_____

_____

_____

_____

_____

put the teaching into practice (completing the teaching and beginning the learning). Here is where you might:
- Teach Elements of Archery Form and Execution
- Hold Competitions
- Make Evaluations/Give Status Reports
- Hold Guest Coach Sessions
- Provide Tournament/Competition Preparedness Tips
- …

Final Third Modules

The last third of any class will necessarily include cool-down and stretching activities, as well as a little fun (in the "leave them wanting more" tradition):
- Put Teaching into Practice (*e.g.* when preparing students to shoot through distractions have one student try to distract another while the other is shooting … but there must be clear ground rules for doing this!)
- Games/Contests
- Cool-down and Stretching Activities
- …

Constructing Classes from Modules This structure is provided to help you design a class session and is not intended to limit what anyone can do. If you have an Olympic coach coming as a special attraction, by all means turn the program over to them, extend the lesson time, improvise, but do make plans ahead of time.

Similarly you may give over one or more sessions to a major in-class competition or opportunity to reach a scoring *Signpost*.

We hope to accumulate modules designed by many AER Coaches on the AER website (*www.archeryeducationresources.com*) for to you to use as you see fit. Some are already available on the AER website, look in Coach Resources. You will also find a template there for submitting your module ideas.

Making Evaluations

Making *Signpost* evaluations (Sometimes? Often? Always?) shouldn't be too difficult, but … there are some pitfalls to avoid. We address some of those here.

Notes _____
_____
_____
_____
_____
_____
_____

Too Easy/Too Hard If you give out "Oftens" too easily, students will think they are making fast progress when they really aren't and can get in over their heads. They will be advancing to more subtle skills when the basics haven't been mastered which will lead to frustration, back tracking. and quitting. If you give out "Oftens" too rarely, students will think they are making no progress when they really are, which will lead to frustration, back tracking. and quitting. Obviously, you are striving for the middle ground. Typically, you will have some archers racing through, while others struggle. Focus on the middle set of students to gauge the pace of any group.

Not Being Sure Sometimes you aren't sure as to a student's evaluation. This is normal. We recommend you err on the side of caution with "Always" ratings and err on the side of the student for "Oftens" ratings. Students don't need to get "Always" to move through the curriculum, but they do need "Oftens." Be honest, but if you aren't quite sure, consider the general progress of the student and whether your rating would help or hurt that student's development. We always want to help.

Jawboning Quite a few adults and youngsters are used to improving their situations by wheedling, cajoling, browbeating, etc. their teachers. Succumbing to their pleas will only lower your stature in the eyes of the other students (and encourage them to do the same). You need to find a way to deal with these annoying students. Maybe ask them to demonstrate for the entire group and let the group evaluate them, then the potential humiliation may keep them from doing this, but this technique can get out of hand as some of these students are attention hounds, so be judicious in its use.)

Conflicts Occasionally there may be a conflict between a student's upbringing and a *Signpost*. Be aware that you and your student can modify their Individual Curriculum Plan (ICP) if any part of it conflicts with their religion, personal mores, or fundamental beliefs. Do have a discussion with them ahead of making a decision. There may just be a misunderstanding of what is being asked of the student.

Details We like to date each evaluation (write the date in small numbers near the box on the student's ICP). By doing this you can keep track of how fast they are making progress and how you are pacing your evaluations. If a student is sitting on a "Sometimes" but it has been several weeks, maybe you need to evaluate them in that *Signpost* again, or maybe you need to remind that student they need to work on

Notes _____

_____

_____

_____

_____

_____

_____

that *Signpost*.

Keeping Track of ICPs However you do it, you need to keep track of student's progress and the ICPs can help. Of course, no student is going to be working on just one thing, so the range of things they are working on stretches from their previous "Often" or "Always" to their latest "Sometimes." A quick scan of a student's ICP should enable you to direct them as to what they need to work on. If there is no drill available, you might recommend that they do that just part of their shot they are working on, *e.g.* taking their stance over and over. This repetition can get tedious, but a certain amount of it is necessary to get over the little humps in the road, as it were. Use your judgment and, often, all that is required for motivation is that there is a gap or hole in their performance keeping them from progressing.

This means you have to have the ICPs with you during classes and you need to consult them, probably before and during your sessions.

We know this is a lot of recordkeeping, so if you come up with a better way to do this, please let us know.

Equipment You Can Make

A fair amount of program support materials can be made quite inexpensively. We

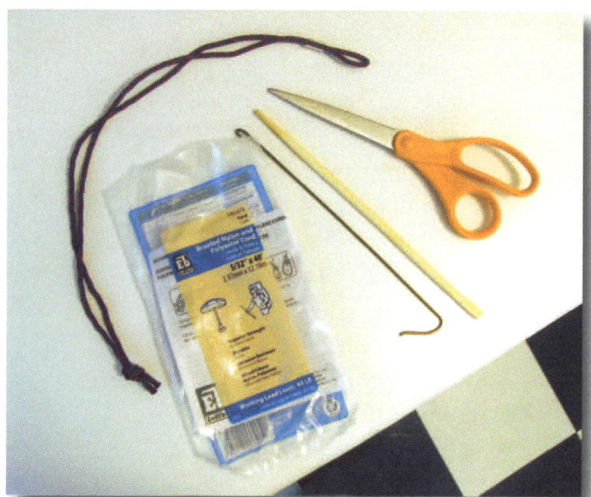

refer you to the Texas State Archery Associations website (*www.texasarchery.org*, click on "Documents") where you can find instructions to build a bow string jig (and directions as to how to make bowstrings), how to tie custom finger slings starting with a shoelace, how to make five or six different target stands and target butts, how to make an arrow backstop (to extend the life of some target butts), and lots of other interesting things.

Below we describe a couple of inexpensive items that can be used as giveaways, fundraisers, etc.

Wrist Slings An inexpensive wrist sling can be made out of nylon clothesline and some plastic tubing. Cut the clothesline into roughly 36-38″ lengths (melt each end a tad to prevent unraveling). Align the two loose ends and tie a simple knot close to their ends. Cut

Notes

a short (³⁄₁₆-¼") segment of ³⁄₁₆" ID flexible plastic tubing. Insert the segment of the loop farthest from the knot through the tubing segment by: (male method) pushing the material through with a chopstick or small dowel or (female method) pull the material through with a crochet hook or hook made by bending coat hanger wire.

To use the sling, insert the tubing end through the loop near the knot and slide bow hand through the hole just created. Pick up the bow and run the tubing end around it and loop the very end around the index finger. Slide the tubing up against that finger loosely. (Alternatively, you can come around the back of the hand and connect with the thumb.) There should be 1-2 inches of slack in the sling either way. If not, retie the knot. When the sling is properly fitted this way, you can cut off the extra clothesline past the knot (melt each end a tad to prevent unraveling).

Arrow Pullers A very effective "arrow puller" can be made from rubber, nonskid drawer liner or light nonskid rug pad materials. Simply cut 6" squares (or circles) out of the material. A piece laid on your hand before pulling greatly assists in removing difficult to pull arrows. It works because so much strength is wasted in gripping a slick arrow that pulling become difficult. The nonslip surface makes gripping easy and pulling your arrows easy in turn.

End of Manual

Notes

Notes

www.ingramcontent.com/pod-product-compliance
Lightning Source LLC
Chambersburg PA
CBHW040909020526
44116CB00026B/11